Diva

THE TOTALLY
UNAUTHORIZED BIOGRAPHY OF

WHITNEY HOUSTON

Diva

THE TOTALLY UNAUTHORIZED BIOGRAPHY OF

WHITNEY HOUSTON

by Jeffery Bowman

with an introduction by
J. RANDY TARABORRELLI

Edited by
JOHN NIENDORFF

HarperPaperbacks
A Division of HarperCollins*Publishers*
Produced in association with
ROSE❦BOOKS

HarperPaperbacks   *A Division of* HarperCollins*Publishers*
             10 East 53rd Street, New York, N.Y. 10022

Produced in association with ROSE❦BOOKS

Cover photograph by DMI.

First printing: February 1995

Printed in the United States of America

HarperPaperbacks and colophon are trademarks of
HarperCollins*Publishers*

❖ 10 9 8 7 6 5 4 3 2 1

This book is dedicated to:
Valarie, Barbara, Karen,
Rooney, and to Tab.

acknowledgments

Deepest appreciation to Geoff Hannell, Katie Tso, Matthew Martin, and everyone at Harper-Paperbacks for their confidence and assistance.

Thanks, and much gratitude, to Rose Books, Inc.: J. Randy Taraborrelli, Sven Paardekooper, Bart Andrews, and everyone else at Rose who made *Diva* possible.

Special thanks to John Niendorff for his many editorial contributions to this biography.

And *very* special thanks to John Passantino, whose research material was invaluable to the creation of the book. His in-depth knowledge of Whitney Houston's life and career helped ensure the accuracy of the text.

Thanks also to Katy Wallin and Kelly Taylor—my love and appreciation for your unwavering friendship, knowledge, support, and love.

A nod to Jim Cruse for his aid.

Thank you Laurie Feigenbaum, Abner Stein, Octavia Wiseman, Roger Houghton, and Ron Monitz.

Thanks also to those associates of Whitney Houston's who were interviewed for this book, and whose requests for anonymity are respected in these pages. And a nod of appreciation, also, to the following individuals for their support in tangible and intangible ways: Maudie Bowman, Elaine Klearman, Darryl Shelly, Alice Chauke, Pauline O'Dell, Ms. Jaskowski, Debbie Heath, Susan Tweed, Tiffani and Matthew Heath, Vida and Bill Strunk, Reverend Leonard Leslie Bowman, Jack and Virginia Bowman, Lauren Weissman, Ken Kilpatrick, and Rosie Maynard.

Thank you, also, to David McGough, Leslie Craigmile, and Scooter McGough of DMI for many of the excellent photographs found in this book.

introduction

BY J. RANDY TARABORRELLI

I first met Whitney Houston in November 1984. Clive Davis, the legendary starmaker and president of Arista Records, invited journalists to the record company's headquarters near Beverly Hills to meet their "latest discovery" (to quote the printed invitation). Whitney was twenty-one years old at the time. She had been under contract to the label for almost two years and now, finally, her first album was scheduled for release in three months.

Over the previous several years, I attended many such events at Arista's West Coast headquarters. Indeed, Clive Davis—along with the high-level executives of every other record company in town—was always introducing the press to a "discovery," someone "on the verge of stardom." And I, as a busy music-industry journalist, seemed always to be traipsing off to press conferences to meet them.

They were engaging, cordial, and talented, and—the women among them, anyway—were touted as "the biggest thing since Diana Ross." As if they were slices from the same wondrous sugary confection, all of them "once sang in the choir," promised not to "change" upon becoming successful, and had put "a lot of time and energy" into their debut album. And all were *enthusiastic*.

A decade later, I can still remember some of their names (Angela Bofill, Rena Scott, and Karen Silver were among them), but I don't know what became of them. I remember a singer named Judy Cheeks. I remember another one named Darcus. Then there was someone named Kellee Patterson. There were Ullanda, Teresa, Ren Woods, Lalomie Washburn, Deborah Washington, and on and on and on. They were lovely, personable, and talented . . . and all of them, for reasons no one may ever understand, have been forgotten.

I distinctly recall that I would have skipped the Whitney Houston event, except the Arista invitation mentioned that she was the daughter of a personal favorite of mine, rhythm-and-blues/gospel singer Cissy Houston. (In the mid-sixties, Cissy was lead singer of a vocal quartet called the Sweet Inspirations. I was a big fan of hers and interviewed her several times.) So I went to the press conference to see *Cissy* Houston, not *Whitney* Houston. However, Cissy did not appear.

The attractive woman standing before the press corps and fielding questions didn't particularly impress me or anyone else in the media that day—not that I can recall, anyway. Physically, Whitney Houston was average and not as glamorous as many other female recording stars I'd interviewed. Clive Davis claimed she'd been a model, but I recall thinking that she certainly didn't seem the type. Her hair was short and curly; she wore just a little makeup. She was reed thin. Carrying an air of cool amiability, she had a winning smile but didn't seem very approachable. In other words, Whitney Houston clearly didn't possess any special qualities that suggested superstardom was in her future. She wasn't even exactly enthusiastic. Hell, *Judy Cheeks* had more enthusiasm.

We in the press didn't have much to ask. So, in turn, Whitney Houston didn't have much to say. She spoke a bit about her childhood, her steadfast belief in "my Lord and Savior," and she recalled the process of recording her first album (yes, she "put a lot of time and energy" into it). Clive Davis brought up the fact that Dionne Warwick was her cousin. He also mentioned that Aretha Franklin was a "family friend." This was intended to impress a roomful of veteran entertainment reporters.

Finally, Clive Davis informed us that each member of the press was to receive a cassette tape of songs Whitney had recorded. "When you hear this tape, you'll know why I am so enthusiastic," he announced with pride.

After the press conference, Davis, always a charmer, continued holding court; members of the media swarmed about him, asking questions. When I noticed Whitney standing in a corner, alone and looking quite out of place, I went over to her and attempted to engage her in a conversation. It wasn't easy.

"So, you sang in church?" I asked.

"Yes."

"Where?" I inquired.

"New Jersey."

"Oh, I'm from the East Coast, too," I said.

"Hmmm," she said, with what seemed to be genuine indifference.

Not until I mentioned her mother did her face light up. "Oh, let me tell you, she is my greatest inspiration,"

Whitney said with sudden warmth. "I only hope I am *half* the singer she is. I love her so much, and I respect her. I really do."

Then we discussed Cissy Houston's group, the Sweet Inspirations. As we talked I felt something in her opening up to our conversation.

"I can't believe that you, a white guy, know so much about the Sweet Inspirations," she told me. "I didn't think any white people knew about her group. That was their biggest problem. No white fans. They never 'crossed over.' It was a shame. My mother should be a huge star by now."

I agreed.

As I was getting ready to leave she extended her hand to me. With a firm grip, she said, "Thank you for coming. I really enjoyed talking to you."

To my surprise, I felt the same way about her.

Then, because I was late for another appointment, I rushed out without my copy of the tape Clive Davis mentioned earlier. I realized it just before I got in the elevator. But I thought, "I don't need an advance copy. It'll wait. I probably won't have time to listen to it, anyway."

Can you believe it?

I just didn't know.

Who did?

Well, Clive Davis, for one. (But even now, after reading Jeffery Bowman's absorbing biography, I realize that Davis wasn't really that impressed by Whitney, either. He almost fell asleep the first time he heard her sing. Only after he realized that she was about to sign with a competing record company did he decide to offer her a contract.)

As I watched Whitney nervously mumble answers to questions in that press conference a decade ago, I never would have predicted that this young woman would one day break records (for consecutive number-one singles) set by the Bee Gees and by arguably the most phenomenal pop group of all time, the Beatles.

And yet:

Her debut album, *Whitney Houston,* sold over thirteen million copies, the most successful solo debut in history. Her second single, "Saving All My Love for You," won a Grammy for Best Pop Female Vocal.

She started at the top . . . and went up from there.

Her second album, *Whitney,* featured four consecutive number-one singles ("I Wanna Dance with Somebody [Who Loves Me]," "Didn't We Almost Have It All?", "So Emotional," and "Where Do Broken Hearts Go?")—more than any other female artist ever had from one album. *Whitney* also marked the first time a female singer entered the charts at number one.

Expectations from her prior success were so great that when her third album, *I'm Your Baby Tonight,* sold *only* seven million copies, the press described its sales as "disappointing" and suggested her career was on the wane! (That album produced two number-one singles.)

In November 1992, Whitney's biggest album, the soundtrack to her film *The Bodyguard,* was issued. It would go on to sell over twenty-six million copies and generate the song that stayed at number one longer than any other song in the rock era, "I Will Always Love You," spending fourteen consecutive weeks atop the charts.

Though she is first and foremost a singer, *The Bodyguard,* her motion-picture debut, in which she costarred opposite Kevin Costner, grossed more than $400 million worldwide. After her initial film, she became that rare Hollywood commodity: a bankable star, whose name alone attached to a project would guarantee major studio financing.

Today, Whitney Houston, who makes $45 million a year and is the centerpiece of an enormous entertainment enterprise, finds herself the object of public fascination, something her record-breaking sales alone simply cannot explain. Many other singers—Toni Braxton and Mariah Carey come to mind—have hit records and lots of dedicated fans, but they don't monopolize the cover of the *National Enquirer* or *The Star* the way Houston does.

She has become something more than a star or even a superstar. She's a *phenomenon,* a force, an international icon so famous she can be identified almost anywhere by her first name alone. She belongs to that exclusive VIP one-name club, those people for whom no additional identification is required: Cher, Liz, Elvis, Roseanne, and Michael.

Why is the woman so endlessly fascinating? What makes her intriguing enough to be the subject of a published biography, though she is only thirty-one and in the early years of a career with future heights that even the most optimistic forecasts cannot anticipate?

Of course, it starts with her prodigious talent. And her fashion-model looks are part of it. Some of it may be the controversy that continually surrounds her—rumors about her marriage, her sexuality, her "bad attitude" toward her fans.

Then you check out what you can *feel* about her. She's self-assured, almost cocky. In fact, you realize that, amazingly, she actually doesn't seem to care what people think of her. (The strength of someone not ruled by insecurity can be very attractive.) Then, just when you think you have her figured out—that she's frosty and aloof—her face suddenly lights up with the biggest smile you ever saw, she erupts into delighted, carefree laughter, and just seems to glow with life.

Maybe *that's* it, you realize. Of course! She's free, a free woman. Free being whoever she is. A natural woman, happy with herself, living a good life, not because she's *trying* to be good, but because the way life comes out of her is good. It's the very thing we all wish for ourselves: to be who we are, fearlessly. We sense that about Whitney Houston, and it may be what makes her so beguilingly attractive.

She doesn't fit into the usual categories, though. Put her in one, and she won't stay.

In an agnostic age where school prayer is forbidden and being "religious" is usually regarded as something for celebrities to keep quiet about, Whitney Houston does the unthinkable. She speaks out publicly on her certainty that a divine force guides her life and career.

"I believe in God, the Almighty," she told *Ebony* magazine in July 1986. "If you just anchor yourself with God, you can resist a lot of temptations. Prayer helps a lot."

Her strong religious upbringing has been an invaluable foundation in the shaky world of superstardom. Her spiritual values give her the confidence to make difficult decisions in her career and private life. Even if an observer thinks a particular decision by Houston is wrong ("She married *who*? She said *what*?"), that observer should understand—if only because she's explained it so many times in interviews—that she feels she's on the right path because God is her spiritual manager. Her certainty about what she does comes from an unwavering belief that—trite as it may sound—she never walks alone.

Her parents, especially her mother, Cissy, also instilled in her the belief that you have to please yourself before you can please anybody else. So Whitney Houston remains on top by the sheer power of an inner voice that seems to say, "Trust yourself." This is not to suggest that she is neurotically self-involved. The list of charities and charitable causes she actively supports, that she goes out and performs for, is long and impressive.

Whitney Houston knows something about who she is. As a result, she doesn't suffer fools gladly. In fact, she doesn't put up with them at all. She has such powerful self-confidence that an audience of 18,000 people booing her in Miami in 1993 (because she banished an autograph seeker from the lip of the stage in a most imperious manner: "Your ticket *does* say seat on it, doesn't it?") didn't seem to bother her. "I've been booed before, and it really doesn't faze me," she told the crowd.

When I saw her perform at the Anaheim Arrowhead Pond in Anaheim, California, in August 1994—nearly ten years after our first meeting—I found her to be intriguing. Of course, her performances of her hit records—in a two-hour show it seemed as if she performed *everything* she ever recorded—were superb, as was to be expected.

She has great authority: when she's onstage, you pay attention. More fascinating to me, though, is the fact that her act was loaded with tantalizing references to her personal life—tantalizing mostly because she keeps insisting during interviews that none of what happens offstage is any of our business, yet she delights in talking about all of it when she's onstage. Jackie Onassis and Greta Garbo actually *meant* it when they said, "I want to be alone." So they disappeared into Manhattan, a city of eight million people. Whitney Houston says the same thing: "I wish people would just leave me alone.

Love my records, love me onstage, but don't pry into my personal life." But she doesn't really seem to mean it. In fact, going to one of Whitney Houston's concerts is like stepping into an extraordinary living, breathing, pulsing, dancing virtual-reality encounter with everyone in her whole extended family.

While she entertained, her husband, singer Bobby Brown, sat on the side of the stage throughout the entire show, and acted as master of ceremonies. ("Let's hear it for my wife, y'all, Whitney Houston!")

The star angrily denounced tabloid stories about trouble in her marriage. She told the crowd, "I am a woman in love. And my man is in love with me. Why? Because I give him *every reason* to stay home."

Bobby then brought out two-year-old Bobbi Kristina, their daughter, to great applause. Later, Whitney also brought onto the stage two of the three children Bobby had fathered with other women, out of wedlock, before his marriage to Whitney. (One of these children was born while he was engaged to marry Whitney.) She hugged and kissed them both.

She brought out her mother-in-law, sang to her, and embraced her. ("She's the best mother-in-law in the world.")

She introduced her sister-in-law, who is one of her dancers, and hugged her, too.

Bobby joined her for a final number. (As the couple left the stage to thunderous applause, he announced, "I'm taking my wife home with me, y'all.")

Everyone seemed to be content. In fact, it was practically impossible for me to imagine that there was any discord—even though that's what is constantly being reported in the press and I know better than to disregard everything I read about Whitney and Bobby.

What I found most interesting, however, is that

Whitney Houston hasn't forgotten where she came from, her roots. In one segment of the show, she paid eloquent tribute to her mother, Cissy Houston, and to Cissy's group, the Sweet Inspirations. She carefully explained to any uninitiated audience members how the group was started, and why its contribution as background singers to Aretha Franklin's early hit records was so important. Then, she sang versions of Aretha's "(You Make Me Feel Like a) Natural Woman," "Do Right Woman," and "Ain't No Way." Whitney's three onstage female background singers emulated, practically note by note, the original backing arrangements that were composed by Cissy.

Whitney then sang two gospel songs—"Wonderful Counselor" and "Blessed Assurance"—a nod to her beginnings in church. Listening to her sing these emotional songs, I understood clearly that she is nothing if not a masterful vocalist. But more—she loses herself in her song. Somehow she becomes the song, and the song becomes her. When she sings, when she's really immersed in the performance, she might as well be completely alone onstage, enchanted. It's almost as if she's praying.

Sportswriters have reported something that happens occasionally to star athletes. It's called "flow"—when everything comes together without warning and what they're doing seems to occur almost magically. The impossible shots get made. The pass that's just out of reach gets caught. The same thing happens with entertainers, usually the really accomplished ones like Whitney Houston. They get caught up in what they're doing and, at that point, something else—something *bigger* and more *powerful* than they are—seems to take over. This transformation is particularly evident with great actors, but singers and musicians do it, also. It's powerfully emotional, not only for the entertainer, but also for any observer who is keen to it.

As Whitney sang "Blessed Assurance," that age-old gospel tune about religious devotion, I saw it happen before my eyes. And I was transfixed. Indeed, a divine wind blew through Whitney and exploded, bursting out of her by way of that amazing voice. It attested to a breadth that far transcends mere technical competence, evidence of an artistic reach inspired from places the merely mortal do not often go. When she's onstage, she's her own best creation, completely at one with her art, herself, and her God.

Ten years after I first met her and thought of her as a shy, young girl, she has become a bold, glorious woman, who sings with a bold, glorious voice. When she reaches up to the heavens for inspiration to sing, inspiration comes down to meet her. It makes for a unique, almost spiritual experience, a holy creativity.

Having started life simply in Newark, New Jersey, Whitney Houston rose to the top of the world. She was not propelled by tragedy; she does not fit the mold of the tortured artist. She had parents who loved her, a mother who encouraged her natural talent, exposed her to some of the great soul and gospel singers of the time, and unselfishly gave her daughter the kind of training no one could have bought with a billion dollars. Whitney grew up in the church, sang in the choir; she was a "good girl." But when the forces of life moved in on her and demanded that she embrace a larger world, she went for it.

So the "good girl" became a person of the past. A younger part of her was sacrificed in the fires of growing up as Whitney found her soul and claimed it rightfully as her own. Now she has a renegade husband, a baby daughter, a reputation as a person who's sometimes damned difficult, and a career that regularly redefines what it means to be on top. Because to Whitney Houston, the top is a place where you stand as you get ready to go even higher.

foreword

November 1975.

New Hope Baptist Church, Newark, New Jersey.

Twelve-year-old Whitney Houston stood next to the choir, waiting for her turn to sing her first solo. She straightened the white pleats of her blue sailor dress, then made a slight face at a scuff mark on her white Mary Janes, one that had not been there when she and her family left the house only an hour before. Her hands could not still themselves; she finally clasped them together behind her back. She knew in advance that she would be singing without a microphone, but suddenly, as she later recalled, the thought of having nowhere to put her hands during the song sent her heart racing.

For this big moment, Whitney and her mother, popular rhythm-and-blues singer Cissy Houston, who was also the church's choir director, had chosen "Guide Me O Thou Great Jehovah," a gospel standard. It was a stirring song, and performing it right required skill and a deep emotional commitment. (Cissy, who was fulfilling an obligation to perform in a club out of town, was not able to be present at church that Sunday. Whitney's father, John, was there, however.)

A smile—but no introduction—from a choir director who was substituting for Cissy brought Whitney to the pulpit. The young girl stood before the congregation, visibly shaking as she looked out at the rows of expectant faces. She saw signs of support from her friends and relatives, but many of the faces staring back at her seemed to say, "Well, go on. Let's see you do it."

"I stood there, stiff as a board," Whitney has remembered. "No one in the congregation moved. It was like they were in a trance. I just stared at the clock in the center of the church."

As if to test the waters before truly diving in, Whitney opened her mouth, hesitantly at first, the sounds barely emerging through her lips. The traditional gospel number called for clear, sweet notes, many of which were held and rounded at the end of each phrase. A tentative approach was definitely not called for here. It was time to sing.

And young Whitney Houston sang. As she stood very still and, with increasing confidence, did what she knew how to do, the rustle of paper fans in the pews seemed to quiet itself and people began to pay attention. She was good. She was very good.

Each breath brought forth more power. Each verse of "Guide Me O Thou Great Jehovah" produced a voice that grew stronger and more sure. As Whitney sang, the choir seemed somehow to validate her performance, their combined voices prompting Whitney to deliver with even greater force.

The astonished choir director turned slightly in order to watch the young girl become part of the music. Whitney's hands embraced the emotion and she raised them to the heavens as the song ended. With the last sustained note, she swung them back to her sides with triumphant finality.

After a moment of breathless silence from the congregation, the applause rang up loud and full. So *this* is what her mother felt like, singing at the Apollo or at Philharmonic Hall when she stole the show, Whitney must have thought. *This* is how it feels to be so swept up in the emotion of the song and of the audience that the music seems to soar from a place deep in your heart and soul, a place where nothing else exists except God-made stuff.

Whitney clearly relished her first taste of performing before an audience. "The people went crazy," she has remembered. "They were clapping and crying. There was a joyful noise unto the Lord. It was wonderful."

Minutes later, she was asked to sing again. They wanted her back. They wanted more. Indeed, in a manner of speaking, this was her first "curtain call." By the closing verses of young Whitney's rendition of the next gospel song, the congregation was on its feet, swaying and shouting back praises—not only for the Lord but also for the sweet soul of twelve-year-old Whitney Houston's voice.

"I knew then and there that if this is what I can do with what God gave me with this gift, my *voice*, then this is what I will do," Whitney concluded. "It was a done deal. I knew God had blessed me. I knew I had to sing. . . ."

one

Summer in Newark, New Jersey, can be described as a "slow season." Oppressive heat and high humidity make life miserable and soggy, with most citizens seeking relief by simply remaining indoors or spending the day at air-conditioned movie theaters.

August 9, 1963, found Newark in one of the hottest summers anyone there could remember. The streets sizzled under a blistering sun and many shops in the main business district closed their doors for the day, the owners preferring to stay home, where the air was generally cooler, more bearable.

That dog-day afternoon, John Houston brought his wife, Cissy, into the emergency entrance of a local hospital. Cissy Houston, in the last moments of pregnancy, wiping the sweat from her forehead, was quickly admitted, then wheeled down the long, tiled hallway as her husband watched from the waiting room. Soon, the heat was far from John Houston's mind, for he learned that his wife had delivered their third child, a daughter. Cissy named the child Whitney Elizabeth.

Whitney has said she was named after television actress Whitney Blake, who played the role of Dorothy Baxter on the sitcom "Hazel," starring Shirley Booth. According to Whitney, her mother happened to be watching the program from her hospital bed and chose the name because Blake's character on the program was the elegant wife of a corporate attorney; Cissy thought that was a classy thing to be.

The world into which Whitney Elizabeth Houston was born was, for most black Americans, one full with future, if not present, possibilities. The air in 1963 carried the scent of an oncoming civil-rights movement, an expression of intense collective passion that would be marked by violence, death, and finally—in the eyes of some—victory. It was a time of change, a time of real and deeply felt struggle.

Life for John and Cissy, at least economically, was not as oppressive as it was for many other black families. Both of them were working—John in a blue-collar job and Cissy as a singer. But not just an average singer. She was, in fact, a superb vocalist, prompting one observer to declare that she had "the voice of angels." At the time of Whitney's birth, she was pursuing a dream that had begun many years before in a Newark Baptist church.

One of five children, Whitney Houston's mother was born Emily Drinkard in Newark in the early 1930s. Her family attended church regularly, participating in all church-sponsored activities and enjoying nothing more than singing in the choir each Sunday. At home, the five Drinkard children were encouraged by their parents to sing; daily, harmonizing voices filled their home. For the Drinkard family, every day was a celebration, not only of a spiritual way of life but also of the strong familial ties that bound them to one another.

Emily, who was later nicknamed "Cissy" by her parents, has many memories of the importance of music in her childhood. "I can remember our playing out in the sun with the other kids, and my older sister Marie would make us stop and come in for a rehearsal," she recalled. "We didn't have microphones or anything— when we rehearsed, we had to use brooms or mops as our microphones."

A family friend, Mildred Dickenson, remembers how the neighborhood children, some of whom viewed Cissy and her siblings as aloof and different, often teased them. "Some of the other kids in the neighborhood used to get on them because they weren't allowed to do things the other kids could do—like they couldn't date until they were much older," she remembered. "But we never got the impression that they were unhappy or that they were being forced by their parents to sing, as some talented kids are. They loved it."

"They appeared to be peculiar," another friend said, "because they were so antisocial. Music was the only thing they had on their minds. Emily was picked on a lot when she was young, picked on by neighborhood bullies because she was 'different,' not always out there in the streets with the other kids. But she loved to sing. . . ."

Maybe it seemed that way, but Cissy later admitted that secretly, she had no interest whatever in singing. "I never wanted to sing," she recalls. "I hated it. But with three sisters, two brothers, and a father who were always singing, I had no choice. I was singing in church by about the age of five."

Mildred Dickenson recalled that the Drinkards spent much of their time in worship. "Sometimes all day," she said. "God-fearing is the word, for sure. They went to church, sang in church—they were good kids. But they were taught to mind their own business. They were very private people, a close-knit family. Their father made sure they stayed to themselves." This single-mindedness in regard to church activities—combined with the elder Drinkard's reluctance to allow strangers into the family's inner circle—was bound to make an impression on Cissy and influence her in later years, when she was raising the daughter who would one day become an international superstar.

"My parents were good people—especially my father. But he didn't take no mess," Cissy recalled. "We all had things to do around the house, chores and the like. Talking back—rolling your eyes and all that crap—was not tolerated. He wasn't hard on us; he simply taught us the meaning of respect. And that's how I tried to raise my kids, too."

Her religious convictions were a comfort to the sixteen-year-old when her father suddenly passed away in 1948. Of all the children, Cissy was the closest to her father, and she grieved deeply over his death. But she knew in her heart that he was now in God's hands, and she was comforted.

"Within the love of God, all things are possible," Cissy said in a 1984 interview with J. Randy Taraborrelli. "I received Jesus into my heart when I was fourteen. I can't describe it. I have been pretty peaceful since then. Listen, I can't expect you to understand," she added. "It's a special relationship, between me and my God."

In order to make up for family income that was lost as a result of her father's passing, young Emily was forced to find work. And she did—at a local dry-cleaning establishment, where her tasks included such dreary things as removing the paper from clothes hangers. After that, she worked at another go-nowhere job: in a toothpaste factory. But at the same time, she—along with her sisters and one of her brothers—had also started a group called the Drinkard Singers, and she was now beginning to enjoy the diversion of those precious moments when she sang with them. Performing in different churches on weekends, the Drinkard Singers soon developed a following, becoming fixtures on the East Coast gospel circuit, and they actually recorded a few songs for RCA and Savoy, working at both studios as background vocalists.

"There was no money in those records," Cissy has said. "We had to keep our day jobs. But we sang. And we sang it *out.*"

When she was seventeen, Cissy formed a choir for the young adults in the church; it eventually grew into the New Hope Baptist Church Young Adult Choir. Before long, she was also singing with several other gospel groups, all the while developing a powerful voice that lent itself well to traditional gospel singing. Eventually, Cissy put together a new edition of the Drinkard Singers with her sister Marie, her cousin Lee Warrick Drinkard, and Lee's daughters Marie Dionne Warrick and Dee Dee Warrick (all from East Orange, New Jersey). The new group began to perform on the gospel circuit in the New Jersey area, quickly becoming popular with their soulful renditions of gospel-music standards.

Rehearsing with the group day and night left Cissy little time for a personal life. Her interest in men had waned somewhat after a brief, disastrous marriage. But because she was personable and attractive, she was courted on many occasions, though she usually chose the company of family and friends.

Her introduction to John Houston came through a friend who had been urging her to date and develop other interests besides singing. Though reluctant at first, Cissy finally gave in to the persuasive charm of this handsome, charismatic six-footer. Soon, she was dating him steadily.

Born in nearby Trenton, New Jersey, John Houston had dabbled in the music industry for many years as a singer and artist's manager. He was a great match for Cissy and they found they had much in common, most importantly their love for gospel music. John, in fact, felt Cissy could be a major star; he even predicted that she would one day want to leave the gospel world for a more commercial career. He filled her head with marvelous dreams of the glorious things they could do together as a team—with himself as her manager and, when she finally had enough time to devote to her career, her as the star. It was strong stuff and—from Cissy's point of view as she began to catch the dream—not at all unreasonable. She knew what she had to give; she knew what she felt inside about her singing. And here she'd met a man who could help her express that talent in a larger world than she was now reaching. It added another kind of excitement to a relationship that, on a personal level, was already intense and passionate. For them to commit themselves to a life together probably seemed the closest thing to perfection.

Thus, they were soon married. (Cissy already had a son from her previous marriage, Gary, who lived with the couple. Her first child with John was a son, Michael. When Whitney was born, she therefore had two older siblings: a brother and a half brother.)

Cissy worked in the recording industry throughout her pregnancy with Whitney. "Mom said the producers were real jittery," Whitney has recalled with a gentle sense of merriment. "But she just told them to quit worrying and get on with it."

In addition to working with the Drinkard Singers, Marie Dionne paid her musical dues by singing on the demos of various songwriters and producers. For this, she usually earned forty dollars per song. A few doors opened up as a result. Burt Bacharach, one of the songwriters with whom she worked, was completely taken by her voice and her emotional interpretation of his music . . . which led to her making a few small changes. Like dropping the name "Marie." Like turning "Warrick" into "Warwick." A few small changes. But maybe not a bad idea. She might have a future as Dionne Warwick.

"I was working in this act with Cissy, and we were good," Dionne recalled in an interview. "But Burt Bacharach and some other people surrounding me at the time—including Florence Greenberg, who was president of Scepter Records—convinced me that maybe I should try my hand at secular music. It was a tough decision. You know, a gospel girl like me faced with the possibility of burning in hell over the singing of pop songs. Or at least that's what we had been raised to believe. But, in the end, I knew I had to find my own place. . . ." And, of course, she did, striking gold with the soulful, pre–feminist movement anthem "Don't Make Me Over," then making show-business history when Bacharach and partner/lyricist Hal David began to write music specifically for her range. The resulting formula took her repeatedly to the top of the record charts with such hits as "Message to Michael," "Do You Know the Way to San Jose?", "I Say a Little Prayer for You," and "Alfie."

• • •

When Dionne decided to leave the Drinkard Singers to embark on a solo career, the group's local popularity and success were seriously threatened. "People thought the Drinkard Singers would fold when [she] left," remembers John Houston, who had taken over as part-time manager of the act. "But we replaced Dionne with her mama, Lee Drinkard Warrick. And with Cissy taking an even bigger role in the group's vocals, they had a whole different sound. They began to wipe out all of the other competing background singers in the recording industry, and they were also doing well on the road with their gospel act."

Cissy—whose experiences as a performer would profoundly influence her daughter—recalls the early days of on-the-road gospel singing. "Things are different now, but when I started out, there was no real money in gospel," she has said. "We were singing those songs and getting a lot of attention, then we'd go back home to our full-time jobs. In my day, gospel was a great way to get your voice together, but it was hard to make a living doing just that."

Dionne Warwick remained close friends with Cissy Houston and often thought of her when she was unable to make a scheduled demo session. Cissy gladly stepped in. "If what they wanted was someone who could take instructions from a producer in the booth or a guy at the piano," says Cissy, "then I figured, 'Hey, I can do this.'" Soon, she became a favorite on the sessions circuit, always working steadily.

Magnificent Montague, a flamboyant sixties disc jockey, hired her to sing the theme song for his then-popular radio show in the New Jersey area. When that theme became a local favorite, he asked Cissy if she would allow him to market it in record stores. But Cissy decided she did not want her name associated with a nongospel recording. Like Dionne, she had been raised to think of secular music as wrong, even evil.

"Growing up, mine was a pretty narrow road," she has said. "I had been brought up strict, to think that all of it, rock and all, was the devil's music. But if God gives you a gift, if He gives you a *voice*, well, I don't think He's going to discriminate on how you best put it to use. I didn't always feel this way, though. Not at all . . ."

And that's why Cissy's song was credited to "Allison Gray," and she found herself in the odd situation of being a local success . . . without anyone's knowing about it.

After a short time, the Drinkard Singers disbanded. But Cissy Houston thoroughly enjoyed her taste of success and had no intention of giving it up before she discovered if something else might be in her future—like a whole banquet. So, as a way to advance her career both creatively and financially, she recruited three members of the church choir—Myrna Smith of Newark; Sylvia Shemwell of Fayetteville, North Carolina; and Estelle Brown of Los Angeles—and formed another singing group. "We were just trying to see what we could get off the ground," Estelle has recalled. "Rehearsing all the time, working on our blend, getting ready—but for what, we didn't know. We just knew we'd make it. We believed."

And that—*believing*—was a big part of everything Cissy Houston did. "I believe in the magic of believing," Cissy told J. Randy Taraborrelli. "In fact, at one point, I recorded a gospel album with Dionne [Warwick] called *The Magic of Believing*. Because I love the Lord, I know He will take care of me. And in my believing that, a certain magic happens, and I *am* taken care of *because* I believed."

Indeed, Cissy always did seem to be taken care of, as far as her career was concerned. She was almost never out of work.

Following the birth of Whitney in 1963, Cissy went back to work as a singer. John Houston, in addition to managing a few other acts and doing part-time jobs for the City of Newark, was involved in the business end of his wife's career, advising her on both financial and creative issues. According to Joe Patriani, an engineer on many of those East Coast recording sessions, John was the perfect man for Cissy to have in her life at that time. "The music industry is treacherous. When you're in it, it's hard to find someone who will stick by you, let alone someone willing to learn the ever-changing business and help you stay on top of it," he observed. "That's what Johnny seemed to be doing for Cissy and her group."

"John Houston was inexperienced," said one of the singers with whom Cissy was working at the time. "But he cared. However, I must say that his inexperience would be the cause of a lot of problems for us. It goes without saying that he wouldn't have been our manager if he hadn't been Cissy's husband, and had she not been the one who formed the group. You deal with the cards you're dealt, I guess."

Whitney—nicknamed "Nippy" by her father—was growing into a beautiful child. Her eyes had taken on an almond shape, inherited from her mother; neighbors spoke glowingly of her sweet disposition. And for reasons that might have been understood only by someone privy to the mysteries of genetics, of the blendings of thousands of unions over countless generations, her skin was lighter than that of many of her friends and associates. It was an iridescent café au lait color that set her apart and made her different, almost exotic looking—but definitely different.

She and her two brothers enjoyed spending time with their father and other relatives while Cissy was on the road touring or recording in the studio. In fact, Whitney and her brothers became accustomed to the frequent absence of their mother, who had to help support her family. It was a difficult situation for Cissy, though; she enjoyed her work but missed her children. And while she was troubled that they were becoming so attached to their father and to other relatives that it often seemed as if they didn't miss her very much at all, she knew she was making the right choice. She was the best mother she was able to be. And she knew, when everything was said and done, that she was doing pretty well at it.

The sixties marked the official birth of an organized civil-rights movement, led by Dr. Martin Luther King, Jr. King preached to African-Americans that they must finally and completely strip off the shackles that held them to their collective past as slaves and rise up, proclaiming their freedom to be equal to the rest of the nation. It was not an easy time. In the summer of 1967, the city of Newark was felled by the winds of a racial hurricane, a five-day uprising sparked by the beating of a black man following a traffic arrest. Two dozen people were killed, hundreds were injured, hundreds more were arrested, and property damage amounted to $10 million.

Overnight, what was once a peaceful neighborhood for the Houston family and their friends became part of the ten-square-mile battleground, with violence and destruction occurring virtually at their doorstep. Much of Newark was in flames, with office buildings reduced to rubble. Cissy and John barricaded themselves and their children in their home, watching the riots on television, afraid to look out the window or open the front door. The family sang to keep their spirits high, praying for the violence to end. Finally, the New Jersey police, along with the National Guard, regained control of the city.

Soon after the riots, John moved his family from their Eighth Street home in ravaged Newark to the suburb of East Orange. The latter city, offering middle-class, mixed-race neighborhoods on tree-lined streets, suited Houston exactly. He knew his children could be scarred for life by the riots, afraid to integrate for fear of rejection or retaliation. He wanted his family to mix with all races and not limit themselves socially.

Meanwhile Cissy was enjoying increasing success. Unofficially known in the recording world as "Cissy's Girls," her group had become an integral part of the recording-sessions circuit—singing backup vocals for various performers.

The group's greatest asset, according to Joe Patriani, was their unusual versatility. Background singers who could provide a producer with the exact sound necessary for a certain track could virtually write their own tickets in the recording industry. The kind of reputation and good word-of-mouth that Cissy's Girls earned meant they never stopped working.

"They could do anything," recalls Patriani. "If you needed female voices to sound aggressively gospel, Cissy and her girls could do it. If you needed female voices to sound very pop—okay, white—they could do that, too."

"We just loved it," Myrna Smith, one of Cissy's Girls, has said. "We were paid pennies for some of those sessions, but when we heard our voices on the records, we sounded so good. It encouraged us to go on. Oh, we were taken advantage of, there's no doubt about it. But some things are more important than money. At least, that's how we felt at the time."

In the 1960s, record producers did not have the benefit of computerized recording equipment, and as a result, the background singers and rhythm section often recorded together in the studios. Today, various instruments and voices are captured on individual tracks—or tapes—and later, using computer wizardry and in-studio know-how, mixed together to achieve a sound that seems to have been recorded on a single occasion. But back in the days when songs really *were* recorded all at once—with instrumentalists, background singers, and lead vocals all present and working together—split-second timing, intense concentration, and great skill were required in order to get everything right the first time. Studio operations were expensive, and producers were not inclined to feel generous about repeated "takes."

Cissy, Myrna, Sylvia, and Estelle—Cissy's Girls—found themselves recording background vocals for many of the top artists of the period, including Wilson Pickett, Dusty Springfield, Dionne Warwick, Connie Francis, Buddy Rich, and Leslie Uggams. "It was good, but we wanted more," said Myrna. "We started to want to be out front, too." The women began feeling strongly that it was time to move beyond the anonymous confines of singing background in the recording studio.

This opinion was only fueled by Cissy Houston's feeling that her voice was superior to those of most other background singers and even those of many top recording stars. Her soulful quality and unique delivery had been praised by many, but other, less secure performers rarely encouraged her to attempt to make it on her own.

"The role of the sessions singer is to make the star sound good," Cissy has stated. "But you'd have to be in the studio to realize how much talent a lot of people *don't* have. The public would not believe how many sessions singers and musicians end up doing the work of the recording artist. It was frustrating to watch someone else take all of the glory for our work."

Both Cissy and John agreed that the time was right for Cissy and her group to break out. And in one of those occurrences that later look as though the cogs and gears of the universe were turning simultaneously to an almost magical effect, at the same time, Jerry Wexler (who had been assigned to work as a producer with Aretha Franklin by Atlantic Records) had noticed the amazing sound of Cissy's Girls when they recorded background vocals for a few of Aretha's songs at Columbia Records in 1965.

Wexler was a mild-mannered man who, although Caucasian, had a great love for the sound of rhythm and blues. In fact, when he was a reporter at *Billboard* in the 1950s, he actually coined the term "rhythm and blues," though he has said, "If I understood then what I know now, I would have called it rhythm and gospel."

In the 1950s and 1960s, Wexler—a man *Rolling Stone* once christened "the Godfather of Rhythm and Blues"— worked with a wide array of singers, including Wilson Pickett, the Drifters, Ray Charles, and Otis Redding. By 1967, he was a vice-president and senior partner of Atlantic Records.

Wexler had been instrumental in redirecting Aretha Franklin's career. While Aretha's former label, Columbia Records, had pigeonholed her as a torch and blues singer, Wexler felt her strength lay in gospel-oriented soul sounds, which Aretha had mastered in her father's church in Detroit. When he worked with her at Atlantic Records, he started to refashion her voice and career—and the result was a string of hit records.

Wexler also realized the importance of background singers to the final product. He had worked with Ray Charles and his backup group, the Raelettes, and marveled at the way that group's sound somehow seemed to bring the best performance from Ray—challenging him, in a sense, to give his all, because, Lord knows, they were giving theirs. Wexler felt that Aretha and Cissy's Girls had the same mutually encouraging rapport in the studio.

Cissy, Myrna, Sylvia, and Estelle cut their background vocals to Aretha Franklin's "Ain't Nobody (Gonna Turn Me Around)" on the evening of June 23, 1967. (The song would appear on Aretha's Atlantic album, *Aretha Arrives*.) That same night, they recorded vocals to the bluesy "Prove It"—which ended up on the flip side of the hit "Chain of Fools."

The evening had been productive, to say the least. Someone sent out for burgers, fries, and milkshakes, as they always did after successful Aretha sessions. Thrilled with the work of Cissy's Girls, Wexler decided to give them an *official* name that evening: the Sweet Inspirations.

"It just fit," he has said. "It was the perfect name. They and their sound—and the way they achieved it—actually *were* inspirational."

Wexler wondered if the group had considered recording on their own. Of course, they had, they replied. "But," said Cissy, "it's so hard to find someone who will give us the chance. Plus, I have other reservations."

Wexler told Cissy he was just the man to offer them

that opportunity. He suggested that Cissy discuss the matter with her partners and get back to him within a few days.

The reservations Cissy spoke of had to do with her own upbringing and the way she, as a gospel singer, was taught to think of secular music. It was one thing to sing anonymously in the background, but to be in front singing pop music was different. This was the same dilemma Dionne Warwick had faced a few years earlier. "Eternal damnation" probably came to mind whenever Cissy pondered the notion of a commercial career.

"That's just the way I was reared," she remembered, in an interview with J. Randy Taraborrelli. "Making the decision to sing pop was traumatic, let me tell you. As far as I knew, the only right way to sing was to sing for the Lord. But I had three children to raise. I had to think about that and what was best for my family. So when I saw the opportunity, I decided it was brought forth by God. Rock and roll, rhythm and blues, and gospel, it's the same thing, let's face it. It's all about love.

"I loved my God, I loved my husband, and I loved my children. And I just wanted to sing out that love for all the world, straight from my heart. I knew what I could do, how I sounded, how I could sell records if I had the chance. And I knew I was wronging my children by not taking advantage of the opportunity God had laid at my feet.

"So when I decided to sign that contract with Atlantic, the Sweet Inspirations were born with God's blessings. I believed in my decision. And the magic of believing gave me peace with that decision."

Wonderful sentiments, indeed. But was it all just a giant rationalization? Wasn't it really that the possibility of getting money by the bagful was sufficiently attractive to lead anyone to the conclusion that all singing was sanctioned by God? "Given what's known about Cissy, it seems unlikely that she would have been quite so mercenary," says her longtime friend Mildred Dickenson. "I believe she did quite a lot of praying about this choice. I think she really was doing what she thought was best for herself and for her family, and that if she thought for a single minute that this decision would somehow compromise her relationship with God, she'd have turned it all down."

In early 1967, when the Sweet Inspirations were recording their first album for Atlantic, the most popular girl group in the nation was the Supremes. That act—Diana Ross, Mary Wilson, and Florence Ballard (later replaced by Cindy Birdsong)—had been formed several years earlier and groomed by Motown founder Berry Gordy, Jr. He had personally supervised their development as recording artists—selecting their material, directing the creation of their extensive wardrobe, and managing the ingenious public-relations hype so his girls would attract the biggest audience. By 1967, Gordy had decided to focus his attention on one member of the group, Diana Ross, who was excited about Gordy's plans—first to increase her importance in the group— renaming them "Diana Ross and the Supremes"—and finally to launch her on a solo career.

While the Supremes had become a major success with a musical style that was decidedly more pop than soul, singing upbeat, radio-ready songs that appealed to the white population, the Sweet Inspirations chose to remain faithful to their roots with a style that combined soul and gospel.

The group released its first Atlantic album, *The Sweet Inspirations,* late in 1967, producing a top-twenty single, "Sweet Inspiration." It's a memorable, startling performance. "You know, there just ain't no tellin' what a sat-isfied woman might do," the ladies wail against a bluesy rhythm. In the middle of the song, a break in the four-part harmony gives Cissy a solo turn. Her voice swoops and soars magnificently. The single release of "Sweet Inspiration" was backed by Ike Turner's mournful "I'm Blue." ("I'm Blue," with new lyrics, would later turn up in 1994 as the song "Shoop" for Salt 'N' Pepa.)

The Sweet Inspirations toured as the opening act with Aretha Franklin on and off for almost two years. "And those weren't glamour tours," Cissy once remembered. "They were one-nighters. We spent all of our time on buses sleeping and on concert stages per-forming, from one town to the next. The dressing rooms were always filthy. There were cockroaches everywhere we went. The food was lousy; we used to eat hot dogs every night."

The Sweet Inspirations also appeared with Aretha on such television programs as "The Jonathan Winters Show," where they sang a raucous version of "Chain of Fools," with Cissy and the girls front and center in appropriate sixties' gear: pink miniskirts, white stock-ings, white pumps. "And we were *wearin'* those pumps, looking great," Cissy allowed in an interview with *Rolling Stone.*

Cissy's group seemed ready to take off, especially after they began headlining in smaller venues. In fact, after the first hit, they were asked to entertain at Bolivian millionaire Antenor Patino's private soirée in Portugal. There, they were treated like stars. Or, as Estelle Brown recalled, "We were the queens of the ball."

For Cissy, the experience must have been wondrous, though traveling overseas was a rarity for her, since she didn't like to leave her family for long.

Aretha Franklin succinctly concluded, "In the sixties, Cissy Houston and the Sweet Inspirations were the hottest—and I'm not kidding, the *hottest*—singers in the business, bar none. Whenever we got together, we knew we were going to be doing some serious singing. We had the same backgrounds—Cissy and me. Different churches but the same God, the same spirit. That's why we got along so well." The Sweet Inspirations recorded countless songs with Aretha, including such major hits as "Chain of Fools," "Think," "Since You Been Gone (Sweet Sweet Baby)," "See Saw," "I Say a Little Prayer," and "This Is the House that Jack Built"—each one an R&B classic.

And this is the environment that young Whitney Houston came to know firsthand. Music. Singing. Good music. Good singing. Terrific music. Terrific singing. All of it an everyday event in the life of a little girl who would one day look back and wonder when music had ever *not* been a part of her experience. How could she grow up and *not* sing?

"Cissy would bring Whitney to those sessions," Aretha once recalled. "She must have been about five years old. And she was always there, in my face. I loved her. She wanted to sing. I knew that even then. She was always watching closely, whispering to her mother. She had great spirit. She sang in the corner, always humming to herself, trying to duplicate the sounds she was hearing. She would say, I want to be a Sweet Inspiration, too."

Estelle Brown of the Sweet Inspirations had this memory of a young Whitney Houston when she was interviewed by J. Randy Taraborrelli in 1983: "We were recording 'Chain of Fools,' I think. The instrumental track was done; we were in the studio trying to work out some intricate background melodies. Aretha was in the corner smoking a cigarette, just letting Cissy run the show like she always did. Well, Whitney—who was about five—wanted to be in the actual studio, not on the other side of the glass watching, as she usually was. Her mother said she could come in just this once and sit quietly, but that she shouldn't make a sound. 'Not a single sound,' she warned. 'And don't you be hummin', either!'

"Whitney came in and sat in the corner on the floor. The tape started rolling, and we started blowing. It sounded strong, real strong.

"Suddenly, this little child squealed out, 'Ooooh, that sounds good, Mama.'

"Well, Cissy shot her daughter a look—and when Cissy gave you a look, you knew you were getting a *look*. The music stopped, the singing stopped, and next thing we knew Cissy was dragging that kid outta there by her elbow.

"'But, Mommy, that just sounded so *good*, I couldn't help myself,' was the last thing I heard Whitney say before Cissy pushed her out of the studio and closed the door behind her.

"'Sorry, everyone,' Cissy said. 'That won't *ever* happen again. I can assure you of *that*.' Cissy was always the consummate professional. She was mortified by that outburst, but we thought it was funny.

"Then we all got back to work as if nothing had happened."

But of course something had happened. Maybe not all on that particular day, for Whitney had been a silent observer during many previous sessions. But that day, it just seemed to burst out—"*Oooh, that sounds good, Mama*"—the result of environment, talent, opportunity, and what the mystical-minded might call destiny. Perhaps this was the night Whitney Houston got a taste of the banquet that would, in the end, never be quite fully available to her mother. And Whitney, liking what she tasted, wanted more.

"I remember one night when I was about five," Whitney has recalled. "My mother and father had gone out. And I was singing in the living room—*R-E-S-P-E-C-T, find out what it means to me!*—and singing so loud you could hear me outside the house. I was performing up a storm, singing along to Aretha's recording. When the music ended, I heard these handclaps behind me. I turned to find my mother and father standing there, applauding. And tears were running down my mother's eyes."

In another interview, this one with writer Perry Stern, Whitney recalled, "Sometimes I got upset wondering where [my voice] was going. I'd say to mother, 'When I do this, hit this particular note, I want to cry.' Or, 'When I sing this way, in a certain style, it sounds really *strange*.' She just laughed and said, 'Girl, you've got a lot of years ahead of you yet. Don't worry about it. Just let it go and see where it leads you.' She was so inspiring."

In May 1968, the Sweet Inspirations appeared in Atlantic Records' annual revue at the famed Apollo Theater in Harlem. Headlined by Ben E. King, the show featured such other Atlantic rhythm-and-blues stars as Solomon Burke, Archie Bell and the Drells, and Dee Dee Sharp. Cissy brought her five-year-old daughter along to see "Mama" in action. Whitney, accompanied by one of Cissy's sisters, stood in the wings—just out of view of the audience—and watched the entire show, awed by the performers and spellbound by the loving way the audience reacted to them.

Estelle Brown recalled, "I remember that night at the Apollo, singing our songs, getting our big applause—honey, we were such *stars*!—and seeing Whitney out of the corner of my eye standing in the wings. We girls had on our big, bouffant wigs and long yellow chiffon gowns, each one with a slit goin' way up to there. And I remember we were singing this Drifters song, 'Sweets for my sweet, sugar for my honey, your tasty kiss thrills me so. . . .' At one point, Cissy took the lead; she would step in front of the three of us with her own mike and just wail, bringing the house down. And on the sidelines, there was little Whitney—just clapping, jumping up and down, so excited. I mean, what little girl wouldn't have wanted this for herself after seeing her mama do it? Lucky for her she could sing, because if she couldn't, she'd have still wanted it . . . but wouldn't have been able to get it."

Noted one observer, "Just look at what Whitney was exposed to and you can see where she came from. All these R&B stars, all of this excitement, the lights, the music. It was sheer magic—the magic of believing, as Cissy would've put it—and any little girl who knew about it would want it in her life. Who doesn't want to be a star?"

"Afterwards," Estelle Brown remembered, "we came off stage, all sweating and tired but so happy. We got two standing ovations.

"Honey, we peeled off those chiffon gowns, took off those wigs and threw them aside, and got ready for a big backstage party. Cissy brought Whitney, who was awake way after her bedtime. She was always immaculate, always the best-dressed girl around, and she had on a freshly ironed white dress. She was just being so cute, mingling with all these performers. She was *five*, you understand.

"Everyone was singing and carrying on, and little Whitney was right there in the middle of it. Aretha was there, too. I mean, it was a serious party," Estelle recalled.

Finally, Cissy told Whitney it was after her bedtime, and that she had to leave. Cissy's sister began looking for their coats.

"But Mommy, I'm having so much fun. I don't want to go," the child protested. "I just want to stay here and sing with Auntie Ree [her nickname for Aretha Franklin]. And you know what? Tomorrow night," she decided, "I'm singin' onstage. *I'm* gonna be a Sweet Inspiration."

Cissy gave her daughter that *look*. "Girl, don't you dare sass me. You ain't singin' *nothin'* tomorrow night, and you ain't gonna be no Sweet Inspiration, either," she told her sharply. "Now *get goin'*."

Whitney didn't like it.

"And don't you be frownin' at me, either, Miss Smarty Pants," Cissy warned.

"I'm sorry, Mommy," little Whitney said as she left the party with her aunt. But not before she had the last word. "I never get to have *no fun,*" the five-year-old muttered under her breath.

Ah, the aroma of that banquet, those bright colors and sweet tastes. *The fun.* How they were beginning to take form and beckon even then. . . .

two

> *On October 13, 1968, Cissy Houston*
enjoyed another triumph when the Sweet Inspirations
practically stole the show from Aretha Franklin at New
York City's Philharmonic Hall in Lincoln Center.
Wearing a pink silk gown that cascaded elegantly to the
floor, and with a matching feather boa draped over her
shoulders, Cissy took center stage to sing the classic
R&B song "Ain't No Way" with Aretha. On no fewer
than four occasions during the performance, the audience cheered Cissy's three-octave range.

Of that performance, a critic from *Variety* noted,
"More than 4,500 fans turned out for two shows
Sunday, ready to clap, stomp and holler . . . and they
got even more than they bargained for in the superb
performance of Cissy Houston. The audience's appreciation of Miss Houston and her group was most strikingly
expressed during 'Ain't No Way.' Four times, the house
exploded with applause for Miss Houston's high soprano
counter-singing to Miss Franklin's lead."

"That was a night to remember," Estelle Brown

recalled. "We all thought Cissy would go on to big things after that night, though I gotta admit we were a little worried about ourselves, about what was going to happen to us."

That evening, Aretha's father, the Reverend Cecil Franklin, came onstage to present his daughter with an RIAA (Recording Industry Association of America) gold record of "I Say a Little Prayer," designating sales of over a million copies. Amazingly, Cissy and the Sweet Inspirations were also presented with gold records for their significant vocal contributions to that recording. For the RIAA to honor background singers with a gold record was rare, but the accolade acknowledged the respect in which the Sweet Inspirations were held.

"Hey, nobody in the world could touch us," Cissy once allowed. "On the East Coast, we were the top. The only competition we had anywhere was the Blossoms, and they were on the West Coast."

In late 1968, Atlantic Records was contacted by Elvis Presley, who had heard and enjoyed the Sweet Inspirations' first album. He wanted the group to open for him in Las Vegas at the International Hotel. The Big Time was at hand.

Between shows, Cissy and Elvis would talk for hours about gospel music. As she recalled in an interview with *Soul* magazine, "Elvis had strong gospel roots. He loved it, was raised on it. He also had a tragic life, and watching him taught me a lot about the bad side of show business, the leeches and the underbelly. All of us girls learned a lot when we worked with Elvis, a sad but so talented man."

As successful as the Sweet Inspirations were in the rhythm-and-blues world, their larger appeal was disappointingly limited. With the exception of their signature song, "Sweet Inspiration," they never "crossed over," were never successful in the pop marketplace. Subsequent albums for Atlantic (*Songs of Faith and Inspiration, What the World Needs Now Is Love,* and *Sweets for My Sweet*) did little to change things, even though, according to most critics, all were superior to their debut album.

Traditionally, girl groups of the sixties who projected themselves as rhythm-and-blues rather than pop stars—such groups as the Glories, Patti Labelle and the Bluebelles, the Toys, and, to a lesser extent, Martha and the Vandellas—had only short, albeit respectable, careers. Actually, the Sweet Inspirations fared better than most industry observers might have predicted, since acts who made a name for themselves as background singers—like the Raelettes and the Blossoms—rarely achieved commercial success with their own singles and albums.

Stewart Green, a music critic of the time, noted other factors that kept Cissy Houston and the Sweet Inspirations from breaking into the mainstream. "The girls could sing rings around someone like the Supremes, but they didn't have a Berry Gordy backing them. They were entertaining strictly on a musical level, but they didn't have the polish required to make it on their own on TV variety shows and such. And that's how you promoted a group on a major level back then."

John Houston, who had continued managing the group over the years, was frustrated because they never seemed to do as well financially as many other groups during the sixties. "They never made any real money, not even with the one big hit ['Sweet Inspiration']. That song was basically to insure that we could get live bookings. The record company made all of the money."

John Houston persevered despite the ultimate commercial failure of the Sweet Inspirations, and he continued to learn about the difficulties and complexities of show business and contracts. He was, and is, a tenacious man. In later years, Houston—who now helps to manage his daughter's career and has supervised recording and engagement contracts that have made Whitney a wealthy young woman—would not make the mistakes he made in the 1960s.

Whitney was clearly aware of her mother's frustration. Upon returning from road trips, Cissy was happy to see her family, though her professional disappointments were never far from her mind. But she was philosophical. "If God wants this for me," she'd say, "then, fine. If not, I will just have to accept it."

By 1969, at the age of six, Whitney had begun to develop a strikingly pure voice and was expressing an interest in show business. To encourage her, Cissy continued to allow her into the recording studio—though never again in the booth with the vocalists—and Whitney was exposed to more of the great singers of her time.

Occasionally, her childish antics made her a nuisance—running up and down the halls, slamming doors, playing hide-and-seek with no one in particular—but she was irresistibly precocious. "I'd be fooling around in the studio, in everyone's way, I'm sure, and talking to my 'Auntie Ree,' who I didn't know was Aretha Franklin, a famous singer," recalls Whitney. "To me, she was just a friend of the family."

"Wherever Cissy went, there was Whitney," said a friend in New Jersey. "Mother and daughter went to all of those sessions together, whenever possible. Whitney was just inundated with soul music, with producers, musicians, singers. . . . What an education that kid got! She was there when the Sweeties—as the Sweet

Inspirations were called by some of us—did backup vocals for songs on Dee Dee Warwick's [Dionne's sister] first solo album. She was there for the recording of solo songs by Cissy that never came out on Atlantic. She was there when Dionne recorded albums for Scepter Records. Whitney was always there, watching and learning.

"Patti Labelle—who is also from New Jersey and was, with her group the Bluebells, also signed to Atlantic Records at this time—came into the studio one day to hear Dionne record something, and I remember her saying, 'Oh, there's that cute little Whitney girl.' And Dionne said, 'She's always here. She's our little good luck charm!'"

Whitney later recalled wishing she could go on the road with her mother, but it was not permitted. Even on those occasions when John joined Cissy on the road to manage her affairs and those of the Sweet Inspirations—especially when they toured with Aretha Franklin—Whitney and her brothers remained behind, sent to stay with friends in the nearby projects.

The Newark projects were typically impoverished and generally unsafe for children—all of which was quite an education for Whitney, a little girl who had become accustomed to a better way of life. Looking around at her surroundings—bleak streets, garbage-filled alleyways, and the unmistakable evidence that life was not valued here in the ways that she understood—young Whitney was surely struck by the differences.

Although she might not have been able to articulate what she felt, she doubtless had a new appreciation of her parents' frequent absences and of the *work* they did, the *work* that kept them and her far away from the kind of life many of the projects' children knew and would never escape.

. . .

By 1970, problems had come up within the ranks of
the Sweet Inspirations.

Marjorie Brookes, who worked for the Queen
Booking Corp. in New York, which scheduled the
group's engagements, remembered, "There was some
friction among the girls as to what direction they should
take, and this was very upsetting to Cissy. The problem,
as I saw it, was that Cissy was the leader, the take-
charge type. The others had to listen to what she said,
and her way—her *sound*—didn't seem to be clicking. So
they wanted to try some other things. But Cissy
wouldn't have it, even though the rhythm-and-blues
style she was into wasn't working. One of the girls, I
recall, proposed something more slick, like the
Supremes. Cissy was cool to that idea.

"Another issue," recalled Brookes, "was that when
Aretha Franklin went to Paris in 1968 to record a live
album at the Olympia Theater, she wanted to take the
Sweet Inspirations with her. But Cissy didn't want to go
because Whitney was under the weather, and she
wasn't going to leave her.

"'Look, I got a family life, too,' she said. 'My child is
sick with the flu, and I'm not going anywhere until she's
better. I'm sorry, but that's the way it is.'"

"The other three said, 'Fine, then we'll go without
you. We've never been to Paris, so we're going.' But
Cissy put her foot down and said, 'No, ladies, this is *my*
group and if I'm not going then *no one* is going.'

"So that was that. Aretha found three other girls—
the Sweethearts of Soul—and went on with the show.

"Myrna, Estelle, and Sylvia were angry at Cissy
about that for a long time. They never got over it. But
Cissy's position was clear: 'There are some things more

important than show business.' That's true, of course, but it doesn't make it easier to juggle things, and for Cissy [the juggling] was becoming impossible."

It was difficult for Cissy to make these kinds of choices, especially since other people's lives and careers were on the line as well. Sometimes, however, bound by performing contracts, she was forced to leave her family and go to Europe when she really didn't want to.

Marjorie Brookes remembers that "when Whitney was five, she was in a school play and was very excited about it. She wanted her mother there, desperately. But we had booked the Sweet Inspirations for an engagement in Italy at the San Remo Festival, where they'd been nominated for a 'Best Performer' award. After we booked the engagement, Cissy told us about Whitney's play and wondered if we could cancel. But it was too late to cancel without facing a lawsuit.

"So Cissy had to go on with the show, though she was very unhappy about leaving Whitney. She explained to Whitney, 'Mama has to work. I wish I could be there for you, but it's just not possible.'"

"Cissy told me that Whitney cried, and was very disappointed. I've always believed that Cissy made a decision at that time that she would leave the group."

Reluctantly, Cissy finally approached John with the idea of venturing out as a solo artist, leaving Myrna, Estelle, and Sylvia to fend for themselves. John said he would support her, no matter what decision she made.

She chose to leave.

Her partners took it hard. "We were crushed," said one of them. "What a blow. Diana Ross had left the Supremes at that time. Do you think it's a coincidence that Cissy left us at the same time? Maybe Cissy was influenced by Diana's decision, I don't know."

"I don't know that Cissy wanted to be a solo star,"

added Estelle Brown, "as much as she wanted more
time with Whitney. The boys, she felt, were okay with
John. But Whitney was getting older and Cissy felt she
was missing out on her growing up. I remember her
saying, 'My little girl is going to be graduating from college before I even get the chance to know her. I can't
let that happen.' So what could we do? We had to just
go on and continue without her.

"We replaced Cissy with a girl from the Bronx
named Ann Williams and recorded one more album for
Atlantic [*Sweet, Sweet Soul—The Sweet Inspirations*]. But
without Cissy, the magic wasn't there, I guess. Soon,
the new girl we hired left the group. So we were left to
carry on as a trio."

(The remaining Sweet Inspirations continued performing, as onstage background singers for Elvis
Presley for the next eight years. They recorded an
excellent album, *Estelle, Myrna, and Sylvia,* for Stax in
1973, then appeared five years later on RSO Records
with the disco-oriented *Hot Butterfly.* That year, the
trio—without Estelle Brown, who was replaced by
Gloria Brown [no relation to Estelle]—toured as an
opening act for the Bee Gees.)

Today, Cissy Houston remains philosphical about
the Sweet Inspirations' career. "As a group, we had
our successes. We carved out our own little niche. All
of our dreams might not have come true, but God did
give us more success than most groups ever dreamed
of. So, we had our time. Praise God, we had our
time."

Cissy then signed with a small, independent label,
Janus Records, and released her first solo album, *Cissy
Houston,* in 1971. While choosing material for the
album, she ran across a song written by Mississippi-
based country artist Jim Weatherly. Weatherly had

recorded "The Midnight Plane to Houston" for his own album and it received moderate praise from the press and fans.

Cissy began to rehearse the song, never feeling completely at ease with the lyrics and tone. Within a short time, she had rewritten it, changing the main chorus and title to "The Midnight Train to Georgia." After clearing the changes with Weatherly, she recorded the song. She and John were extremely pleased with the results, feeling that the song would establish her as a solo artist.

However, even though "The Midnight Train to Georgia" was played on some radio stations and, in fact, received considerable response, it simply did not appear on the best-seller charts. The public was not buying the record.

"That should have been a hit record," John Houston says today. "Everywhere we turned, the song was being played."

Janus Records, however, balked at the cost of promoting the song, thereby effectively halting any chance for it to go "over the top." The Houstons were getting their first taste of the importance of strong and constant backing for an artist by the record label.

"A lousy $5,000 was all we needed to kick it over the top, to do the right kind of promotion," John Houston remembers angrily. "You are really at the record company's mercy if they decide not to plug your album, or if they don't have the money to promote it."

Two years later, in 1973, Cissy Houston watched as her song became one of the biggest hits ever for Gladys Knight and the Pips, who covered it on the Buddah label. Knight's version of the song stayed on the top of the *Billboard* charts for two weeks and sold over a million copies.

"That was painful for Cissy," said a friend. "That was her song. To see Gladys take it to the top—well, it wasn't easy. . . ."

Cissy continued to record, even after the lack of success of her first album. She was not, as anyone who knew her could attest, a woman who was inclined to give up. But ultimately, even Cissy began to have doubts. "I really don't know what went wrong," she says today. "But whatever happened left me feeling disgusted. I'd been in the business for a very long time, and it discouraged me immensely to see people who seemingly started yesterday ride straight to the top. I thought about quitting and just devoting myself to my family and the church for a time. But inside, I knew I would find success."

In 1989, Whitney Houston disclosed her own views regarding her mother's frustrations as a singer. "It just wasn't her time," Whitney has said. "My mother was way ahead of her time—the proof is me. I have the exact singing voice my mother did at my age."

It's true. The star-making machinery that churned out the Supremes, the Beatles, and contemporary superstars like Madonna, Janet Jackson, and Whitney Houston herself was not available for Cissy Houston. And John Houston, though a capable manager, was not a match for the Berry Gordys of the sixties or the Clive Davises of today. He simply did not have the know-how or the connections to turn his wife into a superstar.

By 1973, when Whitney was ten years old, Cissy began to cut back her work schedule to spend more time at home. She has no regrets about any missed career opportunities. "I wasn't worried about how my singing career might suffer," she remembered. "I finally realized how important it was for me to be there with my family."

Despite all of Cissy's heartfelt concern for her children, she was finally to recognize—though not until years later—that parental love can never soften the blows of reality. She did not realize that some of the very standards of excellence she imposed on her daughter were the cause of a torment she had not, and probably could not have, anticipated.

Whitney and her brothers, for example, attended a public grammar school along with the other children of the neighborhood. Whitney, an average but very shy student, was constantly teased by other children, usually because of her lighter skin and the "fancy" clothes Cissy made her wear.

Recalled longtime family friend Mildred Dickenson, "Whitney had a tough time of it. They called her terrible names because her skin was light and her hair was straight. She would cry and run home. She was always dressed in the best clothing money could buy, while the other girls were dressed in old hand-me-downs. Whitney had no older sisters, so all of her clothes were brand-new. She had new shoes, always polished, so she was taunted at school because of that. It wasn't easy for her. She was always such a sensitive child."

"I hated those clothes, those dresses I had to wear," Whitney later revealed. "But my mother made me wear them, no matter what."

"My daughter is special," Cissy would explain proudly. "And she will always present herself as being special."

But children don't want to be that kind of "special" when they're in school. Rather, they seek to conform, to be part of the group. So as a teenager, Whitney developed the habit of bringing old jeans to school, and changing into them before class, without Cissy's knowledge.

Once, she recalled, a thirteen-year-old girl pulled her braids, called her a name, and threatened her. The other girls, who had been watching, all pointed at Whitney and laughed at her. With tears streaming down her face, ten-year-old Whitney went home and announced, "I don't have to go to school anymore."

"What do you mean, you don't have to go to school anymore?" Cissy asked suspiciously.

"Well," Whitney began sheepishly, "the teacher said I was so good, so smart, that I didn't have to go back to school. Ever."

Cissy later recalled, "I wondered, 'Now what kind of nonsense is this?' I asked around and I heard that the little girls were picking on her. I thought it would pass, but it didn't."

"I would never just stand there and just get my ass kicked," Whitney said recently. "I would run. There'd be five, six, seven girls chasing me and threatening to kick my ass. Thank God, I was a fast runner."

On one occasion, when she was eleven years old, Whitney came running home with eight young girls tailing her, taunting her, calling her names, and threatening to beat her up. None of them was older than ten, but somehow they seemed much more mature. Much meaner.

"You'd be surprised at how tough those ten-year-old neighborhood girls were," Cissy once recalled with a laugh. "They'd kick your butt."

Whitney ran into the house, past her startled mother, into her room, then slammed the door behind her.

Cissy recalled, "I went out into the backyard, and there was this mob of girls. I saw the one who looked like the ringleader. A snotty little kid. I could've picked her up and tossed her into the air."

"Now, what has Whitney done to make you want to whoop her?" Cissy asked, trying to be reasonable.

The young girl stuck her chin out defiantly and said, "Oh, she just thinks she's so good. She thinks she's so pretty, she makes us sick."

Cissy walked closer to the youngster, towering over her by at least three feet. "You wanna kick my girl's butt, don't you?" she asked frankly.

"Yeah, I do," came the snippy response. The other seven girls in the posse just watched to see what would happen next.

"Well, you know you're gonna have to whip *my* butt before you'll be able to get past me to get to Whitney. And let me tell you something, little girl"—Cissy squinted her eyes menacingly—"I don't think you can whip my butt. Now, do you?"

The young girl wasn't easily cowed. She stared up at Cissy for a moment, then turned and walked back toward her cohorts. "And let me tell you something else," Cissy shouted out after them as they headed down the street. "Whitney isn't scared of you, either."

Of course, Cissy was lying, and knew it.

According to Whitney, as she related the story later, Cissy came into her bedroom, sat on her bed, and said, "Here's the deal. You are never going to get these girls off your back unless you whoop one of them. And you're going to have to whoop the biggest, strongest one—the ringleader. That's the one who needs an ass-kicking."

Whitney's eyes were big. "I can't do that," she said. "No way. I'm afraid."

"I know you're afraid, but you will do it," Cissy countered, "because if you kick her ass, then all the rest of them will leave you alone. And if you *don't* kick her ass, then I'm going to kick *your* ass."

Mother and daughter looked at each other for one silent beat.

As she got up off the bed Cissy said to her daughter, "I think we have an understanding, don't we?"

With that, she left the room, giving her daughter something to ponder.

The next day, Whitney went to school, and as she tells it, "I had no choice, did I? I had to fight. So I fought. I mean, I fought, man. And I did pretty good," she recalled, smiling at the memory. "To tell you the truth, I was more afraid of my mother kicking my butt than the girls at school doing it. Because my mother was *fierce*."

And the girls in school didn't bother Whitney much after that.

In fact, once she was having an argument with a little Caucasian girl. At the height of the childish squabble, the girl said to Whitney, "Oh, nigger."

Whitney's eyes flashed in anger. She recalled shoving the girl up against the wall. "If you can't call me anything else but my name—which is Whitney—next time, you might get hurt."

Then she backed away from the startled child, who thereafter probably stayed as far away from the girl named Whitney as she could.

Though Cissy's standards may sometimes have seemed too demanding, John was apt to spoil his youngest child and only daughter. "He was so attentive, so affectionate to us children," Whitney related in later years. "As a husband, he treated my mother like a lady, with respect—bringing us both flowers on Valentine's day or on birthdays."

However, Whitney also remembers her father as a stern authority figure. "When he got mad, he laid down the law and we all abided by it. My father slapped me once and, another time, spanked me. I was running off at the mouth and should have stopped while I was ahead. But, mostly he was a softy."

John Houston recalled another occasion of family discipline: "Whitney was about seven and her brother Michael was a couple of years older. They were acting up while I was trying to read. So I said, 'Look, after I finish this book, at exactly four o'clock, I am gonna whip your butt.'"

As John remembered it, Michael turned to Whitney and said, "I don't know about you, but I ain't waiting around here until four o'clock to get my butt whipped. I'm leaving."

"Take me. Take me," young Whitney implored.

So the two youngsters went into their bedrooms and packed small suitcases. They walked out the front door and headed down the street.

Ten minutes later, Cissy came into the living room and asked John where the children were. "Oh, they ran away," John said nonchalantly, still absorbed in his book.

"What!" Cissy exclaimed. "Now, you go on after them."

John winced, got up from his chair, went outside, and saw his two children walking down the street holding their little suitcases. A moment later, a wide-eyed Whitney looked over her shoulder—and saw her father. She quickly turned away. Finally, the two of them arrived at the corner. They put their bags down and looked in both directions, as if to say, "Now, where do we go from here?"

Suddenly, John spoke up, loud enough for them to hear. "You pick up those bags right now and come back in this direction."

The two runaways, exchanging a few meaningful glances, consulted silently with each other. Then, presumably after comparing the benefits of never again having to accede to their father's wishes with the uncertainty of homelessness, they decided to give John Houston another chance. Brother and sister obeyed.

"Oh, we were so cute, he couldn't even whip us," Whitney remembered with a smile. "He just walked us back into the house, said something like 'go unpack those bags and get ready for dinner,' and that was that. That was our big moment. Our big running-away-from-home scene. Mother chose to ignore it, thank goodness. . . ."

A mischievous child, Whitney sometimes got herself into trouble, and once came frighteningly close to a tragedy. When she was about seven, she and her brother were playing in her bedroom. Whitney was "fooling around," holding a wire clothes hanger in her mouth. She remembers, "I was standing there, swinging [the hanger] back and forth, when my brother brought his hand up to my face and accidentally shoved the wire right down my throat."

When Whitney attempted to remove the hanger's stem, she felt something tearing deep in her throat. The thick wire, when she pulled it out, was covered in blood. Blood was also gushing from her mouth, and she cried out in pain and in horror.

The shrieking child was rushed to the hospital by her father. The doctors found that the hanger wire had nearly severed her soft palate, which was hanging by a mere thread of flesh in the back of her throat. Surgery was begun immediately.

Following the long procedure, Whitney's doctor joined John and her brother and stepbrother in the waiting room. He informed the family that Whitney might never speak again, and that only time would tell.

After the doctor left, the family prayed together.

"It didn't look good," John recalled. "There was a good chance she'd never say another word."

Cissy Houston was on the road, but her mother's intuition told her something was terribly wrong back home. She called John, who did not want to alarm her. He said she was mistaken, that there was no problem.

Cissy remembers insisting, "Something is not right. I can feel it. Now you tell me what is wrong with my baby, right now."

Eventually, John related the day's events to his wife. Cissy was horrified, and returned home to Newark immediately. "It was the worst time of all," she would later remember.

In a few weeks, though, Whitney began to speak again.

"It was definitely something to turn over to the Lord," Cissy said. And who, in the face of her daughter's recovery, could argue?

"It's difficult for me to believe that I came so close to losing my voice, the very instrument on which I depend so much," Whitney has said. "My voice is the one thing that has really given me my identity, at least where show business is concerned. To think it could have been lost, that everything from that moment on could have been changed. . . .

"That little incident taught me something very important," she added. "Every moment is precious. In just a thoughtless instant, your whole life can change. I know it taught me to be thankful to the Lord, not just for the big things but for all things—including things that, thankfully, haven't happened. Whenever I think of that accident with the hanger, I get goose bumps. . . ."

In addition to her work as a background vocalist, Cissy was the minister of music at Newark's New Hope

Baptist Church. "You would have thought Cissy was getting paid to be at that church," remembered Memphis Gardner, a onetime member of the congregation. "If you wanted to bring anything to the church in regard to the music, you had to check with Miss Cissy." Gardner continued, "She was very touchy about it, too. But if you were there on any given Sunday, you could understand why. She had those folks singing like professionals. People used to come in from all over New Jersey just to hear her sing."

Thus, as a youngster, Whitney Houston was exposed to the purest form of gospel music. At church and at home, she lived with and was surrounded by its raw emotion and deep feelings.

Tony Heilbut writes in his book *The Gospel Sound*, "Behind all of the dignity, the great emphasis on posture and wardrobe traditional to the black church, is an implicit sense of bad news in bad times. Gospel lyrics may sound banal, but they talk of the things that matter most to poor people. A poor man's concerns are mostly about staying alive—'I could have been dead, sleeping in my grave,' 'It's another day's journey and I'm glad of it,' and so on."

The singing in Baptist churches has a very special kind of beauty and strength. Novelist and essayist James Baldwin describes the power of gospel music: "There is no music like that music, no drama like the drama of the saints rejoicing, the sinners moaning . . . and all of those voices crying together."

Whitney had heard one kind of music and enjoyed a special kind of experience in the recording studio with exciting rhythm-and-blues stars. But this was something different. The music young Whitney heard as she sat on her father's lap at church, watching her mother direct the choir, was filled with even greater emotion and intensity. She witnessed the congregation rising to its feet, calling back to the singers, and shouting out its approval and love. The room would be alive with the pride and fervor of the congregation, seeming, many times, as though it would split the roof open. Whitney's eyes grew wide at the pure passion that swelled from the choir. The Apollo—with the Atlantic Records' Annual Revue—was terrific, but this church experience was beyond description.

And its power was something that Whitney merely observed. One afternoon, John Houston returned from his part-time job as a truck driver to a seemingly empty house, and heard strange noises emanating from beneath his feet. Slowly, he opened the door to the basement and was blasted by sound.

He remembers, "I heard all this hollerin' and screamin' down in the basement, and Whitney was down there with one of Cissy's microphones, singing along with records of Aretha Franklin. I knew her mother was training her [but] I couldn't tell if she had a voice or not. She'd be trying this or that, and her voice would be cracking and then she'd go flat. 'Can you do something about that kid?' I'd ask her mother."

In November 1975, at the age of twelve, Whitney was ready, in effect, to announce her arrival. She would make her debut at the New Hope Baptist Church.

"One day," recalls John Houston, "Cissy said, 'Your baby is soloing in church this Sunday. I'm going to be out of town, so you be there!'"

Of course, John would have gone anyway, but just in case he'd not understood the significance of the event, Cissy had let him know that his presence would be—ah, *required*. No sense in not making myself clear, Cissy probably thought.

That Sunday, young Whitney sang her first solo in

church. "It was never the same for me after that," she has recalled. "That Sunday, I sang and the place went crazy. At first, it was scary. I couldn't believe the reaction. It was an amazing spiritual experience. It was also a turning point. From that point on, I knew I would sing. I knew I *had* to sing."

three ◠

By 1977, it seemed to some industry watchers
that Cissy Houston might finally have found her niche.
Now recording for Private Stock Records, she released
her most successful album to date, once again titled
Cissy Houston, produced by Michael Zager. The album
contained her renditions of several hit songs, all fashioned to highlight her soulful gospel style, including "He
Ain't Heavy, He's My Brother" (originally recorded by
the Hollies), "Make It Easy on Yourself" (also recorded
by Jerry Butler and Dionne Warwick), and a timeless
version of "Tomorrow," the popular song from the hit
Broadway musical *Annie.* Cissy transformed that
lightweight, "up" tune into a gospel-tinged proclamation
of hope for a brighter day—very likely wondering if
perhaps the sun was finally going to "come up" on her
career.

Whitney appeared among the background vocalists
on all but one of the album's cuts. It was her first experience working in the recording studio and was, she has
recalled, "very exciting."

At the same time, Cissy created a nightclub act to showcase her formidable talent and promote the new album. This cabaret act—which she performed in Manhattan—drew capacity crowds; new and old fans alike reserved tables weeks in advance at clubs such as Reno Sweeney's in Greenwich Village and Les Mouches on Eleventh Avenue and West Twenty-sixth Street.

Cissy's career seemed to be on the upswing. A second album was anticipated.

Meanwhile, as Cissy persisted, trying to make it big in the music business, a teenage Whitney continued to sing in church and be coached at home by her mother. During those adolescent years, Whitney alternately succumbed to and resisted the lure of show-business glamour. Certainly, watching her mother's disappointment and frustration had not failed to make an impression on her. Finally, however, when she was about fifteen, Whitney decided that, yes, she wanted to follow in her mother's footsteps. And considering what she had come to understand—that something in her could stir and take form and swell up to express itself through her voice—she very likely couldn't have made any other choice and remained true to herself. Perhaps it was the choice that every truly gifted person makes: *Do I give what I have, regardless?*

Cissy insisted that Whitney be realistic at all times about the business. "She prepared me for all of the things to come," remembers Whitney. "She taught me that fame is not all it's cracked up to be. Sometimes you may love it, and sometimes you may really grow to hate it." At the time, Whitney could hardly have imagined how prophetic that teaching would turn out to be.

As she was preparing her daughter for a music

career, Cissy also found herself confronting what every parent of a teenager anticipates in theory but no parent is quite ready for: the time when the angelic, sweet-smiling child turns into a young adult who discovers the power of grown-up self-assertion—which often means the power of talking back and letting Mom know childhood is over. Thus, Cissy found herself in the role of a sparring partner for her suddenly rebellious young daughter. And it wasn't fun, for not every sound that came out of Whitney's mouth was a song.

A few of Whitney's girlfriends had apparently taught her how to "sass," and Whitney used every opportunity to her advantage as she sought to improve her skills—on her mother. She had talked back only once to her father, for which her reward was a sore backside. Cissy gave her a little bit more room, but once a certain line had been crossed, Cissy was not reluctant to let her petulant daughter know it. All it took was a look—or sometimes a swat.

"My mother always had it in control," Whitney has recalled. "She was the kind of mother who didn't play. She was very strict. And you conducted yourself accordingly. She sort of said, 'Where you tear your ass is where you get it torn.' And she meant it, too. She'd beat your brains out if you didn't listen."

Cissy recalls with a laugh, "She would try to talk back—'try me'—that sort of thing. But I wouldn't tolerate it. She was lazier than hell, stubborn, and opinionated. When she was sixteen, I told her she wasn't gonna make it to seventeen, 'cause I was gonna kill her!

"I'd tell her to make sure those dishes were up and dried, which she hated to do. She hated to wash dishes. In fact, she hated to do anything, so I knew she was going to have to be a star or something, because she was too damn lazy to do anything for herself."

Like most young girls, Whitney found that *she* now wanted to decide how to wear her hair and to choose the clothes she wore to school. She loved nothing more than to have her hair loose and cascading to her shoulders. Jeans were her favorite item of clothing, and when boys became interesting to her, she spent more time with her brothers' friends than with her own.

When Whitney was in grammar school, Cissy and John Houston decided to send her to a private high school when the time came. The Houstons were unhappy with conditions in the New Jersey public school system and feared the rising violence that was erupting in schools across the United States.

Mount St. Dominic Academy in West Caldwell, New Jersey, seemed the perfect place to send their daughter—even though it was a Catholic school. There, Whitney would receive the finest education available and, her parents hoped, bond with girls her own age who would be good influences. (Clearly, while Cissy's career had not brought commercial success at the level she sought, it allowed her to send her daughter to a private school.)

Whitney entered the academy with strong reservations, most of them arising from her feeling about attending an all-girls school. She was shy with strangers, a throwback to the days when she was teased by other children because of her "Anglo" looks and the neatly pressed dresses her mother forced her to wear. The same issues immediately surfaced at St. Dominic. "The girls all had problems with me," Whitney recalls. "My face was too light. My hair was too long. It was a black-consciousness period, and I felt really bad."

Whitney desperately wanted to fit in, but in reaction to being criticized and teased, she became even more of a loner. This behavior was interpreted by the other girls

as "snootiness," and Whitney found herself further
ostracized. "I finally faced the fact that it isn't a crime
not to have any friends," she recalled rather glumly in
1991. "Being alone means you have fewer problems."

While Whitney may have truly believed she was perfectly fine without friends, one can only speculate about
the real pain she was denying, for every schoolgirl needs
friends with whom she can share secrets, laugh at jokes,
and enjoy movies and books.

Of course, her tendency to be a loner was later
intensified by her entering a profession in which genuine friendships are often rare and exploitation in the
guise of friendship is commonplace. "When I decided to
become a singer, my mother warned me that I would
be alone a lot. Basically we [entertainers] all are.
Loneliness comes with life as an entertainer."

By 1977, John Houston had become increasingly
restless and frustrated by his lack of success in the music
industry. Some associates claim that he felt he had
failed Cissy. Although a capable business manager, he
had been unable to guide his wife's career in any positive fashion. When she was working, he was behind the
scenes earning his percentage as her manager. But
sometimes, when she was on the road, he had to find
side jobs, usually with the City of Newark. For him,
such work was less than rewarding, and John was
becoming as frustrated in his life as Cissy was in hers.

Soon, they began to argue—at first over trivial things
and then, eventually, over more important matters.
Should he find a "real job"? Should Cissy quit show
business and find *herself* a "real job"? When Cissy was
out of town, John later recalled, he was glad to have
her gone. And Cissy had told friends she was happy to
be gone. The marriage was in major trouble.

Whitney and her brothers loved their parents and listened through the doors of their rooms, in tears, as John and Cissy battled it out until all hours of the morning. John said he felt neglected; Cissy, in turn, was worried about the lack of physical affection of late. On the surface, the family seemed to continue as it always had, but the Houston children found mealtimes to be increasingly silent affairs, with both Cissy and John rushing away from the table upon finishing.

Whitney felt the pain her parents must have been going through as they struggled to keep the family together. "When times were hard, they fought," she said to *Time* magazine, "which taught me a lot about love and sacrifice. For a while, they stayed together for our sake, but finally they realized that the only way to stay friends was to split." In late 1977, John moved out of the family home and into a small apartment ten minutes away.

Whitney, who was "Daddy's little girl," was struck the hardest by her parents' separation. She dared not speak of it to her schoolfriends, as she was unwilling to give them yet another reason to talk about her behind her back. She armored herself while attending class, smiling politely to classmates in the hall and concentrating on her studies, her heart breaking all the while.

Sister Barbara Moore, a teacher at Mount St. Dominic during Whitney's time there, remembers Whitney as an average student, who kept to herself and seemed to mask her inner pain with comical behavior. "One year the class went to Disneyland," Sister Barbara recalled. "There was a circus, one where the children were allowed to get involved. I walked into the arena and there, walking high on the tightrope, was Whitney—and she was waving at me! I knew the career

plans her mother had for her and I thought, 'If that
child falls and breaks her legs, her mother will break
mine.'"

Teenage Whitney Houston continued her studies—
both at Mount St. Dominic and onstage with her mother, in New York. But she kept to herself, uncertain
about her future. No longer struggling over whether she
should become a veterinarian or a doctor—vocations
she had once mentioned to her parents as alternatives
to show business—she simply accepted that fate would
lead her in a positive direction. Her mother's philoso-
phy about "the magic of believing" seemed to have
sunk in. "I just believed things would fall into place,"
she has recalled. "And when I believed that, they did."

A life in the music business now seemed inevitable.
But at what price? As she lived through the painful separation of her beloved parents, trying to be supportive to
both, she silently wondered if such events were the
unavoidable results of fame. Whitney prayed that she
would someday find happiness—both professionally and
personally. "My mother's theory about the magic of
believing is what I always fell back on," she would later
say. "In believing you will find your way, you *will* find
your way. Or, as it says in the Bible, 'It's done unto you
as you believe.' So I always tried to maintain a positive
attitude about my life and the decisions I had to make.
It wasn't easy, I have to admit. I slipped more than a
few times."

Indeed, according to some friends, her parents'
impending divorce had a devastating effect on Whitney,
causing her to wonder if she could ever trust anyone to
stay by her side or if everyone she loved would disappoint and abandon her.

At Cissy's suggestion, Whitney volunteered to be a
counselor at a local summer camp. She had an innate

love for children, and though she was barely beyond childhood herself, she knew she could be a positive role model for these youngsters, many of whom were from the Newark projects. The camp offered crafts, sing-alongs, and other activities that allowed the children a respite from the unsafe streets of the neighborhoods. Whitney jumped right in and, though fatigued from the nights performing with her mother, found herself truly enjoying the influence she was having on the kids.

When Robyn Crawford, another camp counselor, began to strike up conversations with her, Whitney found, for the first time, a friend who did not judge her or shun her for her looks or talent. Two years older than Whitney, Robyn seemed to understand her on a deep, emotional level. The two of them began to spend time together, and Whitney was finally able to open up to someone and share her dreams, hopes, and pain. "She was the sister I never had," Whitney would later say.

"I did a lot of listening," remembers Robyn, who encouraged her new friend's talent and put up with Whitney's tendency to burst into song in the middle of a conversation. The two became inseparable, leading tongue-waggers in East Orange to speculate about the nature of their intimacy.

"It just seemed odd, these two girls always together," remembered one friend. "They even started to look alike. It got to the point where you couldn't tell where one ended and the other began. They would walk arm-in-arm in public. It all seemed somewhat odd. When they were together, they'd act as if no one else was even in the room. They had their own world. People didn't understand it."

Whitney recalls with a laugh, "People used to say we were gay, because when you saw Robyn, you saw me and when you saw me, you saw Robyn. We were that tight, you know."

Whitney, who was already accustomed to being the outsider in her neighborhood, could not believe that her relationship with her "sister" could arouse such gossip, and she had a number of loud disagreements with other camp counselors about it.

"I remember one particularly nasty fight," said the friend. "Someone accused Whitney of being a 'dyke.' [The person] said she knew for a fact that she and Robyn were lovers. Whitney's eyes flashed with anger. 'Oh, you do, do you?' she shot back. The next thing I knew, Whitney had this girl pinned up against the wall. She was all up in her face. 'If I ever hear you spreading gossip about me, it'll be the last time you ever do,' Whitney warned her. After word of that got around, it was just understood that you didn't mess with Whitney Houston. Her mother had apparently taught her how to fight; she wasn't afraid of anyone. She was one tough girl. And you certainly didn't mess with Robyn Crawford. She was fierce. There were counselors who would quickly walk the other way when Robyn came into a room just because they were afraid they would accidentally say the wrong thing, or imply the wrong thing. Basically, it got to the point where you just let Whitney and Robyn alone."

Still, the two friends were not deaf; they could hear the whisperings around them. At first they shrugged it all off. "This thing kind of followed us," Whitney recalled. "And half the time we'd just say, 'Fuck it. If they think we're gay, let 'em think we're gay.'"

However, the rumors intensified, creating hurt and anger between herself and her friend. "Why are you letting this bother you now?" Robyn wanted to know.

"Because people are starting to know me. I'm not so

anonymous anymore. And it does bother me. I can't help it." Whitney remembers, "It got to be a pain in the ass. No matter how much you try not to let them bother you, [rumors] do bother you."

Robyn understood Whitney's frustration. Still, say friends, she was not about to let any nasty gossip ruin her life. "It came to a showdown between the two of them," remembers one friend. "Robyn finally said, 'Look, Whitney, if you can't handle the fact that people think we're lesbians, if that's so goddamn offensive to you, then, fine, we just won't be friends anymore. See you 'round. It's been fun. Later.'

"'Hey, I can handle it if you can,' Whitney said, boldly."

Weeks went by; whenever the two would see each other they quickly walked the other way to avoid any kind of emotional encounter.

"Whitney's heart was breaking," says the friend. "She missed Robyn terribly. They had shared so much. Finally, Whitney came to her and said, 'I can't do this. It's silly. I wasn't even raised this way, to run from problems. My mother always taught me to face things head-on. We have to be friends, no matter what.' Whitney and Robyn determined to keep their deep friendship alive, deciding that their bond was stronger than small-town gossip." Whitney would later remember telling Robyn on that day of reconciliation, "We're friends. I love you, you love me. Why should we not be friends? Because of what people say and what they think? Look, you gotta live your life. You can't let outsiders ruin it for you."

The young woman had learned a lesson that she would, over and over again, need to remember as her life continued, and as her career began to blossom.

• • •

If self-confidence and pugnaciousness are genetic, Whitney inherited these traits from her feisty mother. In many ways, Cissy Houston was a prizefighter who refused to stay down for the count. She went round after round with her opponent—show business. She remained on her feet through sheer willpower and faith in God. Record after record, show after show, tour after tour—she continued to fight.

Why couldn't she make it? It wasn't a question of talent; her work as a sessions singer had shown the pop-music industry exactly what she was worth. The consensus—at least in the Houston camp—was that a good old-fashioned conspiracy was to blame. "When record companies have wanted to star Cissy," John Houston said in the late seventies, "the big names on their labels—people she's backed—have threatened to split."

This possibility is not without substance. In fact, in a business where many recording artists seem to have as much ego and insecurity as they do talent, it is not uncommon for popular acts to balk privately at their label's signing someone whose musical repertoire, or image, is similar to their own. Indeed, if an artist has been successful enough, that artist may actually come forward to management and log a formal complaint.

In 1991, for example, Janet Jackson signed a record contract with Virgin-America reportedly worth more than $50 million, after recording the multimillion-selling albums *Control* and *Rhythm Nation* for the A&M label. Not everyone was happy about this turn of events. And Paula Abdul, Virgin's hit dance-music artist, made her displeasure clear. She'd been there—at Virgin—*first*, after all. To appease Abdul, the company revised her original contract to include the distribution of Captive, her own label, and the promise that Paula Abdul projects would never play second fiddle to Janet's.

Observed one Columbia Records executive, "There was a black, female star on our label who was put out when—at one point in Cissy's career—Cissy signed on the dotted line. As she put it, 'That woman has sung background for me. If you think I'm gonna stand in her shadow, you're wrong. You'd better make sure she never gets no bigger than me.' That was the sentiment. And that kind of thinking had a big hand in undermining Cissy's career."

Cissy probably didn't help matters by making such occasional self-glorifying statements as the following to the media: "I know that when I get up on that stage to sing background vocals, chances are I can out-sing whoever the star is. I can usually sing circles around the star. It's always been that way. . . ."

"She was always self-confident, almost to the point of being cocky," noted one associate. "And she most certainly passed this trait on to Whitney. Today, Whitney is certain that no singer out there can match her in terms of vocal power and technique."

In early 1978, Cissy decided that Whitney's joining her onstage as a vocalist would be good experience for her daughter—as long as it didn't interfere with her schoolwork. Whitney had become quite the showstopper at church on Sundays, and Cissy felt she was ready for a different kind of audience.

"I basically told her that the opportunity was there for her if she wanted it," Cissy noted in an interview. "I said it was up to her. But I knew in my heart she wanted it."

Upon hearing the suggestion, Whitney at first froze up. Singing in church for friends and family was one thing. But to stand before a paying audience was completely different. Ultimately, however, it was not so different that Whitney would turn down the opportunity. Cissy incorporated her into the act slowly, using her as a backup vocalist.

"My mother is the only person who can make me cry when she sings," Whitney once recalled. "She and Barbra Streisand. My mother has such emotion, such a gift, such presence. She's so warm and friendly onstage. I used to watch her when I was singing background vocals for her. I would watch and see how the people would respond to her. They were so into her, and she was so into them. It was as if she was talking to each one of them personally. That's the kind of entertainer I wanted to be."

Whitney would have her chance when Cissy made the decision to allow her daughter a solo number in the act. It was to be a ballad version of "Tomorrow," from *Annie,* during an engagement at Town Hall on West Forty-third Street in Manhattan. And Cissy is quick to point out that while she obviously had the option to bring Whitney into the act, this was to be no free ride. Her daughter had to live up to certain professional expectations. If the teenager could not hold her own, she'd be out.

Whitney recalls that Cissy sat down with her on the day of her first solo performance and explained the rules of the game. "She encouraged me to make the most of the opportunity," says Whitney. "'Show no mercy,' she said. 'Because if it was me out there, I wouldn't show any for you.' In other words, she wanted me to do my best and not be intimidated by the fact that I was on my mother's stage, sitting on her throne, so to speak."

Cissy remembers asking her daughter, "Whitney, do you believe you can do this?"

"Yes, I do."

"And do you believe in the magic of believing?"

"I do," she said.

And that was enough for both of them.

It was February 18, 1978. The big night had arrived.

Cissy assembled a prodigious fifty-voice choir for background accompaniment just for this engagement. Whitney was added to that choir—just another voice in the crowd. The gentlemen wore plain black suits while the ladies dressed in simple white blouses with black knee-length skirts.

By contrast, Cissy—ever the star—was dressed to kill in a floor-length, hot-pink, bugle-beaded number so resplendent it looked like it cost a million dollars. Her shoulder-length hair was streaked with blond highlights, a stunning contrast to her ebony complexion. When she smiled, her warmth filled the room. When she sang, she brought the crowd to their feet. The audience adored her.

Midway into the show, after her rousing rendition of "Midnight Train to Georgia," the magic moment arrived. "Ladies and gentlemen," Cissy announced, "I have a surprise for you. My daughter is going to sing for you this evening, so make her feel welcome." And then, with a proud smile: "Ladies and gentlemen, Miss Whitney Houston."

There was only a smattering of polite applause. Wouldn't you know it, some of the audience members probably groused, her old lady thinks the kid can sing, so now she's going to foist her on us. We paid good money for this?

Bashfully, Whitney moved slowly to the front of the stage and extended her right arm to her beaming mother. Cissy gently placed a microphone in her daughter's hand. Whitney gripped it tightly. It was as if Cissy had officially passed on the baton. She whispered something—words of encouragement?—into her daughter's ear as the polite applause subsided.

After a moment, the band started to fill the room with an engaging melody. Cissy began the song in a big, proud voice: "The sun'll come out tomorrow. Bet your bottom dollar that tomorrow, there'll be sun. . . ."

After singing one more verse, Cissy took a few steps backward and seemed to vanish into darkness. It was Whitney's turn now. The baby-blue spotlight found her, and the youngster started to sing.

But when she opened her mouth, the first few notes seemed a little off.

A man in the audience cleared his throat. Someone else coughed.

Uh-oh.

Whitney was uncertain. Panic played on her face. She looked back at the shadow of her mother, who was now leaning up against the piano and sipping a drink. Cissy offered no help whatsoever. In fact, her expression seemed to say, "Hey, this is it, girl. And the answer ain't back here."

Whitney turned to face her audience. She closed her eyes for a moment, found her place in the song, and with it a certain confidence. Then two minutes into the number the music arrived at a moment of well-calculated, dramatic modulation. As the choir came in with an authoritative, forceful chord, Whitney's voice started to soar.

Suddenly, she began to sustain a note as if it were the last one she'd ever sing. The choir joined in with the full-bodied thunder of male and female voices. Immediately, the audience was on its feet, where it would remain for the duration of the performance. As

Whitney hit the final notes of the song, she received a standing ovation.

"One more time," Cissy shouted out over the din. "Let's hear that one more time, girl."

The band picked up the song halfway through, and Whitney slipped back into the arrangement where she belonged, the applause seeming to empower her and fill her with even more confidence. "Tomorrow," she sang, her voice somehow seeming much riper than her fourteen years could possibly have permitted. "I love you, tomorrow. . ."

And the audience was right there with her, on its feet, shouting and applauding.

"You're only a day a-a-a-a-a-a-a-a-a-a-way."

Big finish.

Blackout.

Another standing ovation.

Whitney Houston had arrived.

After the song, Cissy just stood in place, stunned. She shook her head, as if even she could not believe what she'd just witnessed, then walked over to Whitney, who also seemed somewhat dazed. The two embraced, as if time itself were suspended. Mother and daughter melted into each other's arms, gazing at one another with tears in their eyes. For them, it was probably as if no one else were in the room.

Then, as Cissy moved to center stage, Whitney went back to her place with the choir.

"You know what?" Cissy asked the audience with mock exasperation as she wiped away the tears and tried to regain her composure. "That girl showed me no mercy."

four

If fifteen-year-old Whitney Houston hoped her performance at Town Hall would generate enthusiasm in the media, she must have been sorely disappointed. Since she'd read rave reviews of Cissy's performances over the years, she probably dreamed the same kind of reaction would greet her own debut. None of the critics, however, gave more than a passing mention to her performance that winter evening.

Soul magazine's critic raved about her mother's "slinky, pink gown, the most smashing outfit she's ever worn," her "blonde-streaked hair," her "streamlined, perfectly crafted act," and her "raucous, well-rehearsed fifty-voice choir." At the end of the lengthy review, in what appeared to be an afterthought, the critic added, "An extra treat was the appearance of Cissy's daughter, Whiten [sic], who successfully sang 'Tomorrow' from *Annie* to great response, even after a lukewarm, somewhat shaky start. 'She showed me no mercy,' exclaimed proud mama Cissy at the end of Whiten's [sic] performance."

The critics may not have taken much notice, but for Whiten—er, *Whitney*—that evening marked a milestone. "What a night!" she has recalled. "I found out that there was something inside of me that made me feel incredible when I am singing. It really is like magic.

"I was pretty nervous [at Town Hall]. I was scared to death, in fact. I just fell in love with my mom that night. She was so wonderful. But I was very, very scared."

Whitney's father, who was employed by the city of Newark at the time, simply observed that his young daughter blossomed whenever she took the stage. "This little girl definitely became a woman whenever she opened her mouth to sing," he said to a reporter, with a smile.

Ironically, just as Whitney was beginning to think in terms of unlimited possibilities in show business, her mother was starting to consider her own limitations. In fact, after that pivotal night at Town Hall, Cissy Houston told a reporter for *Rolling Stone* that she wasn't completely satisfied with the size of the crowds she had been drawing. "I'd just like to know I can command that really big audience," she mused. "Really give of myself and see the people react—like they do in church. When that happens, it's hard to hold back the tears. That's a singer's reward.

"I'm giving myself five more years," she told the reporter. "And if I don't make it in five years, then I'm finished."

Meanwhile, Cissy was faced with other challenges at home. She felt guilty about the breakup of her marriage and the effect it was having on her children. "It's difficult," she told J. Randy Taraborrelli in a 1977 interview. "Raising children on your own isn't easy, especially if you're a show-business mother. I do the best I can, but I feel sometimes that it's not enough. It concerns me that I'm not always available, that I have to tour to bring in money. Sometimes I think maybe I should quit the business and get a so-called 'real' job so I can give my kids all the attention they deserve. When I'm not around, I know they miss me. As far as I can see it, raising your children is a woman's God-given responsibility. But I think you also have to satisfy your own goals and ambitions. So it's like doing a high-wire act, balancing the two."

Although John Houston saw the youngsters often—even watching them when Cissy was on the road if one of Cissy's sisters wasn't available—the Houston household had become a much different place in his absence. When he lived there, John had given the gift of laughter to his family (Whitney's sense of humor was assumed to be inherited from her father). Without John living there, home was a more somber place.

Cissy was, as Whitney has recalled, "all business." Yes, Cissy was the woman who would turn down a trip to Paris because her daughter had the flu, but she also often appeared somewhat humorless to her children, preoccupied with work and other "sensible" matters. And why not? a dispassionate onlooker might ask. Cissy was, in fact, the authority figure in their home, the one who had to deal with the adolescent behavior and the growing pains of two sons and a daughter, and that's not a task for a woman who can't reach goals, set limits, and otherwise do what needs to be done. Nor was she the only one in the house with a strong mind. Whitney loved nothing more than a good battle of wills with her mother. "I had my hands full," Cissy says. "If I wasn't a barrel of laughs, well, hey, that's too bad. . . ."

By 1978, Chaka Khan had achieved great success as lead singer of the rock/soul-oriented group Rufus, her husky voice and vocal range standing out on such late-seventies hits as "Tell Me Something Good." At that time, Chaka was recording her first solo album, and she recruited Cissy for background vocals. Cissy brought Whitney along to the session, and mother and daughter added their voices—though uncredited on the actual release—to the Nick Ashford and Valerie Simpson song "I'm Every Woman," which became a top-ten single for Khan. (Fifteen years later, Whitney would record the song herself and take it to the top of the charts.)

"I'm Every Woman" helped usher in a new trend in popular music called disco, and by 1979, this craze had swept the nation. *Saturday Night Fever* had erupted on the movie screens, sending crowds of people directly from their seats into dance clubs. That 1978 film starred sex symbol John Travolta as a New York Italian-American whose passion for dancing provides an escape from a claustrophobic lower-middle-class existence. The sound-track from the film, featuring the Bee Gees, sold over thirty million copies, making it the top-grossing movie soundtrack of all time—until Whitney Houston's *The Bodyguard* broke that record in 1993.

When the Bee Gees embarked on a year-long world tour in 1979, they were accompanied by the Sweet Inspirations, who enjoyed a resurgence in popularity with a few dance-club hits—without Cissy, of course, and also without Estelle Brown, who had been replaced by Gloria Brown.

Because disco music was driven by a steady beat and rhythm, record producers found that an artist's vocal ability was virtually incidental to the final product. Apparently, all that was required to produce a success-ful disco record was 180 beats per minute and a catchy chorus. Hits no longer depended on radio disc jockeys, but were popularized in the dance clubs. If a song drew enthusiastic crowds to the dance floor, it was a hit. If the dancers seemed indifferent, the record was thrown to the back of the pile.

Although the new musical style sounded the death knell for many artists—people like Johnny Mathis and even Dionne Warwick, who specialized in ballads, were suddenly passé—it spawned an entire new batch of stars. Female voices somehow suited this style of music best. Donna Summer, Vicki Sue Robinson, Evelyn "Champagne" King, Gloria Gaynor, and Thelma Houston are just a few of the stars created by the disco wave.

Established artists who privately cursed the mindlessness of disco found themselves threatened by recordcompany executives who demanded that they sing it or face obsolescence. Clubs were suddenly flooded with disco songs by Barbra Streisand, Dolly Parton, Diana Ross, Rod Stewart, the Jacksons, Aretha Franklin, Smokey Robinson, and even Ethel Merman. Nothing was sacred. Even Broadway shows were plundered, with, for example, a pounding version of "Don't Cry for Me, Argentina" from *Evita*. Ballads were remixed and rereleased with a throbbing backbeat.

It was only natural for Cissy Houston—who remained eternally on the lookout for commercial success—to jump on the disco bandwagon. Her voice, one of the strongest in the business, and her gospel stylings provided a perfect counterpoint to the strong bass beat of the driving disco sound.

Private Stock Records released the up-tempo, religiously fervent "Think It Over," with Cissy as a solo artist. When the song all but burned up the dance floors, the record company rushed her back into the studios to produce an entire album of similar material. But despite its success, "Think It Over" could have been recorded by any female singer; it was not especially distinctive.

The album *Think It Over,* which scored well on both the charts and the dance floors, gave Whitney another opportunity to work as a background singer. The decision to include her on *Think It Over* was the latest phase of Cissy's plan to groom her daughter for stardom. The album would give Whitney valuable experience in the recording studio and teach her about being behind the microphone—with mother standing by to direct and offer support. Although Whitney's voice can hardly be heard beneath the machine-driven melodies, this didn't bother the young singer or detract from the usefulness of the experience.

Unfortunately, success would again be just out of reach for Cissy Houston. As her star began to rise she was given the news that Private Stock was going out of business, once more leaving her without any promotional backing. She went on to record a few disco sides with Columbia Records, but the material was disappointing to her fans; she seemed somehow lost in songs like "Step Aside for a Lady" and "It Doesn't Only Happen at Night." But there was a larger problem. By the time of their release in the 1980s, disco was considered dead. The monster that invaded the village had, it seemed, finally been destroyed by the villagers.

Cissy remained philosophical about her latest brush with fame. "I've been very fortunate in the business," she says. "I've never stopped working, even without a current hit record. Somehow or other, God has made it so that I can always sing."

Thus the theme of Cissy Houston's professional life—"almost but not quite"—was struck once more, as though some imp of the perverse were determined to thwart her. Meanwhile, in what might have been seen as an odd form of compensation, she and her daughter could both discern another, brighter, and more resplendent melody emerging in the distance.

This melody belonged to Whitney.

In 1980, as disco was floating off to a polyester oblivion, the fashion world was breathing a collective sigh of relief. Top designers such as Calvin Klein, Ralph Lauren, and Yves Saint-Laurent, all of whom had kept up with the fad by turning out pleated skirts perfect for that dance-floor spin, openly criticized the culture of dance-crazed "middle-Americans." After the fad died down, designers recaptured their creative spirit and introduced many exciting new lines.

At sixteen, Whitney Houston was growing into a tall, photogenic beauty. Still eschewing anything but jeans at home, she appeared in her mother's cabaret act in slinky, body-hugging gowns that showed off her slender figure.

Then Dean Avedon, a fashion photographer working freelance with many New York agencies—including one called Click Models—spotted Whitney and Cissy as they strolled along Seventh Avenue near Carnegie Hall. Avedon, who had discovered much new talent, approached the two women and handed Cissy his card. She was obviously the girl's mother, so he spoke directly to her, begging her to bring Whitney to the nearby Click agency. Though Cissy seemed willing to hear the stranger out, Whitney was skeptical. As Avedon went into his pitch she remembers saying to herself sarcastically, "Yeah, right."

"Look, we don't have anything to lose," Cissy—who was always open for an opportunity—told her daughter.

And so the two followed Avedon across the street and up the stairs to the agency.

Frances Grill, founder and president of Click Models, remembers the day Whitney and Cissy entered her office. "I loved her," she says. "She was a very pretty kid and she had this wonderful mother with her. It didn't take long to see the potential—so we started her modeling right away."

Whitney began with "editorial" modeling, doing fashion layouts for *Mademoiselle, Seventeen,* and other women's magazines. The agency groomed and refined her natural beauty, teaching her the art of "mannequin modeling"—still photography for print work—and soon she was in demand by many major advertisers. "Everyone loved her," says Frances Grill. "She had a clean-spirited energy. There was no question that she would go all the way to the top. She is a very determined young lady."

As excited as she was about modeling, sixteen-year-old Whitney was concerned that the work would cause her to miss several school days a week. However, the missed class time wasn't what troubled her; rather, she was not eager to call attention to her outside activities, to create a new excuse for her classmates to speak sarcastically about her and to snub her in the hallways.

"She didn't want another reason to be singled out," said one friend. "In grade school she was unique because her mother made her wear frilly clothes instead of jeans. She didn't want attention; she wanted to fit in. In high school, she was faced with the same issue. She wanted to conform, so she kept the modeling a secret from everyone. She never discussed it, ever."

It was an odd and fascinating development. There was Cissy, who struggled for years just on the edges of stardom, with a daughter who couldn't seem to avoid it.

Agency photographers finding you on the streets of New York? Really! Such misty-eyed contrivances are the stuff of adolescent fantasy and beach-blanket-movie plots. As for never discussing it at school, this smacks somewhat suspiciously of Wonder Woman and Supergirl, with their secret identities and glamorous double lives. It was all too unbelievable for real life.

From Click, Whitney switched to a larger agency— the internationally known Wilhelmina—and began appearing in the pages of *Young Miss, Cosmopolitan,* and *Glamour,* and in print advertisements for Sprite and Revlon cosmetics.

Though working as a model certainly gave young Whitney a stronger sense of presence and style, she secretly hated every minute of it—and not because it posed a threat to her life at school. "It was degrading," she said later. She felt that looking good demanded little talent—indeed, she *always* looked good. For Whitney, it was a given, not a goal. In some respects, she found the whole concept absurdly sexist. "What kind of a *mind* do you need to do this?" she would complain privately. "Any empty-headed, good-looking woman can do this work." True, Whitney enjoyed the people she came in contact with, the traveling, and the money, but she found it almost impossible to sit still for the endless makeup and hair sessions. "Too fussy for me," was how she put it. "All you do is stand there in front of the camera and grin." As if every teenage girl in America wouldn't give her eyeteeth for the opportunity to do just that.

There is no doubt that Whitney Houston could have had a successful modeling career. Certainly she is as good-looking and charismatic in front of the camera as Iman, Beverly Johnson, and Naomi Campbell, all top models for many years. But Whitney was finding more and more that what she really wanted to do was sing. *That* was something most people could not do—regardless of their beauty. *That*, to her way of thinking, was something that took real skill and ability, which is why she so enjoyed working with her mother in the recording studio.

Meanwhile, Cissy Houston's recording work continued. In 1980, writer/producer Michael Zager—who, with the Michael Zager Band, had released the hit disco single "Let's All Chant"—invited her to participate in his newest album, *Life's a Party*. And once again, Cissy brought along Whitney. This time, however, Whitney was allowed to sing solo on the album's title track. This now obscure cut holds the distinction of being the first recorded product to present Whitney's voice loud and clear.

Zager recognized the talent in seventeen-year-old Whitney and offered her a recording contract on the spot—which Cissy promptly turned down. John and Cissy Houston had decided that their daughter would finish school before she pursued any career in the music business. Though Whitney was frustrated, she acquiesced to her parents' wishes. "They were adamant that I have a childhood," Whitney has recalled. "They wanted me to move into adulthood in a natural progression. But I really wanted to sing. I was anxious to get on with my career, especially after that first record."

In 1981, Whitney was ready to graduate from high school. The event was a turning point for her, the moment the young singer could finally pursue her dream of singing professionally, the dream she had cherished since that first Sunday she sang publicly in church.

But now, before her graduation, disaster struck. Someone had seen her whirling around at supersonic speed making the magical transformation into Wonder Woman. The dreaded truth was revealed. Despite her attempts at secrecy, word of her achievements had spread. How could her classmates relate to a girl who was not only on magazine covers, but was also the daughter of a famous mother and was now attracting attention as a singer? Did her fellow students, in their magnanimity, admire her from afar, holding her in the esteem reserved for the famous and accomplished, proud to be in her presence? Not exactly. She was, instead, the subject of gossip born of jealousy. "I was miserable," she has remembered. "They absolutely hated me."

And did they have a reason? Well . . . "The truth is that she had a bad attitude," said one former classmate. "Now, maybe she had it because she was resentful about the way she had been treated in school, and her disappointment in the way things turned out for her was misinterpreted to be conceit. She wasn't the nicest girl, however. And she's right; everyone did hate her. She never had any dates. Fellows wanted nothing to do with her, despite her beauty. And she didn't seem interested in men, anyway. I don't ever remember seeing her with a guy, come to think of it."

In fact, only Robyn Crawford stuck with Whitney to the end, attending her graduation and cheering her friend on.

Shortly after graduation in 1981, Whitney sat down with her parents to plot out her future. Her print ads and editorial modeling had brought her some attention, as did the recording with Michael Zager. But she was still unknown. She was in no position simply to choose a record company and produce a hit album.

Thus, John and Cissy began the process of interviewing

prospective managers, who would aid them in pointing Whitney's career in the right direction. They decided upon a New York–based concert promoter, Eugene Harvey. Quick-talking Harvey, along with his partner, Seymour Flics, were venturing into artist management and took the young Houston on as a client.

They were astonished by her voice and had great faith that she would be a successful recording artist.

At least that's what they told her parents.

In retrospect, even they would have to admit that there was nothing incredibly unique or special about Whitney Houston—in fact, there were probably hundreds of young, attractive black women who could sing like she could.

The Houstons met with Harvey and discussed how Whitney's new managers could use their connections to obtain a few small acting jobs for her. Thus, in short order, Whitney began to audition for commercials and television shows, landing a commercial for the soft drink Canada Dry, then a small guest role on the sitcom "Gimme a Break," then a featured role on "Silver Spoons." (Producers of those two programs would later be hard-pressed to remember the episodes in which Whitney appeared; her work was not exactly memorable.)

Harvey and Flics also arranged for Whitney to work with disco producers Michael Bienhorn, Bill Lasswell, and Martin Bisi on an album that would be entitled *One Down*. It was projected to contain eight songs, each featuring a different lead singer—a formula that had worked well in the past for top producers such as Quincy Jones. Because Nona Hendryx, formerly of the innovative R&B/pop act Labelle as well as the disco act Chic, would contribute to the project, Whitney and her parents were enthusiastic about it. However, they and the management team were adamant about showcasing her voice on a strong ballad rather than a glossy, up-tempo, and instantly forgettable disco track. So Bienhorn and Lasswell chose a sentimental song, "Memories," which proved to be the perfect vehicle for Houston's young, soulful voice. When the album, which has long since been forgotten by everyone but the staunchest Whitney Houston fans, debuted, the *Village Voice* reviewed her effort favorably. Wrote the critic, "Guest stars Whitney Houston and [saxophonist] Archie Shepp transform 'Memories' into one of the most gorgeous ballads you've ever heard."

While continuing to model and join her mother in studio background singing, Whitney became the featured guest on an album by flamboyant songwriter/producer Paul Jabara. Jabara was best known for writing the song "Enough Is Enough," recorded by Barbra Streisand and Donna Summer. (According to showbiz lore, he wanted so much to have Summer record the song with Streisand that he locked the reluctant disco diva in the bathroom of his house until she would listen to the track. One can only guess what he had to do to get Streisand to consider the idea. Nevertheless, when he finally got them both into the studio, he reportedly had to intercede several times to prevent the singers from ripping each other's hair out.)

Jabara's next project was to be with Izora Armstead and Martha Wash, two robust singers who went by the name the Weather Girls and also recorded as Two Tons of Fun. Jabara had produced the ladies' hit single "It's Raining Men" and was now planning an album that would feature them. He enlisted the services of several other vocalists and produced an album entitled *Paul Jabara and Friends, Featuring the Weather Girls, Leata Galloway and Whitney Houston*. Whitney gamely recorded another ballad, "Eternal Love," written by Jabara, and the critics again singled her out for her performance on a record that was to fade quickly from the popular memory.

Wrote a critic for the rock-and-roll bible *Billboard* magazine, "Whitny [sic] Houston performs the song in a workmanlike fashion. She shows some potential." It would be a while longer before that name, correctly or incorrectly spelled, would really catch the attention of anyone who worked for *Billboard* magazine. . . .

Guided by her mother's firm and experienced hand—and with a couple of recorded songs under her own belt—Whitney Houston continued to sing one or two featured solos each night in Cissy's cabaret act. In fact, she was becoming so well liked in the show that some patrons, before making reservations, asked specifically if she would be singing that evening. To this day, many longtime friends and associates speak of Cissy's unselfish love for her daughter, which led her to permit Whitney to take advantage of her mother's hard-earned reputation as a cabaret entertainer to further her own career.

A friend and vocalist who worked with Cissy and Whitney in New York remembers watching Whitney blossom onstage. "Cissy would stand back and let Whitney sing a song or two, and the crowd would go crazy," she recalls. "Of course, Whitney wasn't as good as she is now, but it was still something special to see a kid with a voice that big. Plus, she seemed to have a real appreciation for legitimate songs—the kind of Broadway and standard stuff that her mother would do in her act."

On one occasion, as Whitney performed at Reno Sweeney's nightclub in New York, the friend remembers someone leaning over to her and saying, "I wouldn't care if that girl was my daughter, ain't no way I'd let her get that kind of time on my stage."

"Sometimes," the friend remembered, "Whitney would give Cissy so much heat, I couldn't imagine how Cissy would be able to recapture the audience. I mean competition is competition, whether it's a trained dog, a clever kid, or your daughter."

Cissy seemed mostly unconcerned about the fact that her daughter's popularity was beginning to eclipse her own among local audiences . . . that she was actually being upstaged by her own child. Rather, she gladly relegated herself to the background, sacrificing the attention that many entertainers cling to so tightly, in favor of her daughter's growing ambitions.

Judy Garland occasionally did the same for her daughter Liza Minnelli, most notably when the two played the London Palladium in the mid-sixties. But while Liza later admitted feeling strong competition and insecurity on the stage that evening, all was harmonious between Whitney and her mother. (Of course, Judy really had little to do with Liza's career; Liza paved her own way. In fact, the idea of that show at the Palladium was a clever promoter's, not Judy's. Cissy Houston, on the other hand, devoted herself to her talented daughter's career.)

As for winning back her audience after a stunning performance by her daughter, Cissy was always the master of her own game. She would just return to center stage, graciously acknowledge her daughter's accomplishment, then take back her show. Her sense of professionalism and cool confidence made it clear to the crowd that this was *her* stage—*her* night—and Whitney was simply a guest performer.

Cissy expected her daughter to honor the fact that

she—*mother*—was the star of the show and that she deserved a certain amount of respect, if only in recognition of her many years in show business. For Cissy, this didn't have to do with insecurity; it had to do with appropriateness and professionalism. And when she needed to administer a mild, attention-getting swat, Cissy wasn't reluctant to do so.

Thus, one evening at Reno Sweeney's, Whitney seemed determined to upstage her mother by performing vocal acrobatics and quite plainly showing off. Cissy was incensed. "It simply was not necessary," she would later recall.

After her daughter's performance that night, Cissy, the consummate professional, allowed no one in the crowd to see her indignation. Rather, she smiled and applauded her daughter's song. For several weeks thereafter, however, Whitney found herself without a solo.

And so it was made clear. Mother giveth, and if such is deemed needed, mother taketh away.

five

In the record business, as in the entertainment field in general, talent is rarely enough to guarantee success. The old adage "Superstars are not born, they're made"—which was most likely coined by a publicist—contains more than a bit of truth. In show business, singers/actors/writers must not only be born with talent, they must also work endlessly to develop it. A hefty dose of luck is also an advantage.

Besides natural talent, some of the biggest stars of our time have powerful behind-the-scenes people who mastermind their careers. These starmakers often find themselves in a curious position vis-à-vis the star they have made—reflecting their glory (or their infamy, depending on the circumstances) and acquiring a peculiar and often exploitable celebrity of their own. For instance, record producer Phil Spector fashioned the career of his wife, Ronnie Spector, and her group, the Ronettes, in the 1960s. Sonny Bono nurtured the ability of his then-wife, Cher, transforming her from homely waif to international superstar. According to

Tina Turner, record producer Ike Turner physically pummeled her into submission, and then on to stardom. Michael Jackson credits his father, Joseph, with much of his success (and is not unwilling to note that many of his psychological problems stem from Joseph's abuse). In the process, Phil Spector, Sonny Bono, Ike Turner, and Joseph Jackson all became well-known in their own right.

Berry Gordy, the creative force behind Motown Records and the careers of Diana Ross and the Supremes, the Jackson Five, Marvin Gaye, Stevie Wonder, and many others, is another man who shaped not only the careers of his stars, but also their public personas. In doing so, he, too, became famous and has been the subject of many magazine features and books, even being honored as the subject of an Emmy Award–winning special, "Motown 25: Yesterday, Today and Forever."

As Gordy's fame began to wane in the late sixties, another record-industry executive's was waxing. Born in 1932, Clive Davis, a Harvard Law School graduate, used his knowledge of the law to gain a position in the entertainment industry. While his overall accomplishments are undeniable, his career has been marked by a certain amount of controversy. No article appearing since 1973 has mentioned that he actually began with CBS, the then-parent company of Columbia, or that he was fired by CBS for alleged misuse of company money.

Davis joined the music division of CBS Records in the early sixties as its legal counsel. By 1967, he had ascended to the position of president of CBS Records, building his reputation through his development of such performers as Janis Joplin, Bob Dylan, Sly and the Family Stone, and Santana. Davis was known in the

industry as an artist-oriented executive, willing to utilize
without limit the company's money and resources to
back an act he believed in. Much of the label's success
during this time was due to his leadership.

Although he is an astute businessman, Davis's love of
the high life also won him some notoriety. Known for
his extensive wardrobe and eccentric jewelry, he was
often seen tooling around town in expensive cars. But
his reputation took a serious hit when, in 1973, he was
fired from his $350,000-a-year position at CBS for the
alleged misuse of over $87,000 of company funds.

Other industry executives doubted that the charges
brought by CBS were the only reason for Davis's dis-
missal. In an industry where expense money—and lots
of it—is thrown around like empty gum wrappers, his
alleged indiscretions hardly seemed catastrophic. It is
therefore no surprise that some insiders speculate that
Davis was a fall guy—a scapegoat who was sacrificed in
order to quash the possibility of a large-scale investigation into other record-industry sins. As *Time* magazine
concluded in a 1973 article, "Davis has retreated into
the silence of his redecorated apartment and retained a
criminal lawyer. There is speculation in the industry
that the incident could touch off another version of the
1950's payola scandal if the activities of other freewheel-
ing record executives are investigated."

But by 1975, Clive Davis was back. The details of
his eventual settlement with CBS were never made public; the industry eventually forgave and forgot. In fewer
than four years, Davis reappeared as the new head of
Bell Records, a division of Columbia Records—the very
same company that had disgraced him publicly by
accusing him of misuse of company funds. Clive Davis's
past is not without relevance, for one must marvel at
the resourcefulness of a man who can make such a

miraculous comeback. Such resilience would come in handy again as he mapped out plans for the career of an up-and-coming singer, the tall and beautiful Whitney Houston.

Clive Davis's first official act at Bell Records was to change its name to Arista Records, reportedly the name of the New York City school system's honor society, of which he was a member. Monday mornings at Arista Records became "morning music meetings," with Clive Davis at the helm. At these fabled executive gatherings, potential singles would be played and voted on by the promotion and marketing teams. Davis encouraged democratic process; everyone's opinion was considered. However, when a single that carried Clive's blessing failed to evoke a positive response from the rest of the team, the song would be played over and over until the others saw it "Clive's way."

The key to Davis's success lies in his knack for keeping his finger on the pulse of what is happening in the industry—who is appearing where, who seems like a comer, and who does not. He made it clear to his employees that they should always keep an eye out for new talent. Davis's first protégé at Arista was discovered when he was playing in a bathhouse in New York as an opening act for Bette Midler. A lightweight pop singer named Barry Manilow, Davis turned him into a household name.

In the early eighties, Davis hired young Gerry Griffith as Arista's director of A&R—artist and repertoire. Griffith's job was to scout out talent that would be appropriate for the label. He was required to attend weekly meetings that focused on the goals of the company, new acts, and discussions of the status of established acts who were with competing labels. If word got out that a successful act was unhappy with his or her label, or that a singer's contract was about to expire, a game plan was quickly improvised, and the artist and manager—if all was successful—were wined, dined, and signed by Gerry Griffith.

Flashback to June 1980 . . .

Gerry Griffith was representing Arista at the opening night of one of the company's acts, pop/jazz flautist Dave Valentin. The smoke-filled Bottom Line nightclub in New York City was filled to capacity with a smartly dressed, racially mixed audience who had come to see not only Valentin, but also his opening act—Cissy Houston and her family, including daughter Whitney and son Gary.

Whitney Houston had no idea that Griffith was in the audience. Nor, most likely, would she have cared. She had already been approached by Elektra Records and planned to sign with that label as soon as she, her parents, and her managers negotiated the contract.

Ironically, when she finally began to sing on that June evening, the magic wasn't there for her. When she did feel the spirit—when that wondrous meeting of heaven and earth occurred, as it usually did—Whitney seemed able to turn night into day with her voice. But she had a tendency to sound bored and disinterested if, for some reason, she was having an off night. If she and her mother just had an argument or if she was exhausted from a day of photo shoots and interviews, the paying audience would only see an attractive girl with a nice voice who seemed oddly introspective if not downright withdrawn. To be fair, it is a rare performer who can always turn on the magic, regardless of what may have transpired prior to a performance . . . but still, what'll get the attention of the good people who've paid their money is a roof-raiser of a show, not something that looks like a walk-through.

Gerry Griffith was not impressed by Whitney Houston's performance at the Bottom Line. "I'd never seen or heard of Whitney," he has recalled. "She did the song 'Home' [from *The Wiz*]. I thought it was good, but that was about it. I didn't think any more about it."

Then, two years later, in 1982 . . .

Gerry Griffith received a telephone call at his offices, informing him that the girl he had seen at the Bottom Line, Cissy Houston's daughter, was getting ready to sign a record deal with Elektra. He still didn't have much interest in Whitney, but a tip was a tip and his job was to follow it up. No performer is more desirable than one who is in demand by others, and if Elektra Records saw something special in Whitney Houston, well, he'd give her another chance—realizing that if she turned out to be a winner and he didn't sign her, or at least pursue her, he could lose favor with Clive Davis and a chance for greater prestige in the industry.

Griffith heard that Cissy Houston and family were performing at the Seventh Avenue South club in Greenwich Village. When he learned that Whitney and her older brother Gary were still featured, he decided to attend the show. "She had grown so much!" he says today of Whitney's performance that evening. "She did 'Home' again, and 'Tomorrow' [from *Annie*] and wiped me out."

After the show, Griffith sought out Whitney's manager, Eugene Harvey, and informed him that Arista would probably be interested in signing her. Harvey noted that Whitney already had a firm offer from another label, but that he and his client would be happy to discuss other options.

When Griffith finally met with Whitney the next

day, he was—to put it gently—not bowled over by her personality. She had become accustomed to being courted by record-industry types and wasn't impressed. In fact, she was distant and seemed infinitely unknowable. "She was nice," he recalled, "but she never showed any emotion, any excitement about the possibilities. She displayed what I guess you would call 'a cool confidence.' I'm sure that, by then, she was used to people telling her what a good singer she was. She just took it all in stride." Nevertheless, at that meeting, Whitney agreed to a private performance for the Arista executives.

The next morning, when Gerry Griffith informed Clive Davis of his discovery of the "most incredible singer," he was met with a blank stare. "He didn't exactly jump out of his seat," Griffith remembers, though the apparent indifference did not really surprise him. "Anyone who brings a new act in always says they have found the greatest thing since sliced bread, so [Davis] was a bit nonchalant about it." Davis's response was simple—"show me something."

With that, Griffith began to create the showcase for Whitney that he hoped would impress Clive Davis. Special songs were selected—only the ones with which Whitney felt most comfortable. She would perform for approximately thirty minutes—her lineup including "Home" and "Tomorrow," the two songs that had most impressed Griffith. Originally, he also suggested "The Greatest Love of All," a ballad that George Benson had made popular and one that Whitney occasionally performed in her mother's act. Ultimately, though, Griffith and the Houstons agreed that the performance should not be too laden with ballads, so the song was dropped. Some choreography was created. Stage patter was polished. A special gown was selected. If anything could be done to impress Clive Davis, it was done. By the day of the audition—about a week after Griffith first saw Whitney perform—everything was in place.

A half hour before the performance, Davis informed Griffith that he was exhausted from work and did not wish to attend. Have her perform, Clive suggested, and "just let me know how she was." A frantic Griffith managed to change Davis's mind and hastily arranged for a limousine to whisk the company president to Manhattan's Top Hat Rehearsal Hall, where the audition was to take place.

At ease throughout the brief act, Whitney performed her songs with great passion and verve. No walk-through stuff this day. No indifferent performer up there projecting a feeling that she'd rather be in the park feeding birds. She was, in fact, better than she had been the night Griffith saw her onstage. She was *on*.

He was excited, sure that Davis would be impressed with what he was seeing and hearing. But when the jubilant Griffith glanced over to his boss's table, his spirits crashed. Clive was sitting poker-faced and apparently profoundly uninspired by Whitney's performance. At one point, he closed his eyes and tilted his head back as if he had dozed off, until a loud note from Whitney jolted him back to reality. After the show, he said a few polite words to the singer and dashed off.

At the office the next day, Griffith met with Davis, who said that he was not really impressed with Whitney. While he agreed that she was, as he put it, "a good singer," he felt she was not "special." He suggested that the company offer her a "singles deal," which is the kind of arrangement Arista often made with vocalists in which the company had no confidence. A singer with such an arrangement would have the opportunity to record two songs—a single and its flip side. If this

were successful, then maybe—*maybe*—he or she would
be offered a long-term recording contract. If it were not
successful, the company would not have made, and
therefore would not have lost, much of an investment.

Griffith knew that the Houstons would view such a
deal as a demonstration of a complete lack of faith in
Whitney on the part of Clive Davis and his company.
In fact, he felt it was an insult. He reminded Clive that
Elektra was not alone in offering Whitney a better,
long-term album contract; so also was CBS Records,
Davis's former employer. "I don't care," was Clive's
response. "All I can offer her is a singles deal. I don't
really believe in her more than that. That's my best
offer. She's just a newcomer. . . ."

A few nights later, Whitney was back at
Sweetwater's, working with Cissy. Bruce Lundvall, president of Elektra, was in the audience, as was Gerry
Griffith. Both executives greeted Whitney before the
show. During the performance, she acknowledged
Lundvall's presence to the audience but never mentioned Gerry Griffith. Her reason was not hard to
understand. Arista Records was competing for her services, but Whitney (with her mother's counsel, no
doubt) was perceptive enough to know that Elektra was
really the main player. Without being rude, she was
simply responding to the suitor who displayed the most
ardor. And why not?

In the week to come, however, Clive Davis continued to think both about the young singer he had seen
and Gerry Griffith's wild enthusiasm for her. In speaking to others in the industry, he realized his view of
Whitney was not generally shared. What he got was
that Whitney was in demand. It occurred to him that
perhaps he had misjudged her. Perhaps he was just
drowsy that night and, as a result, had not been alert to

the force of her true talent. Could such a thing have happened? He decided to reconsider his offer.

Davis called Gerry Griffith into his office a few days later and offered a restructured proposal. He now proposed a deal he felt would be beneficial both to the Houstons and to Arista. According to his new strategy, Whitney would be presented with a one-album deal and would work with four different established producers—each responsible for three tracks. When the album was issued, it would contain, he hoped, nothing but potential hit singles—riding not just on Whitney's voice and presence, but also on the experience and reputations of the producers.

This proposition was immediately presented to Whitney's attorney, Paul Marshall. Coincidentally, Marshall was privy to confidential information about a power struggle between Bruce Lundvall and Elektra's chairman, Bob Krasnow. Apparently, even as the company's president, Lundvall did not have final authority over the handling of the label's talent and therefore he could not really guarantee how Whitney would be treated if she signed. Clive Davis, on the other hand, could make such guarantees. And he was proposing a specific game plan that demonstrated his belief in Whitney Houston. Griffith also promised that Davis would personally supervise each detail of Houston's debut album. The fact that Davis had done the same for Dionne Warwick and Aretha Franklin—both of whom were close to the Houston family and had experienced major career reversals prior to their association with Davis—probably did a lot for his case in the Houstons' eyes. Without a doubt, Clive Davis had breathed new life into the careers of both Warwick and Franklin.

Elektra's offer was better in terms of money, but, as

Paul Marshall now states, "I recommended that Whitney sign with Clive, even if it was for less money."

To sweeten the pot, Marshall negotiated an almost unheard-of clause in Whitney's contract, one that might ease the pain of her accepting less money. Known as a "key-man" clause, it ensures that should the executive most responsible for the artist's career leave the company for another label, the artist is free to accompany him there. This clause virtually assured that Whitney would never be bound to a contract that could fall into the hands of a new company chairman less inclined to give her the extensive personal attention Clive Davis had promised.

Officials at Arista's parent company were not happy with the key-man clause. Presumably, they had not completely forgotten Davis's alleged diversion of funds for his personal use. This clause would allow Clive Davis—in the event that such an unfortunate situation should arise again and force them to dismiss him—to take a potentially important artist with him. If he were so inclined, he could form his own label with her. In addition, RCA executives felt that the contract gave Whitney, should she become a successful act, too much leeway to walk away from the company that had taken the first risk with her.

Whitney remembers how the decision to sign with Arista came about. "Everyone put their bids in," she says. "So I sat down with my managers and my parents and I remember this long, drawn-out meeting. 'What are you gonna do? Who are you gonna do it with?' It was all very tense. I remember stopping the meeting and saying, 'I have to take a break.'"

Whitney went into an adjoining room and sat alone in a chair. Cissy came in a little while later and tried to offer some motherly advice. According to Whitney,

Cissy told her, "I know this is very difficult for you, but I'm going to tell you the truth: You should go where you're going to get the best guidance. You're eighteen years old. You need guidance. Don't go with the company that offers you the most freedom, because freedom is not what you need at this point."

In other words, Cissy was suggesting that Whitney should avoid record-company executives who seemed too eager to please her by allowing her to do whatever she wanted. Whitney and Cissy concluded that Clive Davis would be flexible, but not weak.

Whitney has recounted her conversation with Davis. "Clive Davis said, 'We'll give you this amount of money, and we'll sit down and discuss everything that happens. And as far as the songs that you want to do, I will help you. I will say, "Whitney, this song has potential, this song doesn't."' He assured me that he wouldn't dictate anything to me, but that he would help me make rational decisions about songs."

With these assurances, Whitney chose Clive Davis as the man who would guide her career—hopefully all the way to the top.

Whitney did, of course, want the Svengali touch that Davis offered as president of Arista. But later, when press releases from the company and magazine articles surfaced giving Clive Davis sole credit for "creating" her, she hit the roof. In a 1992 television interview, when she was asked how important Davis had been in her career, she responded rather testily, "Clive Davis was instrumental in matching me with the right producer—picking the right songs. He has guided my record career; but *I* guide my career."

After considerable negotiation of a sort that is not uncharacteristic of the record industry, the deal with Arista was approved. In April 1983, eighteen-year-old

Whitney Houston became an Arista Records recording artist. In a press photo taken on the day of the signing, a satisfied Davis sits next to an incredibly bland-looking Whitney, who was wearing no makeup and whose hair was in a short, unsophisticated "natural." She looks more like a young boy—one could even go so far as to say a presurgery Michael Jackson—than a future diva.

Cissy Houston was elated by her daughter's success. She had advised her, guided her, and made many sacrifices to get to this point, this auspicious beginning. Now, for the first time, one of Cissy's career plans had worked—though it wasn't *her* career that benefited. Still, as she said, "My daughter's success at signing with Arista was my success. My heart was filled with gratitude to God for guiding us to this point. Knowing that we are guided, no matter what happens, to the right place at the right time has always made our lives work for us. Arista was the right place at the right time."

Always one to remain in charge, though, Cissy boldly informed Davis and Griffith that she would not allow her daughter to record songs with a controversial or provocative content. "She's a church-girl at heart," Cissy warned. "And nothing will interfere with that, or her reputation." Davis agreed.

The budget for the first album was set at $175,000, a generous amount of money for the launching of a new artist, and one that would allow numerous producers and guest artists to work on the release.

Gerry Griffith remembers that choosing songs was not the easy task it may have appeared to be to outsiders. "We didn't really know what to do," he told writer Mark Bego. "Now, it's easy to look back and say, 'Oh, yeah—this is the kind of song that Whitney needs.' But back then it was tough. Her voice dictated the goings-on and her voice was overwhelming. The song had to live up to the voice, in other words."

In order to launch his new discovery in the industry, Davis exploited his own renown. *The Merv Griffin Show*, a popular talk/variety show of the time that starred successful television producer Merv Griffin ("Wheel of Fortune," "Jeopardy"), was planning a special broadcast to honor Davis's contribution to the music industry. In a bold move, the Arista executive put his reputation as a star maker on the line by inviting the novice Whitney Houston to perform on that show and introducing her personally. Davis had energetically promoted new acts in public forums in the past, but this was the first time he was promoting a vocalist who had not yet even recorded her first album with his label.

It should probably be mentioned that Clive Davis's interest in Whitney Houston was not based on his belief that she was the greatest singer he'd ever heard. One shouldn't forget that she practically put him to sleep when he attended her audition. Indeed, he was never knocked off his feet by her voice. "Dionne Warwick, now *that's* a voice," he once said when comparing Whitney with other acts. The fact is that Davis is a shrewd businessman. He realized that what he had in Whitney Houston was a special "package." A youthful, attractive woman, a former model, no less; she could sing; had a fair amount of charisma and stage presence; was trained by her mother, Cissy Houston (known by rhythm-and-blues fans to be one of "the greats"); and, to top it off, was related to Dionne Warwick and was even friendly with Aretha Franklin. He probably wondered to himself, "What else can you ask for? If I can't make her a star using some savvy public relations and the right vehicle, then what good am I as a music-industry mogul?"

Griffin's show appealed to a middle-American demographic—in other words, the largest chunk of the American population—and this was the precise group for which Davis was grooming Whitney. The goal of her appearance on the program was twofold: to create a national awareness and excitement about her talent, and to encourage producers and artists to participate in the upcoming album.

When Whitney heard that Davis himself was going to introduce her, she seemed unimpressed. "So, what's that have to do with me?" she asked, almost flippantly. "He should be glad to be doing it."

"It was as if she was being a little diva before her time," noted one observer. "As if she *expected* royal treatment already."

The truth is, Whitney was panicked, albeit secretly. One must remember: *she was only eighteen years old.* Noted one friend, "This was the scariest time of her life. Everyone was depending on her . . . not just to be good, but to be great.

"Plus, all of her mother's hopes and dreams seemed to now be weighing heavily on Whitney's shoulders. Cissy had wanted to be a star for decades. It looked like it wasn't going to happen. Now it was Whitney's turn to make that dream come true, not only for herself but also for a mother who was clearly living her career vicariously through her daughter's. Cissy was thrilled about the whole Arista–Merv Griffin deal. It was as if it was happening to *her.* 'Finally,' she kept saying, praising God all the while, 'it's finally happening.'

"But Whitney? She was like a frightened puppy. So she reacted the way she always does when she's scared. She retreated and acted unaffected and unflappable. She told me, 'Hey, I'm so good, I'm just gonna be great up there onstage and Clive Davis will be glad he even *knows* my ass. Should I be grateful to him? Hell, he oughta be grateful to me and my mother. We could be over at Elektra if he wasn't so lucky.'

"But, privately, I know she was frightened, because one day she completely broke down after a rehearsal in New Jersey for the Griffin show. She was singing 'Ain't No Way' with Cissy and, suddenly, she just sort of caved in emotionally and began sobbing, 'What if I can't do it? What if I'm not good enough? I've been performing all of my life and now here I am. What if this doesn't work? Just, what if . . . ?' She was hysterical. Cissy went over to her to comfort her, whispering some words that no one else could hear. But Whitney just kept insisting, 'It's too much, Mommy. It's too fast. I need more time. I need more time.'"

Afterward, Cissy seemed unaffected by her daughter's emotional outburst. "Oh, she's just a little nervous," said Cissy. "Who wouldn't be? It's only natural. Believe me, she's ready."

The next day, Whitney and Cissy acted as if the incident had never occurred.

six

Because The Merv Griffin Show _was taped_
in Hollywood, Whitney and her family were flown in
from New Jersey for the appearance. When the
Houstons arrived in Los Angeles, they were immediately
driven by limousine to the theater where the show's
taping took place.

Merv Griffin's soundstages were near the corner of
Hollywood Boulevard and Vine Street, once a mecca
for celebrities and fans. From the thirties to the sixties,
"Hollywood and Vine" was fabled as a destination point
for tourists, with the legendary Brown Derby restaurant
as well as Graumann's Chinese, the El Capitan, and the
Egyptian theaters all within walking distance. But what
Whitney viewed from the tinted windows of her limousine that day in 1983 was a Hollywood far past its
romantic prime, whose streets were now taken over by
indigents and the homeless, by prostitutes brazenly
soliciting the drivers of passing cars, drug sellers and
drug users, hyped-up exhibitionists in outrageous cos-
tumes, and anxious rock-and-roll wannabes—all living,

working, and wandering amid grime and garbage. The place made you want to hold your breath, lest you inhale whatever was in the air.

"It wasn't what we expected," was the only comment Whitney made about her first glimpse of Hollywood.

Clive Davis had invited Ray Parker, Jr., to the taping of the Griffin show. A sessions guitarist, Parker was also an artist and producer for Arista. He and his band Raydio had had several mainstream hit records, including "Jack and Jill," "You Can't Change That," and "A Woman Needs Love (Just Like You Do)." His biggest hit, however, was the theme from the film *Ghostbusters*. Davis hoped that after hearing Houston sing, Parker would be inspired to produce several cuts on the planned album that would showcase Whitney's voice and style.

Merv Griffin opened the show in his trademark style, with a lightweight song, sung slightly off-key. Then he introduced his guest. Davis spoke briefly about his successes and upcoming plans for Arista Records. He then told the audience, "In this business, you know who's got it and who doesn't. This next performer has definitely 'got it.'"

Whitney Houston was dressed simply, in a lavender skirt with black-and-lavender stripes; a plain gold chain hung from her neck. Her hair was cropped short. When she took the stage, she brought down the house with her rousing rendition of the ballad "Home." Then she was joined by Cissy Houston, looking every inch the star in a black-and-gold lamé gown. The two performed the Aretha Franklin classic "Ain't No Way," the same song Aretha and Cissy had sung to a standing ovation fifteen years earlier at Philharmonic Hall. But this time Whitney sang Aretha's vocals. The enthusiastic response of the studio audience was precisely what Clive Davis hoped for. (Videotapes of that 1983 appearance show the delighted Arista president sitting back in his seat, grinning incandescently.)

Later, Davis met with Ray Parker, Jr., backstage, anxious to discover his reaction to Whitney. He was dismayed to learn that Parker's first impression was strikingly similar to his own. "She's green," Parker told Davis. Gerry Griffith, who overheard the conversation, recalls Parker telling Clive Davis that Whitney "sang too many notes," and seemed to be trying to show off. He also felt she didn't have much stage presence. In sum, he was not at all interested in working with the fledgling singer.

Other producers also passed on the opportunity to work with Whitney, including George Duke, who would go on to produce Deniece Williams's 1984 hit "Let's Hear It for the Boy."

Gerry Griffith was perplexed. "We thought people would be knocking down the door to work with Whitney—and they weren't," he proclaimed. "The attitude was, 'Yes, she can sing, but so what?' We were flabbergasted."

Then, in researching his list of potential producers, Clive Davis ran across the name of Jermaine Jackson—Michael's older brother—who had recently left Motown and signed with Arista. Stung by the rejection of other producers, Davis approached Jackson.

Jermaine Jackson had the unfortunate reputation of being the "third-most-talented Jackson"—after brother Michael and sister Janet. When Jermaine married Motown founder Berry Gordy's daughter, Hazel, in 1973, most industry observers felt he would be taken under Berry Gordy's wing, his solo career guaranteed—particularly because Jermaine had stuck by Gordy when

Michael and his brothers left Motown, causing a family conflict that lasted for years. But much to Jermaine's surprise and dismay, Gordy and Motown did not turn him into a major star. He did, however, record a handful of moderately successful singles, including the Stevie Wonder–produced "Let's Get Serious."

By 1983, when Michael Jackson's *Thriller* album had turned him into a huge star, Jermaine's career at Motown was going nowhere. Nevertheless, he remained interested in carving his own niche in the record industry—not only as an artist, but also as a producer. Working with Whitney Houston on three songs—including "Someone for Me" and two duets, "Nobody Loves Me Like You Do" and "Take Good Care of My Heart"—would accomplish this.

Also about that time—early 1984—Davis allowed producer Michael Masser (who had worked successfully with Diana Ross on songs such as "[The Theme from *Mahogany*] Do You Know Where You're Going To?", "Touch Me in the Morning," and "It's My Turn") to produce a song with Whitney for an upcoming Teddy Pendergrass album, *Love Language*. Pendergrass—who was attempting a comeback following a serious automobile accident that left him paralyzed from the waist down—and Houston recorded the lush ballad "Hold Me."

In musical terms, "Hold Me" seems inferior, much of it taken up by bland background vocals endlessly repeating the chorus. Whitney appears to be subdued, kicking in only at the end as the song begins to fade out. As for Pendergrass, his vocal cords had been affected by the accident, but his soulful intonations retained much of the sexual quality that had made him a success.

Dull though it seemed, the song was released as a

single from Pendergrass's album and it soared to the top of the black charts. One reviewer called it, "A classy ballad to mark Pendergrass's long-awaited return; Whitney Houston's sweet vocals are an added treat."

Thus, by teaming Whitney with other popular solo performers such as Pendergrass and Jermaine Jackson (the song "Take Good Care of My Heart" by Whitney and Jermaine ended up on Jermaine's *Jermaine Jackson* album for Arista), Davis was establishing an identity for Whitney before her debut album was even released. It was a stroke of genius. The music industry was already buzzing about Whitney Houston, virtually assuring not only a high public awareness when her album was released, but also a fast-selling product.

"As far as Whitney was concerned, she was just glad to be in the recording studio," said one former associate. "This was exciting stuff for her, a great proving ground. She felt that Clive Davis had a plan, and she was just waiting to see how it would all unfold. She was a willing participant in whatever Clive and Arista had planned."

After the Jermaine Jackson and Teddy Pendergrass recordings, Arista Records' public-relations department went into full swing. In spring 1984, the company threw a party for Jermaine at the Limelight disco in New York City. The highlight of the gathering was the appearance of Whitney Houston, singing several songs, including "Home" (an odd choice, since it was not considered for inclusion on the upcoming album). Jermaine then joined her onstage for a rousing version of "Take Good Care of My Heart."

Next came a tenth-anniversary party for Arista, held at the Museum of the City of New York. In attendance along with Whitney were Patti Smith, Alan Parsons, and Dionne Warwick, Whitney's cousin. Houston and

Warwick were asked to perform. (From the beginning, Davis played up Whitney's relationship to Warwick and Cissy. In all press from that period—including Whitney's biography, which was composed by Arista's publicity machine—Whitney is referred to as the "daughter of Cissy Houston and cousin of Dionne Warwick.")

In May 1984, it was announced that Jermaine Jackson and Whitney Houston would appear on the top-rated daytime soap opera "As the World Turns"—another attempt by Arista to make Whitney's name familiar to a broad audience. The storyline concerned a benefit performance for homeless children in the fictional town of Oakdale, with Jackson and Houston performing the song "Nobody Loves Me Like You Do" (which would appear on Whitney's album).

In a column item, the *Los Angeles Times* noted the duo's appearance and described Jackson as a "famous brother of Michael Jackson" and Houston as a "cousin of Dionne Warwick." Indeed, Jermaine and Whitney were a matched set, "stars" whose celebrity was defined by their more famous relatives. (The item also revealed that "Jackson arrived at the studio with two bodyguards and his own make-up artist and was quickly sequestered in a second-floor dressing room." No mention was made of Whitney's arrival or accommodations.)

Kenneth Reynolds, head of rhythm-and-blues product management for Arista, recalled the promotion given to Whitney Houston prior to her debut album. He told writer Mark Bego, "Everyone was aware of her at Arista, aware of the whole big marketing and promotional campaign that was going to be planned behind her career. I don't think that I have ever seen that type of promotion and marketing put into an act before an album was even put out. She was very, very visible, probably as visible as any act with a hit album. . . .

"It was decided at Arista that this was *the* next performer, as opposed to, 'here's just another singer.' We were talking about Whitney as being the next performer in the league of a Diana Ross and an Aretha Franklin."

Beyond the choice of songs for Whitney—which would, in one sense, define her as an artist—Reynolds added that her image was also a hot topic of conversation and controversy at the label. In the music industry, the buzz phrase "image sells" has held true for years. Elaborate makeup, hairstyles, and clothing have overshadowed the musical talents of many singing stars—including Cyndi Lauper, Boy George, and the rock group KISS. This gaudy paraphernalia helped the public form an image of the performer, often leading to a frenzied fashion craze, as was the case with Madonna, whose female (and many times male) admirers wore bras over their clothes and had multiple crucifixes dangling from their necks.

What to do with Whitney Houston?

Although undeniably beautiful, Whitney seemed to have little interest in cosmetics or distinctive hairstyles. She wore only jeans and casual shirts around the house. She had not particularly enjoyed her experience as a model—hours spent before a makeup mirror with strangers arranging her hair, painting her face, and poking at her with their sharp cosmetic pencils. Whitney actually seemed to shun glamour. She quickly rejected the idea of any "look" that would take a lot of time to create. "I just want to be myself," she said at the time. "I'm not happy with all that glamour stuff. I don't want to be fake. I don't feel like a fake."

Kenneth Reynolds and his staff were given the task

of creating several possible images for Whitney and presenting them to Clive Davis. "When you have someone as beautiful as Whitney," Reynolds has recalled, "you are going to get input from everybody, because everyone has an idea. Due to her age, people were torn whether they wanted her to look like a cute little girl or a sexy woman. There was a bit of a turmoil in terms of getting her image together at the beginning."

Clive listened to hundreds of contradictory ideas from his staff, then quietly set down the law. According to Reynolds, Davis told his staff, "Thanks for your thoughts. They're all very good. I'll give each of them careful consideration. Now, in the meantime, here's what I've decided we're going to do." He decided that Whitney Houston was to be considered a class act, instinctively realizing that his young future star needed no elaborate hairstyles or razzle-dazzle clothing to sell her to the public. He wanted a subtle, "young Diana Ross" look. But would Whitney buy it? She did. It was okay as long as it would not involve, as she put it, "a whole lot of glamour work. I'll do what Clive wants," she said at the time, "but I'm not a robot. I still have to feel good about myself."

"I'm me," Whitney once told a reporter for the *Toronto Star*. "When I started off, I didn't want to be Dionne. I didn't want to be Aretha. I learned a lot from both of them and I love them, but I am me."

Photographs of Whitney's "Clive Davis makeover" were released periodically over a six-month period before her debut album hit the streets. Whitney in an evening gown. Whitney at the beach. Whitney in "super summer shorts and a matching tee."

How does Whitney wash her hair? one magazine article wondered.

And what does she wash it with?

And just *how* does she keep her complexion so clear and blemish-free?

What could she possibly eat that allows her to remain so thin?

All of these earth-shattering questions and more were answered for the media by Ms. Houston herself in prepared text that accompanied the posed photos, in which she was beaming and obviously overjoyed. (Well, of course she was overjoyed. Maybe not, though, because of this marvelous opportunity to appear before the world in slick magazine pages offering advice. Maybe it was because she was a former model and knew how to work the camera, turning on a dazzling smile as easily as most people turn on a flashlight.)

All of this is known in the industry as "vanity press," and it is used as a tool by public-relations and publicity persons to pique interest in a new or rising star. In the early days of Hollywood, vanity press was more prevalent—with top stars such as Joan Crawford and Cary Grant often inviting the public into their personal lives by way of carefully posed photos and "puff piece" text.

Arista's campaign for Whitney, however, was remarkable because a large segment of the nation was becoming acquainted with her *before* the release of her debut album. The public was reading about her upbringing, her family, her history with the church, and the way Cissy had handled her when she was "naughty." She was being promoted as if she were a major star—though she still had no album in the record stores!

The whole process was something of which she would eventually grow weary—hearing the same vacuous questions time and time again, and giving the same big-smile answers—though some observers have imagined that in later years, she may occasionally have wished for a return to those days of fluffy publicity. As her career became more intense and controversial she would experience a darker side of the media, which included much more personal and invasive interviews. At one point, she would yell at one reporter, "Enough of this shit! *I'm* even tired of me."

The next step in preparing for the release of the album was the creation of music videos to support the image and the product.

In 1984, the video "art form" was still in its infancy, although a growing four-year-old enterprise called MTV was bringing music videos into the homes of millions of consumers. Record companies jumped at the chance to promote their artists by supplying MTV, free of charge, with increasingly elaborate video productions.

Basically, what MTV (and later, other cable channels such as VH-1 and BET) were offering was a godsend. Record labels were able to advertise their products to the nation without spending a dime on airtime. Where else in the world could a manufacturer of a product find such a bonanza? Thus, Kenneth Reynolds and his staff decided early on that this emerging medium—the music video—was the perfect platform for Whitney Houston. With her striking beauty, she could easily sell herself and her music.

The first single from her forthcoming album to get the music-video treatment was the peaceful ballad "You Give Good Love." As its development got under way nearly one hundred scripts and concepts were submitted by video directors across the country for consideration by Arista. Michael Lindsay-Hogg—the son of actress Geraldine Fitzgerald—was finally selected by Clive Davis as director.

The concept for the video had nothing to do with

the lyrics of "You Give Good Love." Instead, it had a "rehearsal" atmosphere. It was set in an empty club in Manhattan. (The shoot actually took place in an Italian restaurant very near the now defunct Reno Sweeney's, where Whitney had often performed with her mother.) On the first day of the shoot, it was clear that Lindsay-Hogg had misunderstood the concept in relation to Whitney Houston's youthful image. He had envisioned a Las Vegas–like club and hired older extras to play such club employees as a cook and maître d'. But Whitney's manager, Eugene Harvey, objected to the black chef and maître d'—both of whom were in their sixties—feeling they represented an older, stereotypical view of Las Vegas. Eventually, an alternate was chosen to play the cook—none other than Kenneth Reynolds of Arista Records! Reynolds was young and sported an earring; Davis felt he more closely fit the hip image they wanted to convey in the video.

Reynolds has recalled his impression of Whitney Houston on the set of her first music video. "She came in there like a real polished professional, which is a quality I noticed in everything she did. She may have been new to the business, but she conducted herself like someone who had really been around from day one. There's this coolness, always a sophistication about her."

In that video, Whitney sings directly to an on-screen cameraman who moves about the room as she "rehearses." The feeling between Whitney and the handsome black cameraman seems intimate, with Whitney cooing, "Take this heart of mine / into your hands / baby, you give good love."

Upon completion of the first video, a second was soon in production for the song, "Saving All My Love for You," written by Michael Masser. Shot on location in England, it cast Whitney as the Other Woman, content to stay home until the man she loves can get away from his wife—an interesting choice for a twenty-year-old woman touted as having "grown up in church." But no one had made a good case for the possibility that chastity sells records, or given a whole lot of thought to whether such a worldly image had anything at all to do with who Whitney really was. After all, nobody thinks Sigourney Weaver really spends her days in spaceships fighting aliens.

According to sources who worked with Arista at the time, Whitney and her mother initially protested the song's content, but Clive Davis assured them that the song was innocent and that she would not end up with the man in the end.

Although Whitney and Clive Davis chose not to include two of her standard nightclub songs—"Home" and "Tomorrow"—on the album, they did select "The Greatest Love of All." It was also written by Michael Masser (who wrote and produced "All at Once" for the upcoming album as well), and Whitney had performed it occasionally in her mother's act. Jazz singer George Benson had made a hit of the song in the late seventies, so this was the only track on the album that would be considered a "cover," a reinterpretation of someone else's material.

"The Greatest Love of All" is a ballad of personal faith in oneself and the realization of childhood dreams. As part of her mother's act, Whitney had used the song to demonstrate her vocal strength, belting out the lyrics while gracefully sliding up and down the musical scale with her gospel-trained voice. But by the time the song was included in Whitney's album, it had been homogenized into an "easy listening" sound closer to that of sexagenarian Peggy Lee than of the youthful Whitney

Houston. Perhaps Clive Davis had taken to heart the opinion of Ray Parker, Jr., after Whitney's appearance on "The Merv Griffin Show," that Whitney "sang too many notes."

"Davis did tell Michael Masser to tone her down," said one source. "Whitney wanted to be all over the place musically with that song. She was used to hitting high notes and really doing an acrobatic job. It was difficult for her to tone herself down to Clive's specifications."

In an effort to push the rising young star into the mainstream, Clive had, in fact, worked to "whiten" her voice, as Berry Gordy had once done with Diana Ross. Whitney responded to criticism of this by replying to a television interviewer in 1992, "I don't sing white, I don't sing black—I just sing." Whitney even became a target of the Fox network's comedy series "In Living Color," which delighted in making fun of what they clearly regarded as her saccharine and soulless singing style.

Nevertheless, when it is sung today in concert by Whitney Houston, "The Greatest Love of All" is filled with the soulfulness she's always had, with the emotion she never lacked, but that was cleaned out of her early recording as methodically as if it had been run through some kind of giant and heartless commercial song-laundry.

The third video, for "The Greatest Love of All" (also shot before the album's release), is considered by many to be the most effective video ever made for a debut album. The setting is once again a live performance, this time in a grammar-school auditorium. A young girl, representing Whitney as a child, stands backstage, waiting her turn to perform in the school pageant. The young girl's mother—played, appropriately enough, by

Cissy Houston—waits with her in the wings, offering encouragement before sending her off with an affectionate glance.

The scene then switches to an adult Whitney Houston, glamorous in a beaded evening gown, preparing for a performance. The camera then captures the stage from the audience's point of view as the young "Whitney" and her adult counterpart, the real Whitney, enter from opposite wings, meeting at center stage—the young girl dissolving into the adult performer.

The touching video allowed Whitney to thank her mother publicly and artistically for years of support and love, acknowledging Cissy's formative influence on her to the world.

The fourth video—"How Will I Know?"—uses the only dance track on the album, with Whitney showing more energy and enthusiasm than on any of the other songs. This video also marked a transformation for the young singer. Finally, she was given the opportunity to move beyond the staged performance settings and to demonstrate elementary dance moves in a strikingly designed setting of video screens and colored partitions. Also, in this video, Whitney seems much younger, her natural hair having been replaced by a honey-colored mass of curls held up by a dazzling bow. Her slim figure is accented by a tight, sleeveless dress made of metal mesh, reaching almost to her knees and accessorized with matching arm bracelets.

No doubt about it: the woman was really something to look at.

But, as all of this was going on, an onlooker might have wondered what that performer up there in the spotlight was thinking. The woman who, in her midteens, summed up her feelings about being a famous fashion model and cover girl by saying it was all "too fussy"; who asked, "What kind of a *mind* do you need to do this?" What was that person thinking and feeling? Was she stunned by the glamour and by the attention she was getting? Was she starting to assume that she was really something special because all of these people were crowding around her and looking at her and taking pictures of her and packaging her for the world's consumption? Was she *impressed* by all of that?

Anyone who had the slightest knowledge of Whitney Houston might have volunteered a single four-word answer to all these questions. "Don't bet on it."

seven

By early 1985, Whitney Houston's premiere album was almost ready for release. Clive Davis, however, still had some second thoughts. "He was afraid there weren't enough hits on it," said one former employee of Arista. "He almost had her go back in and record some more stuff. But the other company executives were becoming impatient. They wanted the album to be released. The company had spent over a quarter of a million dollars on Whitney, and some of the Arista execs felt that it was time for a return."

To complete the album, one final detail remained—the concept and look of the album package. Whitney's manager, Eugene Harvey, was on the phone with Clive Davis every day, discussing what Whitney should wear on the cover. They battled over whether the art director should be from the West Coast or the East Coast, and whether Whitney should look like a young girl or a sophisticated woman. In all, ten photo sessions were needed to create the final image—an uncomplicated three-quarter shot of Whitney, draped in a soft white gown by designer Giovanne De Maura, with shoulders and arms bare. She wore a plain strand of white pearls around her neck. Her hair was slicked back, her expression one of confident sensuality. The overall effect was simple, classic, and . . . exotic.

In all, the album had taken approximately twenty-four months of work. Much of the time was spent finding producers and material, shooting the first four videos, and creating the prepublicity saturation campaign Clive Davis had so carefully orchestrated. In retrospect, one can see just how risky this publicity program was. By relentlessly foisting Whitney's image on the press and public before she had a product to promote, Arista was gambling that her potential fans and the media would not grow tired of her before they had even purchased her debut effort. But as it turned out, Davis knew what he was doing.

Whitney Houston's debut album, *Whitney Houston,* is a little masterpiece. Despite, or maybe even because of, all the confusion; the dizzying array of producers, arrangers, and writers (every one of whom is listed in the lengthy liner notes); and all the in-house commotion and advance hype, the final result is enjoyable and even memorable. Jermaine Jackson and Kashif produced two songs each, Michael Masser four, and Narada Michael Walden produced one, "How Will I Know?"

The album blended several musical styles (which led some critics to complain that it was more of a "Clive Davis musical sampler" than a showcase of Whitney's singing talents). Four of the songs were solo ballads, two were duets with Jermaine Jackson, and there was a duet with Teddy Pendergrass. Two of the tracks—"Someone for Me," produced by Jermaine Jackson, and "Thinking About You," produced by Kashif and written by him and his partner, LaLa—featured almost interchangeable through-lines and melodies. Whitney's vocals appear in short, staccato bursts—far from a display of her true talent for lush ballads and soulful riffs but a terrific display of her potential.

The songs that truly showcased the young singer's gifts emphasized her voice rather than any production values. On "Saving All My Love for You," "You Give Good Love," and to a lesser degree, "The Greatest Love of All," the listener is allowed to absorb the emotions of the song through Whitney herself, rather than through the welter of computer-generated violins and background percussion.

Years later, Whitney revealed how she felt about her first album's content and style. "I think we had to be very careful with my [debut] record," she said. "I am very happy with the album but—looking back—there are a lot of things I could have done better and wish I could approach differently."

Whitney Houston was officially released in February 1985. Record stores received ad slicks exclaiming, "The critics agree . . . She's Got It!" and they featured bulleted quotes from music writers who had previewed the album:

> *New York Daily News:* "This is one of the most outstanding records that I've heard in at least a decade. A new star has been born."
>
> *People* magazine: "Houston has a sweet, sure voice that she combines with an emotional sensitivity rare for someone of her age—or anyone else's. It will take an act of congress to keep this woman from becoming a mega-star."
>
> *Newsweek:* "Whitney Houston is a little frightening. . . . No one person should have this much star quality. It just doesn't seem fair."

Arista chose to release "You Give Good Love" as the first single. It quickly climbed to the top of the R&B charts, and the label decided to send Whitney on a concert tour to support the album.

Word-of-mouth on the recording was the best that many industry executives had ever heard. One source described the frustration within the company because shipments failed to keep up with demand. "It was crazy," the person said, marveling. "If you can imagine all of these executives at Arista, including Clive Davis, screaming at their secretaries on the intercom, 'Get me Distribution!' As I understand it, the more copies that were sold and reported by the press, the more the demand. It was a definite snowball effect, with everyone in the nation wanting the album their friends had."

The upcoming concert schedule created even more talk as dates were announced and venues quickly sold out. The tour began with smaller clubs, including the Roxy in Los Angeles, the Judge's Chambers in Dallas, Chicago's Park West, and the Warner Theater in Washington, D.C. Later, after the record began to prove itself with disc jockeys and the public, Whitney would appear in larger theaters as an opening act for R&B singer Jeffrey Osborne.

Arista officials booked her as an opening act in order to gauge audience response and anticipate what might occur in larger forums. Many executives feared that her intimate style would get lost on such a grand scale and preferred the smaller rooms. After several appearances, however, it became obvious that the clamor for Whitney Houston was much larger than these executives had anticipated. They realized that only large auditoriums could contain her growing legion of fans.

At home with her family, nineteen-year-old Whitney

prepared herself for a grueling tour schedule. A multitude of details had to be worked out, and though her manager could handle most of them (the tour was, after all, a small one), Whitney did not have a tour manager and other staff support. But she did have something most others in her position didn't. Her mother.

"My mother was my foundation. Remember, she had already done a lot of this, and she knew about all of the bad things that could happen. She just told me, 'Whitney, you stay true to yourself and try to be a good person, no matter what. People will tell you things, and if you just don't agree with them, you tell them and stay strong. Above all, stay strong.'"

Whitney wasn't naive. She'd seen a few things. She read magazines and newspapers and watched television. She knew as well as anyone that sudden success had caused even the most levelheaded performers to self-destruct. And though she had been performing most of her life, the stakes had now escalated to the point where she often felt as though she were standing on the edge of a cliff while unseen hands tried to push her off. Even those of people she knew.

Was it just her imagination that certain associates began to treat her differently after the album's release? Whitney believed not. Longtime family friends suddenly began to tiptoe around her, apparently forgetting that she was still the same girl they affectionately called "Nippy" for so many years. Suddenly, they treated her like "Whitney Houston, Superstar!" Family members were her only refuge during this stressful period. Whitney's father, John, who remained on friendly terms with Cissy, offered a strong, masculine presence, as did Whitney's two brothers, Michael and Gary. Gary (who had a brief career as a professional basketball player with the Denver Nuggets and was now singing professionally) also accompanied his sister on most of her tour dates, singing backup and performing duets with her from the album.

As the summer of 1985 approached, with the dates at the smaller clubs behind her, Whitney began preparation for the next phase of her concert tour. When she became the opening act for Jeffrey Osborne, the venues would be terrifyingly larger. "This was the scariest time," Whitney recalled in an interview. "My life was changing. Suddenly, I was becoming *so* popular. It seemed like it was happening too quickly, yet I knew we had been planning this whole thing, step by step, for a long time. Sometimes I couldn't sleep, I was so nervous. Sometimes I couldn't eat. My stomach was always in knots. I wanted to do my best, but I didn't know if that was enough. I prayed. That helped me get through it. I depended on my mother a lot, someone to talk to, to lean on. In all, it was a good tour, a growing experience. Becoming famous, boy, it's a trip. . . ."

As Whitney's fame escalated, so did her income. The *San Diego Union Tribune* reported that her August 1985 sold-out dates at Humphrey's in San Diego netted her $11,500 per concert. By the time she returned to the San Diego area a year later, performing at the much larger Sports Arena, she was reportedly earning $100,000 per performance, with her fee doubling for many shows later that year.

The reviews of Whitney's major appearances indicate that Arista had worried needlessly that her intimate style might get lost in a huge stadium. *Cashbox* magazine said, "Her poise and confidence onstage are readily apparent." The industry trade publication also praised Houston for daring to perform songs in concert in a way that differed dramatically from the album recordings. That was "most obvious when [Houston] shifts the phrasing of her biggest hit, 'Saving All My Love for You,' completely around, a move which throws some fans off and would be considered a serious risk by less sure young singers." Whitney shrugged off this compliment by saying, "Entertainers often run into people who ask, 'Why didn't you sing it like we heard on the record?' But I am a part of the public, too, and I know it is difficult to sound just like the record, and performing live is a totally different thing. You can do whatever you want."

You can do whatever you want. That comment hints at her frustration over the arrangements of many songs on her first album—songs that, when performed in concert, were no longer "pop fluff," but inspiring individual statements in musical form.

And perhaps what she did best was live performance. Her concert tour generated massive sales. Many concertgoers only bought the album *after* they had seen Whitney sing in person. Indeed, she seemed incandescent onstage. No technical gimmickry was needed. Her natural talent, though still raw, was enough to captivate her audience. Whitney instinctively realized what they had come for: her, without any in-studio sweetening.

As one dazzled fan at the time explained, "Whitney doesn't need special effects. She *is* the special effect."

The young singer echoed that fan's enthusiasm when she told an interviewer during her first tour, "Live is better. There is an energy with the crowd, and they can read you. They don't want anything tired. They don't want to see *you* tired. You have to love what you do. If you love what you do, great. If you don't, then stay home."

Music fans had a new idol. Arista executives happily read the charts every Monday morning, knowing they'd find their new star at the top. Houston's horizons seemed limitless.

But, on occasion, clouds did appear.

For example, in the middle of her 1985 tour, she awoke one morning unable to speak. It seemed the ultimate terror, the stuff of soap-opera plots, as she tried to speak and nothing came out except a strange, raw whisper. Then terror turned to self-pity, and the young girl, far from home and the counsel of the mother she had come to depend on, began to weep.

Whitney's staff, upon learning of this development, tried to comfort her. One wise member of the entourage even suggested that she go ahead and attempt to sing. Whitney, awash in emotions that could just as easily flare into anger, glared at the woman as if to say, "You are out of your mind, lady!"

Finally, in confusion as much as anything, she attempted a few notes. To her amazement, her singing voice was as flawless as usual—and strong! Whitney had forgotten what her staff member hadn't: the strange fact, as she recounted years later during a TV interview, that "the singing voice and the talking voice are two different instruments."

The reason for her problem seemed clear enough. Absorbed in her work, Whitney was exhausted. She had been facing the grueling demands of daily concert dates; when she wasn't in concert, she was in her hotel room giving interviews to an ever-growing group of reporters; and in her few free moments after she completed those tasks, she could be found on a soundstage, shooting a video of another song from the album. With the enthusiasm of a novice who had finally made it, Whitney simply tried to do everything—in the words of her own song—"all at once." And she paid the price.

"I am so tired," she complained to associates. "You

cannot *imagine* how tired I am. Day and night, I'm exhausted. Is this what it's going to be like?" she fretted. "Is this what I have to look forward to?"

Whitney got through the rest of the tour by drinking gallons of hot tea laced with lemon and speaking only when absolutely necessary. "I have to conserve my voice," she told a reporter. "If I can't sing, what then? I'm in deep shit."

During a brief pause in the cross-country tour, Whitney went into the recording studio to perform another duet with Jermaine Jackson. Producer Michael Omartian hired the two to do an upbeat song, "Shock Me," one of the cuts on the soundtrack of a film disaster ironically titled *Perfect*, starring Jamie Lee Curtis and John Travolta. The 1985 film attempted to be a documentarylike examination of the health-club scene. Curtis played an aerobics instructor who had her class exercise to "Shock Me," which had an appropriately pounding beat. The soundtrack did better business than the film, with many critics and fans agreeing that "Shock Me" was the best offering on the album. The song was further proof that Houston's star was rising, while the film in which it appeared nearly killed the careers of Travolta and Curtis.

At Christmas that year, Cissy Houston was asked to host a holiday show on MTV's new sister channel, VH-1. The proud mother accepted, and invited a newly minted star, her daughter, Whitney, to cohost. The format of the segment—insofar as its producers and writers imagined it—was simple. The mother-and-daughter team would introduce videos, many of them starring Whitney, and fill in the gaps with the kind of (mindless) chatter that has come to be called TVTalk.

But Cissy and Whitney were too excited about the

younger woman's skyrocketing career to engage in idiotic ramblings on the air. They threw out the script they were given and turned their hosting duties into an intimate and engaging conversation between two people who had known and loved each other for years. Sitting on stools in front of a Christmas tree and a baby grand piano, they might have been mother and daughter chatting intimately in their own home.

In one touching moment during the show, Cissy sang a song to her daughter, a capella, that seemed especially appropriate, the Helen Reddy standard, "You and Me Against the World: "When all the others turn their heads and walk away / you can count on me to stay. . . ." One can almost imagine Whitney recalling the times her mother stayed with her when she was sick; when Cissy allowed her in the recording studio; when Cissy let her sing in her act; during her school days, when children beat Whitney up for being too pretty, too well dressed . . . too white . . . and how her mother told her the way to deal with bullies: whip their asses.

Then, for a national TV audience, the feisty older woman set the record straight about their relationship with Dionne Warwick—who in recent press reports had been described as everything from "Whitney's aunt" to "Cissy's mother." Cissy looked straight into the camera and said, "Dionne is not my cousin. She is *my* niece and *Whitney's* cousin."

Typically, Whitney didn't allow her mother the last word, especially in front of countless viewers all over America (hardly any of whom are likely to have cared about the genealogy of the Houston-Warwick clan). "My mother and Dionne's mother," she said, "are sisters—which makes Dionne and I [sic] first cousins."

But Cissy had been down this last-word road with her daughter before. She added, closing the book on the mock controversy, "She is my much *older* sister, of course."

And if that conversation didn't speak to the nation's television viewers of love between mother and daughter, nothing ever would. Clive Davis himself couldn't have scripted it better. For the finale, mother and daughter performed a heartrending gospel classic.

It was a charming program. They were human bookends—one woman whose career was mostly over; another woman who, though nobody, not even the confident youngster herself, could have guessed, would go on to become one of the biggest pop stars of all time. At that Christmas ten years ago during their finale, they were just two best friends doing what came naturally to them: praising the Lord in song.

Back in the dog-eat-artist world of the music industry, Whitney was so immersed in the daily grind of the concert tour, she didn't realize that her album was breaking sales records around the world. (Not that she didn't care about finances. One insider insisted that when the time came to talk money, Whitney's voice was louder than anyone's.) In fact, the singer ignored her performance on the charts to concentrate on her performance onstage. Remembered an associate, "Whitney felt that in order to give her best every night of the tour, she couldn't be sidetracked obsessing over gold records or number one songs."

But she would have had to be deaf and blind not to know she was quickly becoming a hot, hot, hot commodity. "Of course, I could see what was happening," she later told *Cashbox* magazine. "You can tell from the audience's reactions to the songs that things are changing. At first, the applause was polite. I knew that they didn't recognize the songs. Slowly, though, I could see that they were smiling and applauding more and more. Even standing. What a thrill it was. But it was also scary."

At one press conference in New York, Whitney noted, "I cry every day. You've got to remember that I'm still relatively young—I'm a baby in a lot of senses."

Indeed, this "baby" was moving quickly up the charts throughout the world. In the United States, while "You Give Good Love" rose to the top of the R&B charts and cracked the Top 40 of the "Hot 100," "All at Once" reached number five in the Netherlands. "Saving All My Love for You" sold over one million units and went to number one in Britain. Houston's appearance on the French TV show "Champs-Élysées" propelled the same single and album to the top of the charts in France. An identical hurricane was reported in West Germany, Australia, and Canada. And in Japan, a long-term promotion with Nippon Phonogram resulted in album sales in excess of 300,000—this in a country where 50,000 in sales for an international repertoire product is regarded as excellent.

By August 1985, Whitney Houston had the honor of knocking a longtime family friend from the number-one spot on the R&B charts in the U.S. Aretha Franklin had spent five weeks at number one with "Freeway of Love" before "Saving All My Love for You" knocked it down to number three.

Clive Davis, meanwhile, was basking in glory, crowing to the press, "To carefully nurture a young artist for two years and then have your dreams come true is like a storybook tale." Indeed, in the eyes of the press and the public, Davis had orchestrated a real-life Cinderella story, with young Whitney Houston as the recipient of the magical glass slippers and Davis himself a rather elderly Prince Charming.

But as Whitney continued her worldwide tour and her album smashed sales marks in the U.S. and abroad, the press grew tired of the Cinderella theme. The first less-than-glowing piece appeared in *Rock and Soul* magazine in early 1986. In an article titled "How Long Will Whitney Last?" Charles E. Rogers carped, ". . . the new superstar's future looks secure. But is it? Is she a victim of star overkill? And will the fickle public, known for its 180-degree turns once it tires of seeing, hearing and being force fed a 'new' face, voice, body, etc., turn off to Whitney Houston?" An Arista Records executive provided the company's answer when he said in another interview, "Whitney is so good that she'll override the burnout syndrome."

Not everyone agreed. A New York–based entertainment journalist who insisted on anonymity predicted the Whitney publicity machine would eventually crash and burn from overexposure. "I've seen this happen before. A star gets treated like a queen, only to be disregarded like yesterday's newspaper when sales fall off on the next album or the one after that. It's usually the case with overexposure, something that Whitney is getting too much of for her own good and the longevity of her career."

So the questions raised by Rogers could not be ignored. Was she overexposed? And was it hurting her?

First of all, one needed to remember that, of course, Whitney herself was not responsible for the press coverage that landed her on the cover of just about every magazine in the universe in 1985 and early 1986. The responsibility for this goes to Clive Davis and Arista. The company wanted to sell records, so the Arista promotion machine generated publicity. As far as anyone else was concerned, where were the evidences of overexposure? In declining record sales? Press disinterest? Whitney's getting blasé and giving evidence of having a bad attitude?

Well, record sales were still astronomical. The press seemed insatiable. And the object of all this attention, Whitney herself, had a pretty *good* attitude. She seemed unfazed by the microscope trained on her every move and thought. Gracious and polite, she answered the same questions over and over again, as though they were being asked for the first time: "What is it like to be so successful?", "How important has your mother/Clive Davis [interchange at will] been in your career?", and "Is this a dream come true for you?"

Was she overexposed? Maybe. Was it hurting her, or anyone else? In one phrase of the day, "Not so's you'd notice."

Whitney later addressed complaints that she was overexposed and that Davis was micromanaging her career. "Let's face it," she said with a laugh. "You make a record, you want people to buy your record— period. Anybody who tells you 'I'm making a record because I want to be creative' is a fucking liar. They want to sell records. As it went on—and it went on—I took a very humble attitude. I was not going to say, 'Hey, I sold over thirteen million records—check that shit out!' My mother always told me, 'Before the fall, goeth the pride.'"

In another interview, Whitney essentially told her detractors that her attitude was, "If it ain't broke, don't fix it." At that point in her career, her record sales and concert fees showed the Arista publicity machine to be in no need of repair.

And with regard to micromanaging and "orchestration": did Arista have too many knobs and switches it was adjusting too often and too finely? "I don't know about 'orchestrated,'" said Whitney. "Everything I have done has worked. I didn't plan to sell this many copies of my record the first time. Arista and I obviously did the right things, and if that's success—and if it is orchestrated—then I want to orchestrate it for the rest of my life."

Clearly, the woman just didn't understand about being insincere and disingenuously humble. She was being who she was, saying what she felt—and she felt good. "If it ain't broke, don't fix it." There was no need for her to concoct dark theories about how the present stratospheric highs might not go on forever. Or for her to try to predict exactly how things might change.

But change they would.

Half a dozen years later—by 1993—Whitney Houston had become more wary of press scrutiny and told *Rolling Stone* that the price of success was high. "It's really strange," she said. "Michael Jackson said it best: 'You become this *personality* instead of a person.' That's what's strange about this image business—the more popular you become, the weirder they want to make you. I read some stuff about myself last year—it's like, 'Who the fuck are they talking about?'"

From the time of her first album and tour, Whitney Houston began to discover the downside of fame—the arbitrary tides of celebrity status and the terrifying unpredictability of the press. No amount of "damage control" interviews would satisfy bloodthirsty reporters who'd detected the provocative scent of prey. If the word got out—probably from a disgruntled ex-employee—that the singer was haughty, ungrateful, and a "diva"—the press reported it with a savage glee. She began to feel betrayed by those same reporters who originally heaped praise on her.

"I've just figured it out," she announced to one

reporter. "I can't trust you guys. I can't trust the press. I tell them one thing, they write something else. I decide what I *don't* want to say, they quote me as having said it anyway. I'm out here working hard, losing sleep, nervous and all about giving great shows. And the media just writes and writes and writes whatever they want to. It's the kind of thing that can make you real fucking paranoid."

Cinderella had discovered that her glass slippers, though lovely, pinched if she wore them too long. And Prince Charming's wondrous palace, where she had intended to live happily ever after, was full of hidden trapdoors and leering strangers and poisoned food.

eight

By the end of 1985, it seemed as if Whitney
Houston had lived an entire lifetime in one year. Sales
of her album were brisk. Every single from it went
straight to number one and kept the album on the
charts, where it went *triple* platinum—with more than
three million copies sold. Apparently, there were no
fans left who didn't own her album, yet it kept on selling. Her tour continued, with larger venues rebooked
many times in the same cities she had played only
months before.

As 1985 drew to a close Whitney took time out to
evaluate her achievements and their impact on her private life. At the tender age of twenty-two, when most
middle-class kids are trying to figure out what to do
with their college degrees, Whitney was a millionaire.
She had been toasted, feted, applauded, and mobbed by
fans around the world—and she was, according to her
own testimony, still the same person who enjoyed
singing in church.

In 1986, she described her "normal" life in an interview with *US* magazine. "I like to listen to music, read books, spend time with my family." Success and adulation, she said, hadn't turned her head. "I don't go out and party, and I like to keep to myself a lot. I know the press is always looking for something to gossip about so I stay out of the whole party scene when I'm not working."

And even if she had wanted to "go out and party," she wouldn't have had the time. An exhausting concert and personal-appearance schedule didn't allow her time to get enough sleep, much less hang out at trendy clubs.

Her friends have said that she was always something of an introvert when she wasn't onstage. In fact, she seemed to put so much energy into her act, she didn't have any left for a private life. Whitney liked to "cocoon," as pop psychologists call it today—to hang out at home with a cup of tea and a good book.

However, Whitney's sensual stage persona often gave a different impression, creating the illusion that she was hot to trot, a fire waiting to be lit by Mr. Right. At least that's what some writers of fan letters seemed to infer, as Whitney began discovering another downside of fame: obsessed fans.

According to associates, she received letters that were alternately scary and creepy. Some particularly frightening ones implied that the letter writer and Whitney were already lovers. Other fans begged for "just one date" with their idol, promising they alone could satisfy a woman they only knew from concerts. Such delusional people apparently hadn't read the dozens of interviews in which she insisted she wasn't "that kind of girl"—or maybe they *had*, and nothing registered. Maybe, in fact, the operative word was simply "delusional." At least the new star could take comfort in the realization that she wasn't alone in attracting the wrong kind of fan.

Psychologists and sociologists have long studied the phenomenon of idol worship. A 1994 article in the *Los Angeles Times* reported, "Americans—through television, the movies and print media, tend to embellish heroes by assigning qualities of perfection to those who are not perfect." The article also noted, "The nature of the medium of celebrity is to make stars seem familiar to us. We think we know them." This phenomenon too often leads to pathological behavior that can be terrifying to the objects of a crazed fan's obsession: Janet Jackson, David Letterman, Sharon Gless of "Cagney and Lacey," and others have been stalked by fans who fantasized romances with a celebrity they have never met. The murder of young television actress Rebecca Schaeffer is proof of how far a deranged fan can go.

"The fact is that some of these fans are downright scary," Whitney once noted. "I swear, I don't know what to think of them, except that something is not right with some of them. It's a big issue. I think it should be taken seriously."

Unfortunately, Whitney did not have anyone nearby who could truly understand her problem. Cissy Houston might offer motherly support but not direct experience, as she had never achieved her daughter's extraordinary level of fame. Even Whitney's hugely successful cousin Dionne Warwick, never found her life discussed in such microscopic detail.

Whitney was horrified to realize that going on a simple date was virtually impossible. In fact, these days, there was no such thing as a simple date. Anything she did in the company of a man led to reams of speculation, not always in the best of taste, about "Whitney's new boyfriend." In turn, she found most men either intimidated by her success or anxious to exploit it to further their own careers.

Still, when she considered the possibility of romance, she was hopeful but practical. When reporters asked her to describe the kind of man she was looking for, Whitney revealed that she wasn't in the market for a man. She said, "I'm not actually looking. I'd be too busy to even if I wanted to. But when he comes along, I think I'll know. I do believe in romance. But I think you can be realistic and romantic at the same time. I like to be able to sit down and talk to a guy, get to know him. Because really, the basis for a long-lasting relationship of any kind is knowing what the other person wants and believes, what kind of person that they are."

While her disclaimers struck many reporters as disingenuous, the fact of the matter seems to be that there was simply no romance in her life at this time. Some of Jermaine Jackson's friends and associates have claimed that he and Whitney shared a brief romance, but there is no evidence to support this.

They did renew their professional association in early 1986, though. Jackson, who had previously recorded three duets with Whitney, joined her in the studio again—this time for a track on his new album, *Precious Moments,* set for release that spring by Arista. The song was a lush ballad titled "If You Say My Eyes Are Beautiful."

According to a music-industry insider, however, Jermaine was not happy to have Whitney as a duet partner on this particular song, and it had all been Clive Davis's idea. Along with some executives at Arista, Jermaine feared that Whitney had been overexposed. He worried that her appearance on this song would prevent its release as a single. Indeed, while listener response to the song as an album cut was positive, Jermaine's unease proved justified: the song, which had all of the makings of a number-one hit, was not issued as a single. "He was really pissed," said the insider.

Meanwhile, despite her disclaimers, Whitney had not remained romantically uninvolved. In 1985, Eddie Murphy caught her performance at Carnegie Hall. After the show, he went backstage to see if she was as gorgeous up close as she appeared onstage. He wasn't disappointed. One observer said Whitney was "thrilled" by the visit and by his praise of her performance. Gallantly, he also tried to console her about an incident that had occurred during the performance.

Whitney had learned that New York Mayor Ed Koch was in the audience and she asked him to join her onstage during a break in the concert. However, because the mayor's popularity had, for a variety of reasons, taken a nosedive in recent years, the audience turned ugly when Whitney welcomed Hizzoner onstage, and cheers turned to catcalls and boos. Brought up by her strict parents to be unfailingly polite, Whitney was shocked by such behavior.

She chided the 4,000-strong audience, "That's not very nice, is it?" Then she turned to Koch and said, "Don't take any notice. Ignore them. I'm very proud to have you at my show."

The crowd continued to boo until Whitney suddenly walked off the stage with tears in her eyes. Ever the trouper, though, she reappeared a short time later and continued the show, despite being visibly upset.

But such rudeness was not easy for her to forget, a fact of which Murphy was surely aware. "That, plus he had a crush on Whitney Houston," said a Houston associate.

When they met backstage at Carnegie Hall, Murphy was on his best behavior and Houston apparently found something lovable about him. Typically sphinxlike in public, all she would later say about their relationship was that they were "closer than most." A friend of Murphy's, however, was slightly more forthcoming when asked about the two. "Sure, Eddie and Whitney were close," he said. "But not like friends. I know they were very attracted to each other—you know . . . physically."

"Whitney brought out the best in Eddie," said a former associate of hers. "Yes, they were intimate. Yes, they had a good time. No, it was not easy.

"Both of them had busy schedules. They got together when they had the time. But Whitney was afraid to fall too deeply for Eddie. She wasn't sure how loyal he was to her when she wasn't around, which was most of the time. She read stories in the tabloids, heard rumors. So she tried to protect herself by keeping a safe emotional distance from him. They had quiet, romantic dinners. They had great sex and they loved each other, but Whitney was purposely cautious."

Murphy's best buddy, Arsenio Hall, often made references to Whitney Houston during his talk-show monologue to titillate the public about *his* supposed affair with her. Though it was all in fun, a leering and lip-smacking Arsenio continued to joke about his "romance" with Whitney. The audience ate it up.

Then, one night, during his monologue, Whitney appeared unannounced from the wings. Arsenio crouched down, hiding his face, while Houston chastised him. It was all clearly lighthearted. "You lie! You lie!" she said, wagging her finger at him. Arsenio finally confessed in front of millions of viewers that, yes, he had exaggerated his tale of a relationship with Whitney.

Because very little remains unscripted on such shows,

Hall was no doubt in on the stunt. But there was a core of truth in Houston's mock rage, as she didn't want anybody, even as a joke, falsely claiming intimacy with her. (She made several more appearances on the program before it went off the air in 1994, and she and Arsenio remain friends to this day.)

"Whitney would never have been dating Eddie Murphy and Arsenio Hall at the same time, anyway," says a source. "She would never pit two friends against one another like that. She loved Eddie. She liked Arsenio. He helped her out a lot by talking about her constantly on his show, keeping her name out there. . . ."

Even if Whitney's "surprise" appearance on Hall's show was a publicity stunt, Whitney hardly needed it. Her album seemed to be the modern entertainment-industry version of the fabled perpetual-motion machine. Once it started selling, it would continue selling forever all by itself.

In *Billboard* magazine's annual year-end issue for 1985, Whitney was cited in no fewer than sixteen "top" categories. She was number one in Top New Pop Artists and Top New Black Artists categories, as well as high on the list of Top Pop Album Artists—Female, Top Black Albums, Top Pop Singles Artists, and Top Adult Contemporary Singles. "You Give Good Love," "Saving All My Love for You," "How Will I Know?", and "The Greatest Love of All" were all top-ten records (and, in fact, all were *number-one* singles except for "You Give Good Love," which peaked at number three).

Another track from the album, "All at Once," received heavy airplay, almost as if it had been released as a single. In fact, Clive Davis decided not to issue it for fear—*finally!*—of over-saturating the market.

• • •

The new year—1986—would bring even more accolades to the rising superstar.

In January, the National Academy of Recording Arts and Sciences (NARAS) announced the nominees for the twenty-eighth annual Grammy Awards, the music industry's biggest and most prestigious awards show. Not that her album needed any more help, but a Grammy win would add longevity to its stay on the charts.

Houston was nominated in three categories: Album of the Year, Best Pop Vocal Performance—Female (for "Saving All My Love for You"), and Best Rhythm and Blues Solo Performance—Female (for "You Give Good Love"). "You Give Good Love" also picked up a nomination for songwriter LaLa as the Best Rhythm and Blues Song.

Whitney was pitted against a formidable array of established artists in each category. Her album was up against works by Dire Straits, Sting, Phil Collins, and (the sentimental favorite) *We Are the World—USA for Africa/The Album*. Whitney must have been especially pleased—maybe the better word would have been "terrified"—by her competition in the solo R&B category: Aretha Franklin and Chaka Khan, both of whom had been her friends since childhood, and whose singing styles had greatly influenced her. And her vocals on "Saving All My Love for You" were nominated along with offerings from Madonna, Linda Ronstadt, Pat Benatar, and Tina Turner.

There was only one glaring omission: Clive Davis, as though taking the view that her three nominations weren't enough, was enraged that his discovery hadn't been nominated in the Best New Artist category. Other newcomers with less spectacular sales were nominated, including A-Ha, Freddie Jackson, Katrina and the Waves, Julian Lennon, and Sade.

Davis sent NARAS officials a letter demanding an explanation. NARAS wrote back explaining that Whitney was not eligible due to her prior appearance on albums by both Jermaine Jackson and Teddy Pendergrass. Davis wasn't satisfied, and he, or more likely an in-house publicist at his behest, fired off a letter to *Billboard* magazine, which dutifully printed the missive from one of its biggest advertisers in the January 18, 1986, issue. The letter was headlined WHAT DOES "NEW ARTIST" REALLY MEAN?

Davis's complaint began, "How is it that a recording artist can be voted Favorite New Female Artist by the readers of *Rolling Stone,* named Newcomer of the Year in music by *Entertainment Tonight,* Top New Artist (in both pop and R&B) by *Billboard,* sell nearly four million copies worldwide of her very first album and *not* be considered a candidate for Best New Artist by the National Academy of Recording Arts and Sciences?" Davis went on to mention his dissatisfaction with the written response by NARAS president Michael Greene to his initial query.

In that response, Greene had written, "The rule that disqualified Whitney is perfectly clear. It reads: 'An artist is not eligible in the Best New Artist category if the artist had a label credit or album credit, even if not as a featured artist, in the previous year's awards.'"

This only seemed to aggravate Davis more. His letter to *Billboard* continued: "Fair enough. Except that, as a former president taught us, 'perfectly clear' is often a matter of opinion." He then cited his own research, which revealed a very liberal interpretation of the rule on many previous occasions: Cyndi Lauper was nominated as Best New Artist even though she had previously been the lead singer on an album recorded by the group Blue Angel; and Luther Vandross had been similarly honored for his solo debut despite a previous recording as a member of the group Change. Davis's hardworking publicity staff even cited Carly Simon's win as Best New Artist in 1971, when, in fact, she had recorded prior to that, with her sister, as the Simon Sisters.

NARAS's response—that Whitney had been eligible for Best New Artist for either the Jackson or Pendergrass album—only further infuriated Clive Davis. He wrote, "Does anyone seriously believe that [Whitney] would have been nominated as Best New Artist on the basis of two guest duet appearances? When someone comes along and makes an impact such as Whitney has, it'll come as a big surprise to quite a few people that, according to the rules of NARAS, sometimes new isn't new."

One could argue that Davis was being greedy, but then why shouldn't he want recognition for his artist? He was surely dismayed that his brilliant plan—featuring Whitney on albums by other artists in order to create a "buzz" about her own prior to its release—had, ironically, ruined her chances for the one award he apparently coveted the most. Certainly it seemed as if NARAS was splitting hairs, as if some bigwig had said, "We don't want to give too many awards to one person."

The American Music Awards presentation in late January 1986 eased some of Davis's pain, however. Although Janet Jackson was considered the front-runner in the seven categories in which she was nominated, she finally won only two—while Whitney was hailed as the evening's big winner, collecting five. In addition to awards for vocals and material, she won in the Video Singles category for "The Greatest Love of All." (Accepting the award, she thanked "almighty God for love and strength," along with Clive Davis and her mother for their incalculable contributions to her life and career.)

As the Grammy ceremony drew near, Whitney was upset about the fuss over the Best New Artist nomination. She told reporters she was thankful for the three nominations and would not address the subject any further. One source, however, later revealed that although Whitney was supremely honored at the three nominations, she was not quite as complacent as she appeared to be in regard to the NARAS slight. According to an associate, Whitney was miffed. "I think Clive is right," she said. "I should have been nominated in that category. I *should* win it."

"She was upset, but she couldn't let the press know that," another source said. "Her mother was pissed off too. Whitney actually had her managers call Arista almost *daily* to find out if NARAS had changed their minds. When it became clear that the music academy was holding pat on its decision, Whitney's family and friends tried to get her to leave it alone, but she was still ticked off. She knew that she was better than the nominees for Best New Artist, and this realization made her omission all the more irritating."

Whitney managed to hide her annoyance while she was at the Grammy ceremonies, where she let go with a scorching version of "Saving All My Love for You." (In fact, *that* performance later won her an Emmy Award.) Before the ceremony, she told *USA Today*, "If I win, I win. It's an honor, of course, but I feel the same as I did before."

Then, when the time came for the Best Female Pop

Performance award, Dionne Warwick had the job of reading the names of the nominees. When Warwick opened the envelope and read the name of the winner, she let out a whoop—because, of course, it was that of her cousin, Whitney Houston. It was a charmed moment.

Despite what Whitney had just told *USA Today,* it *wasn't* the same after she won the award. She ran onstage with a smile that could have lit up all of North America. Again, she thanked God and her parents, "who made it all possible for me." (A cynic later quipped, "If she had her real priorities straight, she should have thanked Davis first, since he was probably more instrumental in her winning than her mother or God.") After embracing Dionne warmly, Whitney strode offstage in triumph. Forgotten in the joy of the moment was the fact that she lost the other awards for which she had been nominated.

Whitney focused on what she won, however, not on what she lost. Backstage after the ceremony, she told a crowded room of reporters, "I feel like a real Cinderella! It is a very emotional time for me."

Despite conflicting opinions as to how deity, Davis, and family should have been ranked in Whitney's success, the fact was that more than any other singer there that night—with the possible exception of the Jackson brood—Whitney had a family who had been profoundly involved in her accomplishments. This was, of course, particularly true about her mother. In addition to her much-publicized connection with cousin Dionne Warwick, Whitney was still being advised both by her mother (Cissy reportedly continued to choose her clothes for her) and her father, who were still not officially divorced. Whitney's brother Gary sang backup on tour and on her album, and brother Michael worked on the

1964. Toddler Whitney.
Even then she had that
glamour face.

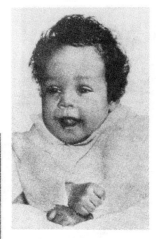

Whitney's graduation
picture. At 16 years old
she was ready to start her
modeling career.

Legendary
Rhythm-and-
Blues singer
Cissy Houston
with her daugh-
ter, Whitney.

One of Miss Houston's first publicity photographs. Her debut album, *Whitney Houston*, was released in 1985.

Posing for the cover of the single "How Will I Know?", her second number-one hit.

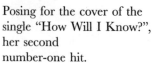

In 1986, Whitney won the Grammy Award for "Best Female Pop Performance."

At a 1986 fund-raiser party for AIDS Research in New York.

Whitney had reason to smile—she'd just won the "Best Female Pop Performance" Grammy Award for the second time, in 1987.

Whitney with her mother, Cissy, and brother, Gary, in 1988.

Whitney is seen leaving a charitable fund-raising party in New York.

A rare picture of Whitney with her mother, Cissy, and father, John, taken at the 23rd Annual Awards of the B'nai B'rith, a Jewish Humanitarian Organization, June 1987.

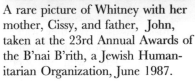

Her second tour, following the release of *Whitney*, resulted in sold-out concerts, including one in New York at the Jones Beach Theatre, as pictured here, in August 1987.

At the 1988 American Music Awards, Whitney walked away with two awards, including one for "Favorite Pop/Rock Single" for "I Wanna Dance with Somebody (Who Loves Me)."

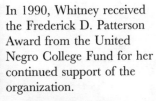

In 1990, Whitney received the Frederick D. Patterson Award from the United Negro College Fund for her continued support of the organization.

© ALBERT FERREIRA/DMI.

John Houston with his "little girl," Whitney, at a pre-Grammy Awards party in 1988.

© DAVID MCGOUGH/DMI.

Whitney Houston with her cousin, Dionne Warwick, in 1990.

© ALBERT FERREIRA/DMI.

Long-time friend Stevie Wonder with Whitney Houston in 1990.

© ALBERT FERREIRA/DMI.

Lena Horne is seen congratulating Whitney on winning the 1990 Hitmaker Award.

© ALBERT FERREIRA/DMI.

Whitney Houston and mother, Cissy, in 1990.

© ALBERT FERREIRA/DMI.

Natalie Cole sang a duet
with Whitney on Cole's
short-lived music series *Big
Break* in 1990.

In 1991, Whitney hosted
Saturday Night Live, with
actor Alec Baldwin. Here,
she is seen rehearsing for
her segment.

Whitney and fiancé, Bobby Brown, attended the 1992 Friars Club Tribute to Clive Davis. Davis is president of Arista Records.

© ALBERT FERREIRA/DMI.

After suffering a miscarriage on the set of *The Bodyguard* in 1991, Whitney tried again in 1992. Did she ask Santa for a boy or a girl?

© ALEX OLIVEIRA/DMI.

Husband Bobby Brown congratulates Whitney on winning two Soul Train Awards in March 1994.

© KEVIN WINTER/DMI.

tour staff, which also included a female cousin as well as best friend/surrogate-sister Robyn Crawford.

Over the years, while Whitney's father had worked for the City of Newark in various capacities, he also became a shrewd businessman. And in 1986, a press release announced that he would be joining Eugene Harvey as his daughter's co-manager. Despite their separation, Whitney came first for both parents, and they put their personal differences on permanent hold for her greater good.

"John wanted to do more," an associate said. "He felt stifled by his less-than-glamorous job with the city and was also a little jealous over the strong bond between his daughter and Cissy. And he dearly loved show business—always had. He asked Whitney if he could co-manage her. She said, 'Yes, absolutely.'"

Cissy, who still had a lot of respect for John, graciously didn't stand in his way when he sought the job. Photos from this period always show Whitney standing between her parents, a living link connecting them. Whatever antagonism they may have felt for each other, they kept to themselves for the sake of their superstar offspring.

Whitney, one must acknowledge, has been truly blessed by her parents' devotion. They provided a buffer against a cutthroat industry that tends to elevate artists to celestial heights, then indifferently regard their earthward plunge when the next "overnight sensation" comes along. And since the adulation a pop star receives can turn even the sweetest of God's children into an egomaniacal monster, it is a sign of Whitney's good sense that to this day, even as her life has undergone radical and sometimes uncomfortable change, she continues to ask for, and to get, her parents' love and advice.

nine

To say that Madonna was the world's most photographed woman in 1986 is not hype. To say that Whitney Houston was a close runner-up is not hype, either. The difference is that Whitney most likely couldn't have cared less. Which is not to suggest that she was indifferent to publicity; it simply means that Whitney probably wasn't keeping score.

Madonna created a grim, synthetic, hard-edged, in-your-face eroticism—packaged it, sold it by the millions of units, and got very rich. Whitney Houston, a "good girl" who learned her craft while singing in the church choir, was sleek, reserved, and elegant, measuring herself out carefully but with a springlike sort of freshness. She also got very rich. (The same opposites were present during the British invasion of the sixties. The Beatles were the nice working-class boys next door. The Rolling Stones were the outlaws you wouldn't want in your bathroom because you were afraid they'd use your towels.)

Considered together, the women represented an

archetypal dichotomy—that of the virgin and the whore, the good girl and the bad girl. From a man's point of view, the woman you marry and the woman you lust after. From a woman's point of view, the woman your mother taught you to be and the woman you fear you really are—or wish you were. Whitney was the virgin; Madonna was the whore. In that sense (and probably *only* in that sense), they were two sides of the same coin. The record-buying and concert-attending crowds knew, if only dimly, that the world of popular music was offering them both face of their personal fantasies—love and fear, clean and dirty, accepted and forbidden, saintly and wicked.

To her credit, Houston's image seemed to be more authentic: what you saw onstage was what you got. With Madonna, what you saw was likely just to be her latest phase, as she moved from one persona to another with the facility of a child playing dress-up in Mommy's (and sometimes Daddy's) clothes. What you got was her latest mood. (Madonna fans, of course, would counter that what you got was simply the latest facet of a complex continually evolving personality.) It might take a roomful of psychoanalysts to fathom the ongoing popularity of Madonna—a woman who herself admitted she didn't have that great a voice and was not a particularly proficient dancer.

On the other hand, Whitney Houston's popularity is easy to understand. She has a powerful, expressive voice, equally mesmerizing when belting out a song or whispering a love lyric. And she is so drop-dead gorgeous she could be a model, which of course she had been.

Issues of popularity aside, however, all was not at ease in the business empire of which Whitney was the centerpiece. And there were subtle pressures from

Arista's marketing department for her to be a little sexier on her videos. But Whitney didn't want to turn into a tease. And if she hadn't held that opinion already—which she did—her awareness of Madonna's relentless publicity seeking would have brought it out of her.

"I find Madonna particularly revolting," she told one interviewer, with characteristic candor. Whitney had very specific views of performers who "used sex to sell albums" and minced no words when it came to the sexually ambiguous Madonna. "Madonna says horrible, nasty things like, 'Go to bed with anyone you want.' She's not really lady-like, is she? I don't know what she has—but I don't like it. In the long term, I'm sure she will just be forgotten."

(People in 1986 thought that prediction was lunacy. Madonna was *the* pop star at the time, earning more than the gross national product of some small South American countries. Even today, Madonna can turn up on David Letterman's show, produce dirty underwear, and get her name and face on the front page. But her sales have slacked off. One wag recalled the assertion that sexually explicit magazines have done what no one in six thousand years of recorded history ever thought would be possible: they've made sex boring. Maybe, he suggested, that's what Madonna did with her relentless overexposure: made *herself* boring.)

During a chance meeting backstage at a music awards show, Whitney approached Madonna, who had just beaten her out of the Best Female Performer Award. "Hey, girl. How ya doin'?" Whitney asked.

Madonna gave Whitney a look that could only be characterized as chilly, the way the inside of an eighty-ton commercial refrigerator can be characterized as chilly. Then she brushed by Whitney and sniffed, "Obviously better than *you* are."

"What is her problem?" Whitney asked a friend later. "What did I ever do to *her*?"

Although Whitney, the former choir singer, makes a striking contrast to the Material Girl, she is no Marie Osmond. She would never end up playing Maria in *The Sound of Music*, unless it was a parody of the musical on '*In Living Color.*' When crossed, Whitney can swear like a stevedore or be as controversial as Andrew Dice Clay or the late Sam Kinnison.

In a 1986 interview with *Rolling Stone* headlined WHITNEY GETS NASTY, she discussed her views on sex and the influence of her brothers during her early years. "I knew all the shit that guys could lay on you from A to Z," she said. "I got to hear how guys talk about girls. It's so ugly! They're going: 'I had her the other night,' 'Well, I had her *last* night,' 'Well, I had her last *week*. . . . ' You know, my brother had one girl outside, one upstairs, one in the basement—and all three of these girls would be waiting for him. It was sick. . . ."

Yes, Whitney Houston's image was a far cry from Madonna's. One can almost imagine her mother/manager whipping her upside the head if she ever pulled any Madonna antics, like, on a video, pretending to masturbate or burning a cross in front of the Houston family's church. Finally, however, the public did insist on viewing her as a sex symbol, not because of any overt behavior but simply because the statuesque singer with mile-high cheekbones was so beautiful. While one might say that Madonna created her fans, one might also say that Whitney's fans created Whitney—or at least they created a lustful longing for the singer.

An industry insider has said, "Whitney is very sexy, but her sensuality comes from the inside. It's who she is, and she doesn't need to roll around or wear revealing clothes to put it across. She simply is sexy."

Whitney would agree with this assessment. Her sexuality is natural, not synthetic. She said, "I have this thing about being sexy—where it comes from. Either you have it or you don't. It's not something you can put on. It has to come from inside." Then, in a not-so-subtle slap at Madonna, she added, "I think when people try too hard to sell records by using sex, they lose the focus. I think there is a certain sensuality that music deserves. But I don't try to use my sex appeal to sell a record. I think my record will sell itself."

Whitney's strong family influence and moral upbringing have encouraged her to set boundaries in the way she promotes her career. Her image allowed the majority of her fans to catch a glorified glimpse of themselves, born and bred in middle-class America. Regardless of the fact that her family had been in show business since she was a child, Whitney remained "the girl next door," who made it and somehow stayed real and true.

And while Whitney wasn't concerned about her significance in terms of pop sociology, she was, nevertheless, enjoying the delightful fruits of her huge popularity. "I'm still adjusting to success," she said. "What is exciting for me is to be able to do whatever I want to do—like traveling, for instance. I recently enjoyed a trip to Europe, and Paris was the best! I did a lot of shopping."

At that time, when she was still living in an apartment in Woodbridge, New Jersey, five minutes away from her mother's house, Whitney, in more than one interview, couldn't help but praise her parents. "My parents, the love and security they wrapped us in, has been most beneficial to my career. My mother's input is major. I think sometimes people move too fast in this business. So I'm taking it slow. Longevity is what counts . . . and I just hope and pray that I'm still here, alive and singing, in twenty years."

Was it all too much—that she regularly thanked and gave credit to God and her family? Didn't it all sound too *decent*? She had to be kidding us, right? It was almost enough to make a person uncomfortable. Except Whitney herself didn't seem to have a problem. So whose problem is it, anyway? One might have wondered.

And what did she think of Los Angeles, the city to which so many celebrities migrate when they become famous? "Oh, *puh-leeze*," she said, laughing in an interview with the *Boston Globe* in July 1986. "L.A. is L.A. and I'm from a different world. I'm not into L.A. at all. I'm your basic East Coast person. I'm a New Jersey girl. I'm very secure here, so I don't want to go anywhere else. This is my home and where my family is. My foundation is here, and I don't want to leave that."

Whitney was asked to perform at the hundredth anniversary of the Statue of Liberty on the Fourth of July and presented a moving rendition of "The Greatest Love of All." After the ceremony, she talked about the lyrics of the song and what they meant to her. "Our young people need to hear that song and realize that it's about loving yourself," she told writer Lynn Normant. "If you can love yourself through all the rights and wrongs and faults, then that's the greatest love of all. That's the message."

The message of love is spread in many ways, and Whitney knew her success would enable her to support charitable causes. In Washington, D.C., she hosted a charity concert for homeless children and asked the ticket holders to bring along a can of food. Children had always been of special interest to her, but she spread her largesse across a whole spectrum of worthwhile causes, raising money for unemployed steelworkers and donating a large sum to a charity that buys gifts for terminally ill children.

Indeed, Whitney devoted so much of her time to various charities that people wondered where she found time to promote her own career. One cause she couldn't help but join was her cousin Dionne Warwick's fight for AIDS awareness. Warwick had scored a number-one hit with "That's What Friends Are For," with Elton John, Gladys Knight, and Stevie Wonder, and had organized a four-day extravaganza to benefit the Warwick Foundation fund for AIDS education and pediatric AIDS care. As one of the song's writers, Warwick donated all her publishing rights to her AIDS foundation. The highlight of the fund-raising weekend was a concert at Avery Fisher Hall, which featured Whitney, Gregory Hines, Gladys Knight, and Cyndi Lauper. Onstage, Whitney was visibly moved. She began to cry as her cousin explained the foundation's impact on the littlest sufferers: "They will be nurtured, cared for, hugged, sung to, cuddled, kissed, and taught there is love."

Arista Records and Clive Davis decided to waste no time in producing a follow-up to Whitney's debut album, which, by the end of 1986, had gone platinum *six* times—selling over six million copies—and had set a music-industry mark as the best-selling debut album ever. Davis assembled much of the talent from the first album, including Michael Masser, Kashif, and Narada Michael Walden. Jellybean Benitez, who had worked wonders with Madonna and Janet Jackson, rounded out the production team.

While several producers laid down initial tracks and compiled arrangements, Whitney took time to return to her hometown of Newark, where Mayor Kenneth Gibson gave her the key to the city. Witnesses to the event say it was hard to tell who was smiling with more pride, Whitney or her family. The mayor, after a brief speech, presented Whitney with a plaque that said, *Whitney Houston, your voice is as beautiful as a Monet painting. You have reached for the stars and now you hold them in your hands. I know we will have the pleasure of hearing your outstanding singing for years to come. Thus, I give you flowers which will last throughout all those years.*

Whitney beamed as she accepted the plaque, looking into the crowd for familiar faces of friends and relatives from the old days. The honor was gratifying, but the event was tinged with sadness for her. Whitney has said she couldn't help but notice the change in old friends. These onetime intimates now treated her like home-grown royalty; she found their deference off-putting and embarrassing. "They no longer call me my nickname, Nippy. Now they call me *Whitney*," she said to *Ebony* magazine in 1986. "When I go to visit I'm treated like some kind of goddess. But I'm really the same kind of girl I was five years ago, with the same morals and values. I do have a lot more money," she allowed, "and I'm a lot busier than I was before. But that's basically it."

Still, it seemed a matter of perception. Whitney felt strange because her friends were *treating* her like a stranger. Then, some of them complained that *she* was standoffish, that she just did not seem the same. "She wasn't what I remember her as having been," said one neighbor when interviewed. "It's like she's another person all of a sudden. Sort of distant."

One Hollywood insider has noted, "Somebody as

famous as Whitney Houston often discovers she has the odd expectation put on her by others to be *perfect*. People expect her to be their perfect mother, their perfect beloved aunt and big sister; their perfect nurse, psychoanalyst, and best friend. Then, when the celebrity turns out to have actual human personality traits, the onlooker is disappointed and is even likely to get angry. How dare she be less than perfect! The celebrity, meanwhile, is left with her jaw hanging, not understanding why this adoring fan is suddenly heaving ripe fruit onto the stage."

Whitney was the recipient of so many honors that she had to divvy up their acceptance among relatives. While she pocketed the key to the City of Newark, her father was in the Big Apple, accepting a New York Music Award for his daughter. Beaming, he joked, "Whitney would probably thank her two brothers for not killing her when they used to fight as kids and for saving her voice."

Whitney Houston's fans were inordinately curious to learn anything about her next album, and *Black Sounds* magazine sent a reporter to the recording session to find out. During a break, Whitney gave the journalist a sneak peek. "People have their own opinions about the record, but it is basically *me*," she explained. "A lot more up-tempo things will be on this album. My ballads are still there—I can never do away with those. There are a few surprises and things."

The interviewer wanted to know how Whitney kept her performances on tour fresh. She responded, "Each night, I don't sing the songs the same exact way I did the night before. And I don't necessarily do the same things I did onstage the night before. We try to do different things to make it more interesting."

While these nightly variations kept her happy and her material fresh, many fans were vocal in their disappointment. They had come to the concert expecting to hear a live duplicate of the album they adored. One fan complained, "I love Whitney's voice, but I went to one of her concerts and I couldn't even recognize most of the songs. She performed them so differently than she did on the album, and although I think she's got a great way of improvising, I felt cheated. I wanted to hear the songs I liked so much. And I didn't."

Some observers felt she didn't "connect" with her audiences, while others called her performances "sterile." "It felt like there was a big glass wall between us," one concertgoer said. "She was nice enough and had energy, but I thought maybe she didn't really like the songs she was singing and that she really didn't care whether we were there or not."

This complaint had been mentioned in several reviews of her live act. An executive at another label placed the blame for Whitney's coldness on Arista and its calculating boss. "The way Arista 'built' the first Whitney Houston album really left little room for the artist. It was all about the songs and the impact they would have on a certain demographic. In this industry, when one goes for a product meant to appeal to just about everyone, something is going to get lost. In this case, what got lost was Whitney Houston, herself.

"When you have an artist, let's say Anita Baker, she brings with her a certain emotion and 'place' that she comes from with the material. The album is then built around that place and the audience is asked to respond to a very specific emotion that deals directly with the singer and themselves. Whitney Houston was not asked to bring anything with her to her first or her second albums. The emotional depth of the recordings is shallow, because the emotions in the songs are not hers. All the listener is hearing is her voice, singing words that someone else wrote that, in most cases, mean very little to her."

Though Whitney has admitted that she changed her songs each night in order to "make them interesting," one reviewer wasn't buying that defense. "If Whitney really cared about the material and truly felt the emotion of the songs, she would not have to make them 'interesting' in different ways each night. They would simply represent emotions she feels and the sounds would come naturally."

It's logical that Whitney didn't feel the full depth of some of her songs simply because she lacked the life experience that would have enriched and deepened her performance. Compare the early Beatles' work, which sounds like bubble-gum music, to their later recordings, material so sophisticated it has been compared favorably with the work of major classical composers. Certain things take time, and much of Whitney Houston's personal and artistic evolution was yet to take place. In the meantime, however, she was giving what she had. And with the possible exception of an off-night (or even a bitchy night), what she had to give was evidence of a remarkable and well-developed talent.

Meanwhile, sales of her debut album had reached thirteen million. It logged fourteen weeks at number one on the *Billboard* charts, making it the longest-running album by a female artist other than Carole King (fifteen weeks at number one in 1971). Who cared if Whitney appeared frosty onstage? She was burning up the charts and sending Arista stock into the stratosphere.

The second album was scheduled to hit the streets

on June 2, 1987, with the first single to be released one month prior to that date.

At a promotional meeting the game plan for that album was discussed in the kind of detail that had earned Arista a reputation as the best record company in town in terms of hustling its product and its stars. The strategy in Arista's boardroom seemed more reminiscent of a military campaign than a publicity campaign.

Each member of the marketing team received a promotional packet that would be sent to every radio station, disco deejay, and important music journalist in the country. Inside the kit was the heading MERCHANDISING MATERIALS, under which the text read: *Look for an all-out merchandising blitz at retail and rack locations throughout the nation!*

Not for nothing was Arista famous for giving its all to an artist. And Arista had thirteen *million* reasons to believe in Houston. A small sampling of the campaign items suggests the blizzard that would descend on consumers and retailers: prerelease announcement streamers; lavish retail kits distributed to five thousand record stores throughout the U.S.; posters, large and small, of the photogenic singer; tapes; videos; and on and on and on.

The only trick the advertising gimmicks seemed to miss was the promise that Houston would appear in person at every record-buyer's home—although some wags joked that Davis was busily trying to find a way to clone his star for just such a purpose.

The first single off the new album was the up-tempo "I Wanna Dance with Somebody (Who Loves Me)," which, per the album notes, was "Loved, produced and arranged by Narada Michael Walden." Radio stations were generously provided with copies of the single, along with a note from Arista's legal department warning them not to air the single until 7:30 A.M. on April 29, 1987. Arista executives had even picked the hour and the minute this new offering could be unveiled to the public. Such marketing control would result in virtually every pop, rock, and R&B radio station in the country playing the new single *simultaneously.*

Whitney Houston was to kick off a support tour for the new album on July 4, 1987, at Tampa Stadium in Florida. *Billboard* magazine, in an unprecedented move, planned to feature a "pull-out 17 x 22 frameable photo of Whitney Houston" in an issue that would hit the stands at the same time radio stations began broadcasting the single.

With all this hoopla, even something as uncommercial as, say, a Gregorian chant would have hit the top of the charts—and Houston's second album did just that, entering the Billboard Hot 100 chart at number one. (It must have been the "frameable" photo that did the trick.) Whitney would become the fourth artist (the other three being Elton John [1975], Stevie Wonder [1976], and Bruce Springsteen [1986]) and the first female artist ever to debut an album at number one.

To die-hard fans, Whitney's second album proved that her debut wasn't a fluke—which was a matter of concern among some, since the music industry is littered with one-hit wonders. Some music purists, however, complained that she had chosen a safe repetition of the lightweight, nonthreatening tracks of her debut album.

But radio listeners didn't care what purists and the critics thought. They just loved (and bought) what they heard.

The first single off the new album, "I Wanna Dance with Somebody (Who Loves Me)," had the dynamic impact Arista anticipated. It debuted at number thirty-eight on the *Billboard* pop charts and soared to number one in seven weeks.

Despite the record's success, however, Whitney's critics had suddenly become harsh. The fashion among "serious" music critics was now to attack the black singer's white-bread musical style. One critic dusted off the famous remark about the sixties' group the Fifth Dimension, calling Whitney the "Lawrence Welk of Soul."

Perhaps the most venomous attack came from Carmen Keats in her review in *Melody Maker* magazine: "Whitney Houston has the vacant gaze of an out-of-use letter-box and the kind of brain—yes, she has one—that thinks up a splendid LP title such as *Whitney*. Whitney can also bore the pants off of me. There, I've said it. Her mock spiritual affectations and her awed assumption that even sexual love is a gift from God (but do you know about Jesus, dear?) make me feel like I'm having pureed Jehovah's Witnesses forced up my nose." Somehow, Whitney had begun to attract the kind of toxic criticism usually reserved for Barry Manilow records.

Other writers, well, played it safe by sticking to the theme "Whitney Plays It Safe." The album was seen as a well-planned, well-executed copy of her first. Once the critics' darling, Whitney had now become the bad girl of homogenized pop. "Trite," "pleasant," "light," "trivial," and "overwrought" were some of the nicer adjectives applied to her second effort. A few writers bucked this pack journalism and insisted that the new album evinced growth, if not in the choice of songs at least in the artist's delivery.

Impartial industry observers—if such people can be said to exist in this volatile, partisan, highly charged business—tended to feel the album's commercial success derived from a handful of songs strong enough to become hit singles.

Others, especially big fans of the singer, felt the second album was superior to the first because it was pure Whitney—no duets with established stars like Jermaine Jackson or Teddy Pendergrass as a form of insurance. And Arista had obviously felt this, too. Because the company truly believed in the artist, it threw her into the marketplace without a life preserver (like Jermaine Jackson) because it felt she didn't need one.

Arista's confidence was not misplaced. The second album reveals a more expressive, more mature voice, and a more evolved artist—Whitney herself, having done the vocal arrangements. Enthusiasts felt their star had overcome the mediocrity of the songs by the sheer force and expressivity of her musical personality.

As one fan said, "When Whitney sings a song, it done stay sung."

"I Wanna Dance with Somebody (Who Loves Me)" is an infectious dance number that achieves exactly what it sets out to. The rhythm is irresistible. It stays with the listener hours later, the way particularly catchy tunes from a Broadway show stay with a theatergoer. In comparison to her debut album's "How Will I Know?" this dance track allows Houston to cut loose from saccharine lyrics and over-orchestrated harmonies.

The strongest up-tempo track on the album is, without doubt, "So Emotional." This hard-driving song about an obsessive love brings Whitney closer to the "inspired soul" of her early mentor, Aretha Franklin, than any other Houston song to date.

"Just the Lonely Talking Again" is another breakthrough—the focus being on Whitney's voice, with a sensual through-line reminiscent of Anita Baker or even the early soul recordings of Whitney's mother.

Unfortunately, however, Clive Davis's much-loved "multidemographic" approach still prevails on the second album, with a cloying "Love Will Save the Day," which seems to have been lifted directly off (or possibly rejected from) a Miami Sound Machine album. And no one would have been surprised if Olivia Newton-John had been credited in the liner notes as composer of the heroically insipid "Love Is a Contact Sport."

Whitney's second album contained a total of eleven tracks, variously produced by Narada Michael Walden, Michael Masser, Jellybean Benitez, and Kashif. In the album notes, Whitney takes no chances and—after God—thanks what appears to be every person she has ever known. The list starts with her mother, her father, her brothers, Robyn Crawford, her producers, and her musical arranger; then goes on to include her cats, managers and road crew, Arista's international affiliates, her band, her staff, and even "every studio I worked in, as well as the musicians who played on this album and especially to the engineers who work that board. . . . "

Oh, "and also Clive Davis . . . "

ten

In 1987, the New York Daily News *reported* that Whitney Houston was worth over $44 million. Not bad for a twenty-two-year-old with just two albums under her belt. Only Steven Spielberg (with $50 million) and Madonna ($47 million) topped her on the list of Hollywood's wealthiest stars. Whitney even beat Michael Jackson, whose net worth was *only* $43 million.

Whitney Houston was rich. She was also young, beautiful, talented, and—lonely? Although she was generally acknowledged to have been involved with Eddie Murphy at one time, Whitney said she had never really been in love.

In a television interview that year, she explained why one of the richest and most beautiful women in America didn't have a date on a Saturday night: "I have felt the feeling of being in love, but I've also turned away from it. 'Cause I've known people who have been in love and how they react and I just ain't got there yet. It's like—'You're about to be losing your mind!' I haven't gotten to that stage yet."

While Whitney insisted she hadn't found Mr. Right, the overeager tabloids claimed she was madly in love with a string of unlikely men. A photo of Whitney and baseball player Darryl Strawberry in the *New York Daily News* incorrectly reported that both celebrities were single, even though Strawberry was involved in a nasty divorce case. When one tabloid reporter popped the question "Are you and Whitney an item?" Strawberry was clearly taken aback and finally muttered, "Yeah, well . . . Aw, I don't want to get into that." Then, as though he wanted to tweak the rumor a bit, he added, "You never know, do you?" The baseball star's noncommittal yet teasing answer was all the tabloids needed to run Whitney-loves-Darryl stories for a solid month.

One of the more unlikely figures linked romantically to Whitney was the Purple One, The Artist—as reporters now identify him—Formerly Known As Prince. (Writers are compelled to use that elaborate descriptive term because most ordinary word processors and typesetting devices can't produce the unusual ankhlike symbol to which the eccentric singer legally changed his name.) But back in 1987, when he was still plain old Prince, he seemed to believe the fiction that the tabloids were printing about his "girlfriend," Whitney Houston.

Prince told a reporter, "Whitney is so different from any of the women that I've been in love with. If I'm going to marry and have kids, it will be with Whitney." The tabloid didn't even bother to get a comment from Prince's putative bride. Maybe the reporter knew how ridiculous the whole story was.

Not to be outdone, the *National Enquirer* upped the ante by declaring that Houston was "in love for the first time." And it claimed the object of Whitney's love wasn't the purple-clad rocker, but a six-foot-five-inch New York restauranteur by the name of Brad Johnson. According to the story, Johnson met Whitney at a party and they immediately made plans to see each other the following evening. "Since then," the *Enquirer* reported, "things have really heated up between them. They've gone out all over New York for intimate dinners and to music clubs." Johnson was quoted as saying, "I love to be with her. We've been dating regularly. Whitney's personality is as warm and open as her singing. I'm glad she likes to be with me."

Whitney and Johnson were sighted at nightclubs "holding hands," and, as a final note of proof, a "source close to Whitney" confided, "The other night I heard her singing to herself. It was the old standard, 'Someone to Watch over Me.' I asked her who she was thinking about and Whitney said, 'Well, I'm going out with Brad again tonight.'"

If the story is true, we may never know because the new superstar was very reluctant to discuss her personal life. In this vacuum—and because she never sued them—the tabloids churned out story after story.

Occasionally, however, the intensely private singer would slip and shed a little light on her romantic life—though the operative word was "little"—as when she admitted in an interview that she and Eddie Murphy were "closer than most." But such glimpses were rare and sketchy. Unlike many of the publicity gluttons in show business, Houston really didn't care to live her private life in public.

As her album sales increased, the legitimate press as well as the tabloids couldn't get enough of Whitney Houston. She found herself in unwanted competition with the likes of Princess Diana, Elizabeth Taylor, Michael Jackson, Don Johnson, Madonna, and

Roseanne Arnold. Putting any of those famous faces on the cover of the tabloids guaranteed an increase in circulation.

Whitney sheepishly admitted that she loved scouring the tabloids and kept a sense of humor about the bizarre fictions they called "news." In an interview on a local New York talk show, she said, laughing, "They're funny. I read them and I think, 'Wow! They're really into me!'" Then she added, only half joking, "I should own part of them. They make a lot of money off of me!"

There was, however, some truth to one rumored "connection," which Whitney substantiated during an interview with talk-show host Byron Hall. Asked about her relationship with actor Robert De Niro, she replied teasingly, "Yeah, he was sweatin' me."

"Bob wanted her to star in a film with him," explains a former associate of Whitney's. "And he also wanted to get to know her personally. Some felt he used the idea of a film project as bait to catch her."

There's a certain logic to De Niro's courting Houston for a possible film role (though Whitney was unhappy with the script he showed her) and maybe for more personal reasons as well. De Niro's romantic interest in women of color is well-known. His ex-wife is African-American actress Diahnne Abbott, and at the time of this story he was dating African-American model Toukie Smith.

De Niro inundated Houston with avalanches of flowers, which arrived with increasing frequency. A friend of Whitney's said, "Every few days, she'd have a big bunch of flowers, roses, or something exotic, from De Niro. Now this was not unusual, except when he just kept sending flowers . . . with his home phone number." When the flowers didn't get a response, De Niro upped the ante by sending her jewelry, including a cuddly teddy bear that happened to be wearing diamond earrings!

"That was it!" Whitney's friend said with a laugh. "When that bear was delivered with diamonds dangling from each ear, I said, 'Girl, this man is after you. Just what are you gonna do about it?'"

Houston was flattered and a little embarrassed by her suitor's ardor. "'I think Mr. De Niro wants more than just my friendship!'" her friend remembers being told.

Finally Whitney called her would-be collaborator and wannabe lover. The conversation was short. "She said he was very nice on the phone," the friend has recalled. "They congratulated each other on their successes and he told her he was interested in the idea of them doing a film together. But she said she was real busy, which she was at the time. That was pretty much it."

According to sources, Whitney *was* swamped with concert and recording dates, but the real reason she declined the overtures of one of the greatest film actors in the world was that she hated the script he had offered, which was about kept women and corrupt filmmakers. And, on top of everything else, mother Cissy was definitely not happy about a possible relationship between her daughter and the actor.

According to one source, when Cissy Houston learned of De Niro's interest in Whitney, she wasted no time stepping in and putting her foot down. "Cissy had ambivalent feelings about De Niro," this source said. "Any time his name came up, she would get a little upset. Cissy was not happy that he was sending Whitney presents and other things. She said, 'That man is twice as old as Whitney.'"

Whitney, however, was intrigued. Still, her mother continued to have a lot of influence over her, and Cissy quite simply forbade her to get involved with the actor. John Houston agreed, and had a heart-to-heart with his daughter, assuring her that "you don't need this in your life right now."

Some Arista executives even got in on the act and reportedly told Whitney that a liaison with a white man would not be the greatest publicity for the new queen of soul. Davis indicated the nature of his concern by using the term "career suicide."

De Niro persisted. He reportedly told a friend, "I've tried everything . . . flowers, notes, jewelry, and even a teddy bear or two. I'm still in the batter's box, but I can't even get a single!" De Niro was clearly smitten with the model-turned-pop-star. "She's the sexiest woman I have ever seen. She is gorgeous. I want her by my side," he confided to an associate.

Whitney told one friend that she had tried everything to get the actor to move on to another potential conquest. "I really don't know what to do about this," she said. "The attention seemed so nice at first. But, even though I am flattered beyond belief, I really don't want a date with him."

De Niro's response was that he was willing to wait. And wait he did.

Sources also now reveal that Cissy had the final word in the matter. "During one conversation with Whitney about De Niro, Cissy became very upset. Whitney and Robyn then left to go to New York and when they walked out, Cissy ran around the house, grabbing all of the presents that De Niro had ever sent to Whitney. She shoved the things, including some really expensive designer objects, and that damned teddy bear, into a giant box and addressed it to Robert

De Niro. She enclosed a note that said, 'Return to sender' and 'Thanks, but no thanks.'"

Reports about the men in Whitney's life (or the men who wanted to be in Whitney's life) circulated with seamy regularity in the gossip mills. But other kinds of stories also made the rounds. Those involved her relationships with women—or, rather, one particular woman: Robyn Crawford. Suspicious minds—and, of course, "inquiring" minds—refused to believe two females could be the best of friends without also being lesbian lovers.

Whitney's intense friendship with Robyn had fueled rumors for years, and both women had denied them for years. But as the young singer's popularity continued to soar, the stories-that-would-not-go-away came back. After all, when you're a journalist dealing with one of the most famous women in the universe, you have certain *obligations,* don't you? Whitney *owes* it to her fans to respond to everything you ask, doesn't she?

Questions about her sexuality and her sexual preference began to emerge in interviews. Reporters and gossips were emboldened to ask the most personal of questions.

At first, Whitney's attitude toward this issue—which, one must recall, she had been confronting since she was a teenager, when her friendship with Robyn began—was consistent with her down-to-earth reputation. She refused to discuss the matter. But then her silence was construed as an admission that the rumors were true.

Respected magazines like *Time* began to discuss the issue. Once that prestigious publication asked if she was gay, other publications felt they, too, had the right to ask, without any sense of embarrassment, "Are you and Robyn lovers?"

Whitney should have just ignored the whole matter. Instead, she responded. . . and responded and responded. All denials, but extremely *vehement* denials. Now she had become the hunted. Taking shots at the famous and formidable and impenetrable Whitney Houston became an approved journalistic sport.

After a while even the levelheaded Houston lost her composure, and exploded at a reporter for *Rolling Stone*. "The media distorts shit. It's never, never what I said; it's never how I said it; it's never how I thought the person perceived me. It's always some other crazy shit—which is why I don't like giving interviews. Because they lie. They just outright lie. You know what? I am so tired of this. I'm really sick of it. People want to know if there is a relationship [between Robyn and me]. Our relationship is that we are friends. We've been friends since we were kids. [Robyn] is now my employee. I'm her employer. And we're still the best of friends. That's what it is. You mean to tell me that if I have a woman friend, I have to have a lesbian relationship with her? That's bullshit. There are so many, so many female artists who have women as their confidantes, and nobody questions that. So I realize that it's like 'Whitney Houston—she's popular, let's fuck with her.' I have denied it over and over again and nobody's accepted it. Or the media hasn't."

But Whitney's profanity-filled response made good copy, and other publications, hoping to enliven what they imagined might just be one more unremarkable interview with a self-absorbed rock star, gleefully brought up the "L" word in their interviews.

Freelance music journalist Kelly Leonard believes that such eminently quotable, vitriolic responses to questions about her sexual identity simply stoked the fires of Whitney-is-gay gossip. "She talks too much, that's the real problem," Leonard says. "Her responses are exactly what we are looking for—it makes for very good press. That's the only reason that the magazine would print it.

"Let's say you ask someone a question during an interview, and they respond with. 'Oh, that—big deal.' We are not going to print that. Who cares? Short, boring answers to questions do not make it to the final cut of the story," Leonard explains. "So what Whitney Houston really does is to keep the story alive by responding with so much anger. She should just shut up. Really, what she should say to the interviewer is, 'Can't you think up a more interesting question than that?'—and then drop it. I guarantee you—the issue would be dropped in no time at all."

And so, what was one to believe? Whitney and Robyn had a strong, long-lasting friendship. A *close* friendship. In an age of embattled relataionships and rampant selfishness, here was Whitney Houston with a truly devoted friend. How dare she!

Were they lovers? Whitney vehemently denied it.

Had they ever been lovers? Whitney vehemently denied it.

Was she lying or telling the truth? We may never know for sure, although if we credit Whitney with some integrity, or even if we just want to respect her privacy, we might give her the benefit of the doubt.

On the other hand, maybe the question needs to be regarded differently. Whitney had a friend she loved, who stuck by her when much of the rest of the world became snarling, stalking, rapacious. Maybe the relationship would last, maybe it wouldn't. Maybe it would change form. Who was to know? And maybe if the rest of us shared the kind of friendship Whitney and Robyn had, we might not feel the need to make arbitrary judgments about the lives of other people, of people who seem to be happy and who are sharing love—whether the love is that of friends or of lovers.

Despite the growing rumors, Whitney's public image was still squeaky-clean enough for her to be considered a role model for the youth of America. A national magazine reported in 1987 that "trash is out and class is in," calling the exhibitionistic Madonna a perfect example of the former and Houston a sterling example of the latter. The magazine quoted the following from Harvard psychiatrist Dr. William Appleton: "Many people are fed up with trash and sleaze. They've become disenchanted with songstresses who dress and behave like tramps." The magazine praised Whitney for her "rewarding approach to intimacy" and her positive influence on young girls who were just beginning to date.

Other publications lauded her religious upbringing and saw her as an ideal for young women seeking a career in the music business. Her popularity spanned many demographics, and pop sociologists praised Houston for bringing numerous disparate groups together through the power of her music. Dr. Tom Greening, a UCLA psychologist, said in a 1987 article, "Whitney Houston is a binding force. Her versatility bonds families together—different generations feel better listening to her, realizing that they have something in common."

Whitney wasn't exactly thrilled to take on the onerous burden of role model to 250 million people, though. Nowhere in her job description had she seen any reference to that task. She felt the assignment was unfair and—as she became more and more famous—somewhat frightening. While she was happy to lend her name and popularity to good causes, especially if they aided young people, she categorically rejected the notion that her personal life was a model for the youth of America to follow. Nevertheless, in the eyes of many, she remained a person to be emulated and idealized.

A sociologist theorized that many of the nation's youth seemed to confer near-godlike virtues upon Whitney Houston because, "Young people are disillusioned, scared, confused, and looking for answers—and Whitney personifies a refreshing romanticism."

Maybe so, but when she read this, she became angry. "My private life is mine," she retorted. "You can't live a life in the public because they rip you apart." And she felt the public had unrealistic expectations of her. "It seems like you're a prisoner of your own fame," Whitney told one reporter. "I try to be normal. I don't want to be a prisoner. I was born free."

The subject of fame and its presumed obligations was a frequent subject in discussions between Cissy and her famous daughter. The elder Houston has said, "I remind Whitney that they build you up just to tear you down. I tell her she is never to drink the perfume, just to smell it." Cissy has also stressed the need for Whitney's continued reliance on two foundations: God and family. Says Cissy, "If she's on a firm foundation with those, no one can destroy her, no matter what."

Very well. But some prophetic hints had been dropped, though no one really caught them. "I try to be normal." Why would a person say that? "I don't want to be a prisoner." Why would a person say that? "I was born free." Why would a person say that?

Then one day in late 1987 something happened. Whitney Houston's fans and admirers may never know exactly what caused it, whether it was something she felt or thought of or heard or read or dreamed or imagined. Whatever the cause, Whitney changed. On tour in

London near the end of 1987, she suddenly seemed to give up. She was tired. She had spent two years traveling the world. During brief breaks, her time was consumed with recording sessions and endless interviews. She was being asked the same questions and was giving the same answers, over and over again.

Backstage before a concert at London's Wembley Stadium, she appeared distracted and pensive. Witnesses later said she actually seemed to resent being required to go onstage and perform. When would she have time for herself, away from the studio, concerts, and the bogus controversies?

As though by force of will, she pushed herself onto the stage that night.

The lights dimmed; a spotlight followed the young singer across the stage. The opening theme song began. The expectant hum of the audience turned to a roar as the fans waited for her to begin. Whitney seemed refreshed by the adulation and threw kisses to the crowd. She took a deep breath. But what came next wasn't a song.

"Hello, London! I have had seven consecutive number-one singles!" she bragged uncharacterstically. Then, in an exercise of questionable judgment on that particular turf, she crowed, "I am bigger than the Beatles!"

The audience turned against her. There were boos. Catcalls. Whitney's attitude? "What's *their* problem?"

"She had no patience for any of it," said one concertgoer. She added, "The show was haphazardly performed. [Whitney] practically sang to herself. When she addressed the audience, she was chilly. It was a horrible concert."

The diva had emerged. Her now-famous truculence had made its first major appearance. Aroused by impossible demands from the public and the nitpicking of the press, Houston began to build a protective shell around herself that very few people, certainly not reporters and fans, would ever crack again. Her behavior from then on seemed to be saying two things: "No more Ms. Nice Girl" and "Leave me alone. I don't owe anybody anything but a good performance."

Following the fiasco at Wembley, Whitney arrived two hours late for a postconcert party, keeping guests like Boy George and Elton John waiting.

After spending only a few minutes with Whitney, Boy George told the *Daily Mirror,* "What a rude cow! I've met most of the Royal Family, including Princess Diana. Yet, royalty wouldn't treat people that way. She made me feel like a nothing."

In retrospect, this concert can be seen as a major turning point in the public's attitude toward Whitney Houston. Back in the United States, reviews of her concerts began frequently to mention her "bad" attitude onstage, a subject that often crowded out praise for her talent. After a concert in Boston, she was described as "tired and a bit grumpy" by a reviewer for the *Boston Herald.*

"Houston started out by complaining about the chill in the air. She stayed unglamorously overdressed in a turtleneck sweater with a leather jacket and gloves. . . ." The reviewer then took exception to her need to control her audience. "When the audience wouldn't cheer quite loudly enough to please her, she insisted that they could do better. Later, in her exactly-90-minute show, she asked the crowd, 'Are you having a good time? That's good, I am too.' She added [this] without a trace of conviction."

In Pittsburgh, the *Courier* noted, "[A] sharp opening pop-jazz performance by Kenny G. with his saxophone was at least partially wasted on Houston by her apparent reluctance to play to the audience rather than her dressing room mirror. . . . Early on in the program, [Whitney] was given two bunches of roses from her loving fans and, almost in complete horror to the packed house, she immediately proceeded to walk the roses over to where the musical director was seated. Smiling, she heaved the long-stemmed flowers like a bale of hay into the pit. 'It's hard to be humble' could be her personal motto.'"

Whitney also began adopting some . . . *eccentricities*.

Before she would perform at one state fair in 1987, she reportedly demanded written assurance that the following would be included in her dressing room: two clothes racks, two matching lamps, a large banquet table, flowers, a hot plate with hot water, fruit juices, springwater, a box of herbal tea, four fresh lemons, a cheese-and-fruit tray, and unprocessed honey. And for her entourage, fifty complimentary tickets, five cases of beer, four dozen freshly laundered bath towels, and a piano tuner.

J. Randy Taraborrelli, author of *Call Her Miss Ross: The Unauthorized Biography of Diana Ross,* sees a familiar pattern at work. "Whitney really was tired," he insists. "You can't really blame her. I don't think she realized the costs of that kind of fame. She probably felt she had no choice but to entertain. She is a singer. Most of her associates agree that she does not like to entertain. However, she was now a major corporation and a lot of people were relying on her—she was supporting most of her family and many other people. The expectations were very high."

Taraborrelli notes that Diana Ross exhibited the same behavior at one point in her career. "After Diana had her children, she didn't want to work anymore for a while. She told this to Motown executives and was

met with a deaf ear. Of course, she had to keep working; she had contracts, she had certain responsibilities.
In that business, you have to strike when you're hot.
And because she had no one else to lash out at, she
took it out on her fans. All of those smiling faces looking up at you and asking for your autograph—she
began to resent them, and it came out in both her live
appearances and in her interviews."

Writing in London's counterculture magazine *Time Out*,
Nick Coleman recounted his experience with Whitney
Houston during a press junket. "She has a blank face. It
registers emotions singly and without apparent movement
between each mask. She smiles; she looks sincere; she
looks bored; and she has a depressingly effective look of
undisguised contempt, at which the corners of her mouth
turn up, her eyes narrow and her shoulders slump in an
attitude of instant and total ennui."

Coleman raised this issue with the star during a press
conference.

"If I am asked intelligent questions and things that I
like to answer," Whitney told him, "then I find it very
enjoyable. If I'm asked things which are stupid and
don't matter, then it's very boring." As she answered
the question, Coleman noted, the superstar refused to
make eye contact with him. The intrepid reporter simply walked over to where she was looking and forced
himself into her line of vision.

"What about gospel, then?" he asked her. "You have
gospel roots; are you likely to record some gospel material?"

Whitney looked at him, rolled her eyes, and stared at
a spot on the ceiling. Then, without moving her body
or her eyes, she said, "Uh-huh. At some point. Yeah."

Coleman asked, "You don't like answering these
questions, do you?"

Whitney finally looked at him and shrugged. "They're kind of boring, you know?" After that, she refused to call on him at the press conference filled with jostling reporters.

Taraborrelli adds, "It happens a lot with celebrities. They seem to want the fame and the money and the glory, but no one really prepares them for the bad news, which is you still have to perform, even when you're not performing. The public does not understand that when you refuse to sign their autograph book, snub them, or worse yet, give a bad performance—you are simply being human. Tired, bored, angry—they're all human emotions, but unfortunately, we as a public do not allow our heroes and heroines to possess these qualities."

During that memorable concert in London, Whitney Houston seems to have decided that she *was* allowed to possess these qualities. No longer would her well-being be in *their* hands, leaving her to fear that *they* would scorn or reject her. Her life was *her* life.

She invited and then faced the fear, every person's fear, every performer's fear—of public scorn, ridicule, rejection. Indeed, it wasn't pretty. It would lead her into moments of extreme self-indulgence, self-absorption, and pettiness. As the world looked on, she would change and grow. But when it was finally over, she would have learned what she needed to learn. She would have walked alone through the fire.

From that night on, a different woman appeared before the public, a woman who, whether her fans liked it or not—or even understood—was reclaiming her own soul.

eleven ◯

In 1988, a reporter for a teen magazine asked Whitney Houston, "What are your plans for the future?"

Her usual response had been "sing, sing, and more singing." But this time she surprised her interviewer when she said, "You know . . . I eventually want to branch out into other things, like acting, acting in films and stuff." Then she added a shocker: "The only part I've considered seriously is playing Diana Ross in her life story. . . ."

Upon learning of Whitney's film plans, *Miss* Diana Ross replied tersely, "Fat chance."

The battle of the divas was under way.

Neither Diana nor Whitney was happy that the media was constantly comparing them. Whitney hit the ceiling whenever anyone credited her success to anyone other than herself or her mother. And Diana's associates claim she was sensitive to the implication that Houston's interest in portraying her in a movie implied that she was either too old or too near the has-been category to play herself.

Rumors in the film and music industries were that Houston's debut film would be an adaptation of the hit 1981 Broadway musical *Dreamgirls,* a thinly veiled fictional account of the Supremes and the sixties group's lead singer, Ross.

Whether or not *Dreamgirls* was an accurate depiction of the group's rise and fall, Ross *hated* it. And the possibility that the younger star would play her in the film adaptation enraged her even more.

Ross had refused to attend the 1981 Broadway premiere, and she went so far as to forbid her daughters and staff to see the show. "I don't want my daughters to see *Dreamgirls* and think that what they see is really how it was," she said.

An associate of Ross said the forty-four-year-old singer was particularly galled that Houston, at twenty-four, was at the peak of her career while sales of Ross's recordings were declining. "I'm sure that [Diana] was somewhat sensitive [about Whitney] from the start," the associate said. "You're a big star, you're minding your own business, and along comes this newcomer and the media is writing that she is the new version of you? That's enough to make anybody mad."

But according to a confidante, "Whitney never really wanted to do *Dreamgirls,* anyway. But she did say that if Diana were to do it, the movie would have to be retitled *Dream-Grannies.* Ouch!"

Whitney did nothing to squelch this feud with her stinging remarks about the veteran singer in the now defunct *Fame* magazine. In an interview, she speculated about the cause of Ross's alleged jealousy. "What happens to people when they get to a certain stage and hear the patter of little footsteps [behind them]? I think

Diana likes the attention. I don't need attention that bad."

Whitney then offered her theory on why Ross's film career was in the Dumpster. "Diana got boring," she said. "*Lady Sings the Blues* was amazing. And then *Mahogany* and *The Wiz*. She got boring. I don't know what happened."

Houston's caustic remarks were especially shocking because stars rarely bad-mouth other stars—at least not in public. The thinking is basically that if simple courtesy isn't a sufficient motive for restraint, the star you are disparaging could suddenly get hot again, you might want to work with him or her, and then where would you be? It's the old adage about not burning your bridges. And an older, more mature performer would have realized this. But the young and blazingly successful Houston didn't.

Whitney's manager, Eugene Harvey, worked on damage control by telling reporters that Whitney had not even seen a script or received a concrete offer to star in the film version of *Dreamgirls*. But he did hint that her debut film would probably be a biography of legendary singer Josephine Baker, who escaped the St. Louis ghetto to become the toast of Paris during the Roaring Twenties.

"It might be interesting to portray somebody historical who is not alive," Whitney later said. "Somebody interesting and real three-dimensional, like Josephine Baker. She founded a kind of orphanage for kids of all colors and nationalities, her rainbow children, as she called them. I think that's pretty inspiring."

These thoughts did not mollify Ross. In fact, they probably irritated her even more than the idea of Whitney playing a fictionalized Ross in *Dreamgirls*. Ross had wanted to play Baker for years. In 1976, she performed a few songs made famous by Baker and even donned the late singer's trademark banana skirt during her concerts that year. (However, she stopped short of imitating another Baker trademark: appearing topless.) And, in 1985, she optioned *Naked in the Feast,* a Baker biography. "I am *very* interested in Josephine," Ross said at the time. "She was an absolutely incredible, multi-faceted woman. There are lots of different areas about her that people don't know about. I get incredible feelings about this lady."

Unfortunately, so did Whitney Houston. Whitney told another writer, "I'm a great admirer of Josephine Baker. I really think the role would be lots of fun. I'm looking forward to doing it."

According to her associates, Diana, of course, went ballistic. Sounding a bit paranoid, she told one associate, "Whitney Houston has no interest in Josephine Baker. She just wants to one-up me!"

Diana was further incensed by a suggestion made by Jean-Claude Baker, one of Josephine Baker's adopted children. "I suppose," he said in 1988, "that a compromise could be struck: have Whitney Houston play my mother as the teenager who stormed Paris in 1925, and Diana Ross play her as a mature woman during World War II." This was clearly not what Ross needed to hear.

The media labeled Houston as "young," "fresh," and "new." Terms like "languishing career" and "once great" were applied to Ross. It is easy to imagine the older singer feeling trapped in some kind of nightmare version of *All About Eve,* with Ross playing Margo Channing to Houston's Eve Harrington.

Was cherubic, choir-singing, God-fearing Whitney Houston toying with the media? Was she purposely stoking the fire to perpetuate a "feud" with Diana Ross?

As much as she criticized the invasiveness of the press, many felt Houston was fast learning how to manipulate the institution she claimed to loathe. Insiders speculated that the entire Robert De Niro affair could have been kept under wraps if Whitney hadn't leaked information to the press. Even the usually media-shy De Niro felt compelled to say of Houston's disclosures, "I feel like I've been used."

Diana Ross apparently didn't feel used, however. Whether her rage was real or feigned, Ross got more mileage—and publicity—out of her spat with Houston than she had received in quite a while. In fact, some friends of Ross started their own campaign of leaks and innuendo. Soon reports began surfacing that Diana was planning a comeback in order to "topple Whitney and reinstate [herself] to her rightful place as queen," according to one of Ross's partisans. In view of the disappointing sales of Diana's latest album, *Workin' Overtime,* a little conspicuous scratching and howling with Whitney wouldn't have hurt.

It all seemed to get out of hand, though, perhaps prompting Whitney to try to set matters straight by saying to writer George Hadley-Garciaone, "Diana's a wonderful role model for young black kids. She got out of the ghetto and made it big. We're not friends, but we never feuded. I admire a lot of what she's done, but I don't really know her. I've heard rumors about her temper, the 'call me Miss Ross' thing. I don't know what's true and what isn't." And then, as if to keep the so-called feud going, she added, "It's true that her record sales are not what they used to be, but isn't she fifty or something?"

In the end, Ross never got to play Baker. And neither did Whitney. Actress Lynn Whitfield played the singer in an HBO film.

With her film stardom still in the future, Houston once again found herself a winner in the music industry. Her second album not only debuted at number one on *Billboard*'s Hot 100 chart, it also spawned a string of number-one singles: "I Wanna Dance with Somebody (Who Loves Me)," "Didn't We Almost Have It All?", and "So Emotional." In 1988, the album earned her a Grammy for Best Pop Female Artist—for "I Wanna Dance with Somebody (Who Loves Me)"—and two American Music Awards. (Was anyone paying attention to the fact that she had won five awards for her debut album, compared with only three for the second? Who are we kidding? There were probably *hundreds* of people in *dozens* of meeting rooms all over the world trying to figure that one out.)

With these accolades in hand, Whitney had the courage to tackle an even bigger name than Diana Ross—though in this case, the focus was a collaboration not a catfight. In a televised interview, Whitney revealed, "Of all of the people that I would like to do a song with, Michael Jackson would be on the top of the list." She also mentioned that she had talked to the elusive superstar on the phone, but didn't have the nerve, despite her own celebrity, to ask him to record an album with her. The increasingly media-savvy young singer also couldn't resist the temptation of hinting that she and Michael were an item. One reporter fell for the ploy and wrote, "Whitney seems to be trying very hard to get in good with Michael Jackson. She seems to be everywhere that he is—a coincidence?"

Indeed, Houston did seem to pop up in Michael's life at regular intervals. In 1988, she was spotted at various functions that Jackson also attended. She made sure they were photographed arm in arm at the

Grammys, and she spoke of Jackson fondly in interviews. In March of that year, Michael was awarded an honorary degree of Doctor of Humane Letters by Fisk University in recognition of his generous donations to the United Negro College Fund. Houston attended the ceremony, which was held at the Sheraton Center in New York, and a camera caught the two stars beaming at each other.

Houston's presence at the event could be explained by the fact that she was also a major contributor to the United Negro College Fund. But the smile she shot Michael when she came onstage to sing the unofficial black national anthem, "Lift Every Voice and Sing," suggested her motives were more than philanthropic. That suspicion was confirmed when she made sure the paparazzi photographed her with Jackson.

Houston didn't give a speech, but Jackson's friends Elizabeth Taylor and Liza Minnelli did. One industry insider who was present said, "It was funny the way Taylor, a notorious publicity hound, and Minnelli, whose career was practically nonexistent at the time, were practically trampled on by the paparazzi [on their way to] get to the *real* stars, Michael and Whitney."

Later that year, Whitney flew to California to present Jackson with the Life Achievement Award for Video, which was broadcast as part of the "World Music Video Awards." After the ceremony, Jackson further fueled rumors of a romance with Houston by inviting her to lunch at his family's compound in Encino, California. That the superstars' relationship was less than romantic was suggested, however, when Jackson also extended the invitation to the entire production crew of the televised awards ceremony. One pundit wondered dryly if Michael invited that whole crowd of people so they would be de facto chaperons "in case Whitney got frisky. . . ." After lunch, Jackson gave Houston and the rest of the party, a personal tour of the grounds, *on horseback*, as though—the same pundit joked—he hoped to keep at least a horse-length buffer between himself and Houston.

So, finally, there was no romance, no scandal, no lawsuit, no bickering, no hatred, no exchange of nasty accusations, not even any vicious, depraved rumors. Almost, from a public-relations point of view, a total failure. But not really, because a lot of photographs got taken.

Selling millions of records? Having the media hang on your every word? Snubbing reporters at press conferences? Being pursued by Robert De Niro? Hanging out with Michael Jackson at his ranch? Whitney Houston was having quite an amazing life, and it all seemed to have happened so fast.

Whitney, however, displayed a certain sensitivity about things earned and unearned when the press implied she had come suddenly "from nowhere" to attain her stardom. As she said in an interview to promote her first album, "This was not any overnight success. I have worked and trained for over ten years to get to where I am today. I am very lucky to have the family support that I have, and to have someone like Clive Davis helping me to direct my career. But if I was born with none of these things, I still feel that I would have been successful. It took hard work and a lot of decision-making. I earned it. All of it."

Whitney always made sure to include her family's love and support when citing the reasons for her success. Her family had, in fact, remained a strong influence in both her professional and personal lives. Unlike so many other stars, who replace friends and family with high-powered agents and attorneys, Whitney maintained her relationships with her mother, her father-manager, and her best friend, Robyn Crawford.

But no matter how close they may be to their mothers or fathers, children must finally break away and establish their own identities. Some psychologists call this important process "individuation." Lots of people think of it in terms of rebelling, but whatever you call it, it's just growing up.

Much of this process usually takes place during the teen years. Many child stars (Jodie Foster and Brooke Shields come to mind) have such a strong bond with their mothers, who also serve unofficially as their career guides, that the separation doesn't occur until much later. In Shields's case, it was in her twenties. And Foster recently told *Vanity Fair* that at the ripe old age of thirty-two, she had finally broken free from her mother's influence.

Similarly, at age twenty-five, in 1988, Whitney was often seen finding fault with Cissy's hands-on approach to her career. Whitney and her mother began to argue—the kind of mindless squabbles that usually occur during the teen years but that, in their case, had been delayed for a decade. At first they disagreed about minutiae like appropriate clothes and hairstyles. But soon their differences became more substantive, involving such issues as Whitney's friendship with Robyn Crawford.

That battle involved three very strong personalities.

Whitney loved her mother and felt grateful for the advice she received at the start of her recording career. But as she grew older and more self-confident she began to have ambivalent feelings about Cissy, who still treated her like the ten-year-old who needed tips on dealing with playground bullies. Back then, getting her mother's blessing to "whup their behinds" may have been comforting, but at the age of twenty-five it was more than a little annoying to have Mother vetting her relationships, whether they were with men or Robyn.

Robyn was proving herself every bit as willful as her boss and her boss's mom. Robyn's official job description was "personal assistant," but her influence on Whitney went much further than this designation might suggest.

And Cissy seemed to be fed up with her superstar daughter. "She has turned my hair white," Cissy said in 1988. "It was never easy. But Whitney has always had her own personality, and I wanted her brought up strictly, which wasn't always her idea of a good upbringing."

A family friend claimed that Robyn was now in charge of Houston's career, supplanting Cissy. Whitney had a domineering personality, but Robyn's was even stronger. "It's easy to see who's the boss when they're together," the friend said. "But Whitney is strong, too. It's just that Robyn is the more dominant one."

According to one source, Robyn repeatedly urged Whitney to "cut the apron strings and take charge of your own life, girl!" And a family friend in the Crawford camp said, "Robyn wants the best for Whitney and right now that involves untangling the . . . strings that exist between Cissy and her daughter."

According to one source, Whitney didn't want any part of the Robyn–Cissy rivalry. But she nevertheless found herself in a quandary. On one hand, she had only one close friend and confidante from her childhood. But she also felt indebted to her mother, whom she credited with guiding her through the shark-infested waters of the music industry.

"She never wanted to be in the middle," said this source. "Whitney hoped they could work it out themselves and had no intention of making a decision between the two. Whitney appreciated the influence of both in her life and for good reason. Although she was not related to Robyn by blood, Robyn was her 'sister,' the only [such person] she had while growing up with two brothers. And in many ways, Cissy was more of a sister-confidante than a mother. Whitney felt she was standing between two sisters pulling on opposite ends. Whitney handled it by *not* handling it. She let that period go by, hoping it would work itself out—and it eventually did."

At that time, Whitney bought a huge estate in Mendham Township, New Jersey, not far from her mother's home. The five-acre estate was valued at over $10 million. One wing of the main house contained her master bedroom; on the second level were an exercise room, hot tub, steam room, and guest room. In another wing were a lounge, recording studio, and three-car garage. In the center of the massive complex was a circular two-story living room with a skylight, a bar with solid-gold fixtures, and an oversized stone fireplace. The main wing included a restaurant-sized kitchen and dining room. Members of Whitney's family were frequent visitors, usually staying in a separate guest house, which featured a bedroom suite, sauna, spa, and bath—all overlooking the swimming pool.

With all of this room to move about in, Robyn and Cissy could easily have avoided one another if they had so chosen. But even the cavernous mansion wasn't large enough to contain the ballooning rivalry of mother and friend.

While the two women battled over Whitney, the singer herself took refuge in the comfort of two other friends—man's (and woman's) *best* friends—in this case, two dogs, Akitas named Lucy and Ethel. And the way her mother and Robyn were going at it, Whitney may have felt they were her *only* friends, at least the only friends who weren't fighting over her.

twelve

   The Soul Train Music Awards, while less prestigious than the Grammys or American Music Awards, have evolved over the years into an important event, thanks largely to the participation of major black recording artists and the enthusiastic support of record labels. Created by Don Cornelius, who hosts *Soul Train,* a black TV show similar to *American Bandstand,* the event recognized the important contributions of African-Americans at a time when they were either lumped into inappropriate categories by the Grammys and other music organizations, or ignored altogether. The Soul Train Music Awards often recognized black artists who felt unappreciated by the Grammy Awards committee.

  In 1989, for instance, Michael Jackson's *Bad* album was nominated in several Grammy categories, but failed to win a single award. However, at the Soul Train Awards ceremony that same year, Jackson won Best Album of the Year, while the title cut picked up a statuette for Best Single by a Male Vocalist.

Also that year, Whitney Houston was nominated for
a Soul Train Music Award for Best Album by a Female
Vocalist. The nomination must have been particularly
gratifying to the singer, since it was symbolic proof that
she hadn't "sold out to the white establishment" with a
"white-bread" style, as many critics and black activists
had charged.

Whitney showed up at the awards ceremony with a
small entourage, including Robyn Crawford. She hadn't
been asked to perform, so when she arrived at the
Santa Monica Civic Auditorium she felt unpressured
and in good spirits.

When her category came up, she was announced as
the winner of the award for Best Album. Delighted, she
clapped her hands and skipped toward the stage. But
halfway there, she suddenly stopped and looked at the
audience in shock. The unthinkable was happening. A
large portion of the mostly African-American crowd was
booing her. Others shouted at her the ultimate racial
insult, "Oreo!" (Like the cookie, black on the outside,
white on the inside.)

Whitney pretended to be unshaken by the catcalls
that were being televised nationwide. Appearing unruf-
fled and delighted, she gave her acceptance speech and
made no mention of the people booing her. But inside
she was seething.

When she returned to her seat, her friends tried to
console her. One friend insisted good-heartedly that
only a few people in the 3,000-strong audience had
booed. But Whitney wasn't fooled by the friend's well-
intentioned lie; she just sat there, stone-faced. A member of her entourage noticed that her hands were
quivering, the only indication of her inner devastation.

Besides being cruel, this incident was unfair and
misplaced. Indeed, her two albums were more popular

than soulful, yet they had set a number of sales records, which could only make the white-dominated recording industry more receptive to signing new black artists.

Her first album had outsold any other debut album by a female artist. And the follow-up album was the first by a woman, black or white, to debut at number one on the charts. That latter distinction, however, may have only infuriated her black critics more, since the album had hit the top spot on the *pop* charts. But Houston's trailblazing was already helping other black women in the recording industry, such as Mariah Carey and Toni Braxton. African-American activists, no matter how much they disliked her less-than-funky style, couldn't deny that the singer had performed at dozens of benefits, raising millions of dollars for the United Negro College Fund and many other black nonprofit organizations.

Further, Houston was hardly the first black artist to sing "color-blind" music. Both her mother and (especially) her cousin Dionne Warwick had "crossed over" to a less ethnic sound. In fact, Warwick's enthusiasm for Broadway show tunes had earned her the mean-spirited sobriquet, the "Julie Andrews of Soul."

While Whitney remained silent about the boos at the Soul Train ceremony, her fury over the incident erupted during a later interview. The strong-willed singer attributed the boos to jealousy, not race. "They've just gotten sick of me and just didn't want me to win another award. No, it does not make you feel good. I don't like it and I don't appreciate it, but I just kind of write it off as ignorance."

Now, *that's* the way to stop the hunters before they even get their rifles loaded.

Ironically, however, the awards show proved to be a

crucial and positive event in her life. After returning to her seat, she was quickly distracted from her public humiliation by an electric performance on the stage by Bobby Brown, an up-and-coming solo artist, formerly of New Edition. Brown had earned a reputation as the bad boy of R&B. His body movements onstage were X-rated, and he had once been arrested for simulating masturbation during a performance. For the Awards show's TV audience, however, Brown had toned himself down to an R rating. (If he hadn't, the former church-going gospel singer's reaction to him would no doubt have been entirely different.)

A friend later revealed Whitney's assessment of Bobby Brown. "She had met him, sort of, before. But didn't really know him. When he started dancing and singing with that sweet voice of his, Whitney really went off. She couldn't take her eyes off of the stage and she kept looking around, as if to say, 'Do you believe that?'"

Whitney later told *Rolling Stone* her impression of Brown that evening. "He was kicking 'Don't Be Cruel,' and he was hot. He was on fire!" After Brown's set, he returned to his seat in the audience, which happened to be directly in front of Whitney. By now, thanks to her friends and, more important, to Brown's hypnotic gyrations onstage, she had virtually forgotten her earlier humiliation.

Whitney has recalled the scene: "[We] were sitting behind him. I was hugging [my friends] and laughing and I kept hitting Bobby on the back of the head. Robyn said, 'Whitney, you keep hittin' Bobby, he's goin' to be mad at you.' I leaned over and said, 'Bobby, I'm so sorry.' And he turned around and looked at me like, 'Yeah, well just don't let it happen again.' And I was like, 'Ooooh, this guy doesn't like me!'"

Brown made it clear to her that he wasn't impressed by her fame, nor by her odd way of expressing approval, namely whupping him upside his handsome head.

Whitney was intrigued by Brown's indifference. With her model's good looks—not to mention her celebrity status and all of her money—Houston was used to men falling all over her. Bobby's unusual behavior was a challenge. "I always get curious when somebody doesn't like me," she later admitted. "I want to know why. So I said [to one of my friends], 'I'm going to invite Bobby to a party.' And I did." Despite his apparent lack of interest in the megastar sitting behind him, Brown accepted her invitation.

It turned out to be the first act of a drama that led to the altar.

At that time Whitney was only slightly less dazzled by her encounter with another singer, longtime family friend Aretha Franklin. Despite her legendary status, sales of her albums had been shrinking for some time, and she needed something to jump-start the album she was then recording. A duet with Houston, she imagined, might be just the thing.

Some critics later complained that Franklin had done more than merely elicited Whitney's assistance. She had, they suggested, also appropriated the younger singer's style. Critics said Franklin's 1989 album *Through the Storm* was a desperate attempt to duplicate Houston's pop success.

Only one song on Franklin's album was unequivocally praised by critics—the final cut, a duet that was a perfect match, a raucous musical dialogue between Aretha and Whitney. The lyrics for "It Isn't, It Wasn't, It Ain't Never Gonna Be" had the older and the younger woman fighting over a boyfriend. Their obvious affection for each other sweetens the track and brings the otherwise bland album to life.

The *New York Times* reserved its praise for that final song. "Ms. Franklin and Whitney Houston engage in a catfight that is as alive as anything either singer has recorded in years. The battle, by turns fierce and playful, could easily be for musical supremacy, and the singers' voices do the contest justice. These are two of the most talented singers of their respective generations."

Despite the critics' enthusiasm, however, the duet, released as a single, didn't burn up the charts and stalled at number sixty-six, the worst performance by any Houston single ever.

This disappointment couldn't have come at a worse time for Houston. Arista was negotiating a third album deal with her, and the sluggish sales of the Franklin duet must have been nerve-racking both for label executives and for the singer herself.

In July 1989, a Los Angeles concert by gospel singers BeBe and CeCe Winans was interrupted by a "surprise" visitor. BeBe announced that a "good friend" of theirs was in the audience; it turned out to be Whitney Houston. (The Winanses had long been good friends of the superstar and represented a link to her roots. BeBe Winans once told an interviewer, "When I first heard her sing, I said to myself, 'This girl could have only come from the church—a voice like that comes from the church.'") The concert audience roared—with enthusiasm, not boos—as Whitney made her way to the stage, where she was warmly embraced by the brother-sister act. She performed two contemporary gospel songs with the Winans's, then delighted the crowd by modestly joining the backup singers for the rest of the show.

The press cynically suggested an ulterior motive for Houston's rare appearance. Music columnist Steven Ivory wrote, "Some observers view Whitney's spate of visibility in this fashion as retaliation to cries that she has somehow forsaken her R&B roots. Proof that Whitney and her company realize this, say the critics, is the news that the singer is busy recording a new album that is supposedly more R&B than her past efforts."

Thus, the shaping of the third album was beginning to draw attention.

In addition to a sound that reflected Whitney's roots, another influence in this album was the hip-hop/R&B style of her new friend Bobby Brown.

Whitney had, in fact, run into Brown a second time backstage at the Winans concert. She later described this meeting in a *Rolling Stone* interview. "After the show, BeBe had a party, and we all went out to dinner. At the end of the dinner, Bobby walked up to me and said, 'If I asked you to go out with me, would you?' I was dating someone at the time, but it was kind of 'ehhh.' So I said, 'Yeah, I would.' And he said, 'You really would?'—he's so cool. And then he said, 'I'll pick you up tomorrow night at eight.'"

When Brown showed up at Houston's twenty-sixth birthday party, to which she had invited him when they were backstage at the Soul Train Awards, the popular entertainers had yet to become, in Whitney's term, "intimate." Whitney said later, "See, our whole relationship started out as friends. We'd have dinner, laugh, talk, and go home. It wasn't intimate. And then it kind of dawned on us, 'What's going on here?'" That was a question a lot of their friends—as well as the inquiring minds of the tabloids—were asking themselves. What *was* going on between the handsome rapper and the gorgeous pop star?

Whitney's birthday party was an A-list gala at her New Jersey estate. One guest later said, "Whitney looked great; she looked as if she were really having a good time and didn't seem uptight at all." Over four hundred guests showed up, among them Natalie Cole, Freddie Jackson, the husband-and-wife duo of Ashford and Simpson, Narada Michael Walden, and basketball great Isiah Thomas. Whitney, looking resplendent in an all-white outfit, beamed as Stevie Wonder led the guests in singing "Happy Birthday."

Another attendee remembers that several guests flirted with the birthday girl. "There was Eddie Murphy, who Whitney had been dating for some time. And Whitney was wearing this big ring she admitted Eddie gave her." (The giant sparkler on her right hand looked like a diamond engagement ring to some, but Houston still insisted she and the film star were "only friends.")

Meanwhile, the bad boy of rap, Bobby Brown, was definitely behaving himself. A guest said, "Bobby Brown stayed pretty quiet at the party. He had some friends there and he mostly talked with them, but whenever Whitney would enter the room, he literally could not take his eyes off of her." Brown, though, didn't fare any better than Houston's other wannabe suitors. The handsome rapper was also "just a friend" of the self-sufficient diva.

Whitney started 1990 by promoting several charities close to her heart. In February, she joined Frank Sinatra, Bill Cosby, Eddie Murphy, Bob Hope, Michael Jackson, Dionne Warwick, and others in paying tribute to an ailing Sammy Davis, Jr., who would eventually succumb to throat cancer. The gala was broadcast on ABC. Whitney did her umpteenth rendering of "The Greatest Love of All," and the camera caught Davis weeping as he watched Houston's emotional performance.

In May 1990, Whitney accepted cousin Dionne Warwick's invitation to perform at an AIDS benefit, the highlight of which was a star-studded rendition of Warwick's hit "That's What Friends Are For." Joining Whitney and Dionne were Chevy Chase, Jane Curtin, Melanie Griffith, Jermaine Jackson, Whoopi Goldberg, and many others. Burt Bacharach accompanied them on the piano.

She spent the rest of the year touring—it seemed as if she was *always* touring—and recording her third album for Arista. In the fall of 1990, Whitney released the album, *I'm Your Baby Tonight.* Critical reaction was generally negative, with many music writers speculating that she had dramatically changed her singing style to counter criticism that she just wasn't black enough.

The *Rochester Democrat and Chronicle* complained, "Whitney Houston's new album may be R&B *inspired* and gospel *influenced,* but it doesn't convincingly display much of anything other than lackluster pop crooning."

Critic John Leland analyzed things this way: "Houston is no longer square. As a marketing strategy, it sounds great, but on record, the pickings are mixed. The music is all contrapuntal rhythm doodads, pops and whistles. . . ."

In a classic case of damning with faint praise, the music critic for the *Philadelphia Daily News* said, "Whitney Houston's third album shows how easy it is for even a superlative singer to falter when she's interpreting unsuitable material."

Another critic, however, Kelly Leonard, saw past the

"Is she black enough?" debate and actually reviewed the album, not the sociological bric-a-brac surrounding it. "In reality, *I'm Your Baby Tonight* would have made an outstanding first album for Whitney Houston. It has all of the elements that make an album great—the songs are all strong in their own right, and they don't try to stretch for different demographics, as the songs on the first two albums did. It is essentially an album of great songs sung by a very talented singer. It far surpasses both previous albums." That last phrase must have been especially gratifying to Whitney.

Leonard's observations were accurate, but they got lost in a certain backlash against the superstar's overexposure. The point seemed to be that the public may not have been tired of Houston's singing, but they were tired of the hoopla surrounding her. One overburdened fan groaned, "If I walk into a grocery store and see Whitney's mug on one more magazine cover, I'm going to stop eating so I don't have to go to the store anymore."

The fan would also have to avoid the local record store, where Houston's face was plastered all over giant cutouts and, of course, avoid the jacket cover of the third album itself. The jacket photo showed Whitney sitting on a huge black Harley, looking almost angrily into the camera lens as if to say, "Get off my back! Gimme a break, will ya!" The insert photos tried to present the "real" Whitney Houston, whoever that was. Backtracking right past the earlier glamour poses, they showed a woman grimly determined to be judged on her real talent, not on political fallout.

The production lineup includes Narada Michael Walden, Michael Masser, and Luther Vandross. And as though to suggest an unofficial African-American seal of approval, Whitney's idol Stevie Wonder produced one of the tracks, "We Didn't Know" (which was recorded as a Houston/Wonder duet).

Whitney told *Jet* magazine, "I have always dreamed of singing with Stevie. It was just a dream come true to sing with a man that I admire, someone I look at as a musical genius. I had such a good time. There was no ego-tripping, it was two artists coming together as friends . . . every second was pure joy. If I didn't have the track to play back, I'd have thought that I'd dreamed it!"

The title track, "I'm Your Baby Tonight," was produced by her longtime friends L. A. Reid and Babyface, who also happened to be two of the hottest producers in the business at that time. No one could ever accuse those two of being "too white." The cut, which lacked the trademark "sweetening" of Houston's previous efforts, was most notable for its hard edge. "I'm Your Baby Tonight"—although not many people may have recognized the fact—was pure, raw, unvarnished Whitney.

As usual, the liner notes on the album thank the many contributors to Whitney's work and life, only this time Robyn Crawford is lumped in with her manager, Gene Harvey, and other *business* associates. Previously Whitney listed Robyn with family members. This subtle change echoed the statement she made in an interview. "Robyn and I started out as friends, and we still are. But now we have more of an employer/employee relationship. I am her boss and she works for me."

In life, Whitney seemed to be saying, unapologetically, that things change.

The interview was also noteworthy because she mentioned the increasing difficulties in running a corporation largely staffed by family members. She said, "It is hard having your family working for you. I have fired them all several times. But I always end up re-hiring them."

This was the same theme showing up more and more frequently in Whitney's life. *Things change.*

thirteen

In 1978, when Whitney Houston was still a
teenager, a treatment, or synopsis, of a feature film was
making the rounds of the studios and agencies in
Hollywood. Of course, she couldn't have known it at
the time, but that treatment would become a script, and
that script would be made into a film, and that film
would turn into a huge blockbuster that would have a
powerful impact on her life.

It was titled *The Bodyguard*.

The eight-page treatment described the romance
between a black female pop star and the white security
man she hires to protect her after receiving a a series of
death threats.

Interracial romance, even in the liberal, post–civil-
rights era of the 1970s, was still a touchy subject.
Though the movie industry likes to consider itself pro-
gressive, the story's depiction of a black woman and a
white man in love made the studios uneasy—not so
much because of the racial theme itself, but because studio executives feared that less liberal elements of the

public would reject the film and ruin its chances for success. And if that happened, the people responsible for okaying the film's development might very well find themselves looking for work.

One person in Hollywood wasn't intimidated by American squeamishness, maybe because he wasn't American. Thus, in 1978, British director John Boorman acquired an option on the treatment and managed to communicate his enthusiasm to actor Ryan O'Neal, who became actively involved in finding a studio to finance the project. In addition, O'Neal and Boorman agreed on the perfect person to play the female pop star—the legendary Diana Ross, who had just finished filming an African-American remake of *The Wizard of Oz* called *The Wiz* (which turned out to be a major box-office failure).

Though Ross read the treatment, she found the violence and the inclusion of a nude sex scene distasteful. O'Neal, however, began a campaign to woo the singer. According to Ross's associates, the two began an affair, and Ross eventually fell in love with O'Neal. But, as it turned out, O'Neal was more interested in a film collaboration than a personal relationship, even though he did give the singer an amethyst engagement ring on her birthday in 1978.

According to J. Randy Taraborrelli's *Call Her Miss Ross*, after Diana felt secure in the relationship she told O'Neal that she really did not want to costar in the movie with him. He promptly broke off the relationship.

By the early 1980s, screenwriter/director Lawrence Kasdan had written a script loosely based on the original treatment of *The Bodyguard*. Finally, in 1990, the script landed on the desk of Kevin Costner, a personal friend of Kasdan who had worked with him on *The Big Chill* and *Silverado*. Costner loved the script and wanted to star in and perhaps even direct it. But before he could spend any time developing the project, another small matter required his attention: directing, producing, and starring in *Dances with Wolves*.

After *Dances* was released (and grossed more than $250 million worldwide), the handsome young actor found he could pick just about anything he wanted for his next major project, and he wanted to do *The Bodyguard*. Warner Bros. outbid all the other studios for Costner's pet project, a chancy film with a controversial theme that had the possibility of turning into a colossal commercial dud.

One of the actor's first tasks was to select someone to play the female lead—the pop star, Rachel Marron. The script described her as black, beautiful, sensuous, bitchy, and young. Initially, Costner had the same idea as O'Neal—to hire Diana Ross. But he finally realized the singer, at forty-six, was now a bit too old for the part.

Costner came up with another idea. He wanted Whitney Houston.

The only problem was that Costner had no idea whether the pop star could make the transition from songs to celluloid. He was well aware of the many disasters that had occurred when recording-industry stars attempted to act in movies. The Rolling Stones, the Bee Gees, Peter Frampton, and even Michael Jackson had all laid eggs on-screen.

The studio was less excited about Houston than Costner. An executive even tried to dissuade the superstar by mentioning Madonna for the role, even though her film work had become the joke of the industry. Costner was cold to the idea. "Kevin was not a Madonna fan," said an insider. "She had mocked him horribly in her film *Truth or Dare*, made him look like a naive fool just because he had come backstage after one of her concerts and said the performance was 'neat.' He was furious about that, felt it was a cheap shot. He said he would never, ever work with Madonna."

Costner had never met Whitney Houston, but he had seen her videos. "She's right for it," he insisted. "I have a gut instinct about her." When he remained firm in his casting decision, Warner Bros. caved in, as the respected and powerful actor hoped it would. Then, according to Houston, Costner began to woo her in early 1990. But unlike O'Neal with Ross, Costner—a happily married man—was up-front about the nature of his interest.

And so one day, the phone rang in Whitney's New Jersey mansion. Kevin Costner was calling to ask if she would like to costar in a movie with him.

Of that conversation, Whitney recalled, "I went, 'Yeah, sure.' So then I called my agent and she said, 'It's true! They want you to do this movie. Take it seriously.'"

"My God!" Whitney observed. "Can you imagine this! Kevin Costner calls me up out of the clear blue sky and asks me to be in a movie with him. Who would believe this?"

Without even reading the script, Whitney was willing to take her chances. If one of the biggest names in movies thought she was right for the part, who was this novice actress, who had done nothing beyond music videos and a guest shot on TV's *Silver Spoons* to disagree?

Of course, she *had* contemplated acting before, and it mostly led to trouble. But proosals were still presented to her and discussed. She simply made it clear that she wanted nothing to do with any project that involved Diana Ross's life, *Dreamgirls,* or Josephine Baker.

"Enough is enough," she said privately. "I'm sick of this thing with Diana Ross. I don't even fucking *know* Diana Ross. And here I am competing with her, and she's competing with me. I'm sick of it."

"Right now, I don't want to do film bios, not of Miss Ross and not of Josephine Baker," Whitney told a reporter in 1990. "Maybe one day, if the part's well-written and the person is dead, I'll consider a biographical film."

"But not the Miss Ross story?" the reporter asked.

"No! No way! Never! And no comment!" Whitney replied firmly.

Until now, Whitney's exhausting schedule of concerts and recording left her little time even to think of acting. But she made time when a film project involved Oscar winners Costner and Kasdan.

Her enthusiasm for the project, however, was diluted by two concerns: fear that the public would reject her acting efforts because she came from the music industry and fear that her film debut would be such a high-profile role. "I was concerned that people would dog me before they gave me an opportunity to do the job," she told *Rolling Stone*. "I wanted to do some acting, but I mean, I never thought I'd be co-starring with Kevin Costner! I thought, 'I'll just get this *little part* somewhere, and I'll work my way up.' And all of the sudden I get this script, and I said: 'I don't know. This is kind of . . . big.' I was scared."

Soon, a third concern surfaced. As she read the script she found a lot she didn't like. But instead of walking away from the project as Ross had done years earlier, Houston had the temerity to ask the multiple Oscar-winning actor/director to make some changes. The biggest problem with her role, she felt, was that Rachel was obnoxious. Or as Houston later explained, the original Rachel was "very rough, very hard—a little bitch."

She was determined to make the film, but she also insisted on a kinder, gentler Rachel. "I knew it was the right project, but Rachel's character had to be fleshed out a bit. In the first draft, she was just mean and bitchy all the time. I mean, we all have our days, but I thought she should be a bit warmer."

In this regard, Whitney showed she was a canny script doctor. In the final draft, Rachel does start out as a cranky, self-absorbed celebrity, but gradually, as she falls in love with her bodyguard, she becomes more considerate and less egotistical. Or in Houston's words, "a bit warmer."

For the moment, though, Whitney Houston was swamped by music commitments. "Look, I want to do this movie," she reportedly told Costner. "But I have to find a way to work it into my life and schedule. I'll get back to you. I promise."

In fact, the biggest name in Hollywood would have to wait until Whitney Houston could take a break from her primary career. She had a new album and a tour to deal with.

Despite the negative reviews, *I'm Your Baby Tonight* went double platinum. Double platinum sales would represent a major coup for any other artist, but not Houston, whose previous albums had sold many more copies. Thus, only by comparison were her third album's sales disappointing, but such comparisons weren't to be discounted. Regardless of where it started, if the line on the graph on the wall of the executive offices is headed down, that's not good.

Reporters began quoting unnamed sources at Arista who called the album's performance "dismal."

But Whitney felt that Arista was responsible for the

disappointing sales. As she told *TV Guide,* "I know a lot of folks who would like to sell as many records as *Baby Tonight* sold. What disappointed me was that my record company did not do what they should have done to make *Baby Tonight* more of a success. They bungled."

The title single reached number one on the pop chart, but a week later fell to number two, and the press—ever compassionate in its assessments—suggested that Houston's career was faltering. Reporters didn't mention that this was Houston's eighth number-one song, tying the record set by Madonna, whom no one in the press was calling a has-been.

Happily, Whitney's full schedule didn't allow her sufficient time or emotional energy to dwell on negative press or on the usual fiction being printed about her in the tabloids. (The headline of one tabloid story screamed, WHITNEY HOUSTON PREGNANT WITH EDDIE MURPHY'S BABY. The text claimed, *Whitney Houston and Eddie Murphy are getting married this spring! And if that's not enough to quell the rumors of Houston's sexual preference for women, Murphy is tying the knot with her because she's pregnant with his child!* The story also claimed that Murphy originally got involved with her to stop the rumors about the singer and her personal assistant, Robyn Crawford.)

One of Whitney's close friends insisted that not only did these flights of pseudo-journalistic fancy amuse the young singer, but also that she and her public-relations staff were now taking part in planting the stories. (According to Frank DiLeo, one of Michael Jackson's former managers, Jackson and his publicists often plant stories in the tabloids, as do other entertainers. Apparently, some stars—like Roseanne—realize that approximately ten million people a week buy the so-called rags. That's *a lot* of publicity, good or bad.)

Whatever the truth of these reports, Whitney felt it was much more important to respond to criticism of her new album in the legitimate press. She told *Music Express,* a small trade publication, "If you really want to know, I don't give a damn what the critics say. I don't care what they write about. I care what the people say. And what they told me is that they loved the songs I was singing. They loved the way that I look. They loved everything, whatever I did. And that means more to me than some *schmuck* sitting there criticizing me. I'm about the people, and the people tell me what they like and they don't like."

Meanwhile, rapidly escalating tensions in the Persian Gulf were making issues like the critical response to Whitney Houston's third album seem petty and trivial. As the United States prepared for war, memories of Vietnam erupted and, even as a national debate about American involvement in a Gulf war raged, Americans rallied to the idea of "supporting the troops." Organizers of the 1991 Super Bowl hoped to capitalize on the resurgence of patriotism by hiring America's premiere diva to sing the national anthem before the kickoff. The Super Bowl's 100 million TV viewers would be the largest audience for whom she had ever performed.

Whitney Houston's understandable nervousness was undetectable when she grabbed the microphone with both hands and sang "The Star-Spangled Banner." Her performance was so riveting that afterward, one could see a gradual reversal of the negative tone of her music reviews.

The respected *Entertainment Weekly* summarized this shift in attitude: "Every so often, a singer comes along and reclaims 'The Star-Spangled Banner.' Now, with her stirring Super Bowl rendition, it's Whitney

Houston's turn." The usually staid *New York Times* was ecstatic: "A full orchestra accompanies Ms. Houston's sinuous, sultry voice, which makes the national anthem voluptuous; under the last note is the whoosh of F-16 jets flying overhead."

Whitney later described the overwhelming emotional impact of the Super Bowl experience. "At first, I just started to sing the song, and I was happy to be there. And then, I looked at the faces of the crowd and I saw the parents of men and women who were over in the Gulf and it really made me think. It made me say, 'This song is for them.' It made me very emotional and I cried. This is something that my children can look at in the future and be proud. And I am proud of that."

Master showman/businessman Clive Davis could hardly stand the idea of letting go of his artist's 100 million viewers after only one performance. Arista Records thus announced it was releasing Whitney's performance of the national anthem as a single. As it turns out, this idea was not an afterthought. A source close to Davis insists that long before she stepped up to the microphone, the music mogul had planned to capitalize on the patriotic fervor. How else can one explain the presence of so much electronic equipment trucked into the Super Bowl stadium, enough to ensure a release-quality tape of the song?

The plan was kept under wraps to forestall the notion that Davis was trying to make a buck off the Gulf War, which of course he was. The decision to exploit the commerical possibilities of the Super Bowl and the war had to be seen as a spontaneous gesture *after* the fact, inspired by Davis's patriotism, not his balance sheets.

The first gambit was to explain the souped-up recording facilities at the Super Bowl as part of the company's plan to send free copies of the song to the servicemen and women in the Gulf. Davis may have fooled the general public but not the press when, in response to being asked about plans to sell the recording in the United States, Davis said, "If there is a demand, we'll release it." Considering his star's megapopularity, the record executive might as well have said, "If the sun comes up tomorrow, we'll release the recording."

And why shouldn't the public have believed Davis's interpretation? After all, he had promised that all profits from the single and the video would be donated to a war-relief charity "to be chosen by Ms. Houston at a later date." Never mind that the generous donation reaped millions of dollars of free publicity for the singer, who just happened to have a new album whose sales were relatively disappointing.

But no amount of promotional wizardry could overcome an embarrassing leak a month later when Bob Best, chief of the Super Bowl's pregame entertainment, revealed that Houston had actually taped the single in a Los Angeles recording studio called the Lighthouse several days before the game. It wasn't Whitney's live performance but a souped-up, sweetened studio production that was played at the Super Bowl then sent to the troops in the Gulf. Whitney, in fact, had sung along with the track into a dead microphone. While it was no recording-industry Watergate, this revelation dampened some of the goodwill generated by Whitney's performance.

The more excitable newspapers, however, acted as though Houston and Davis *had* burglarized Democratic headquarters. The *New York Post* editorialized, "The biggest 'fake' of the Super Bowl may have happened before the kickoff—when Whitney Houston's widely hailed rendering of the national anthem was actually heard on pre-recorded tape." The pregame producer, Best, quickly explained that Houston *had* actually sung the anthem live, but nobody farther than a few feet away from her could hear it, because her microphone had been shut off. What the 100 million listeners heard was the recording.

To Whitney's horror, her performance was being compared with a much more egregious lip-synching scandal—the disclosure that all the supposed live performances of another Arista act, Milli Vanilli, had been prerecorded. Of course, whereas Houston's live performance had been replaced by a recording of her voice, Milli Vanilli's tracks had been recorded by entirely different artists.

The singer's press agent, Sylvia Weiner, tried to put the best possible spin on the debacle, saying, "This isn't lip-sync-gate here. As far as Whitney knew, she was singing it live."

The press was not mollified. With visions of sugarplum Pulitzers in mind, reporters asked, "What did Whitney know and when did she know it?"

Whitney was perplexed about the whole controversy. "Who cares about this?" she said privately to one associate. "This is ridiculous. What are they trying to imply? That I can't sing? *Please!*"

Was Houston involved with the minor deception before the event or after the fact? Did she acquiesce to Davis's scam, or did she find out after the singles were released and keep silent in the hope that no one would find out?

Experts suspect that she knew all along. She was famous for never singing a song the same way twice. What came out of her mouth at the Super Bowl must have sounded subtly but unmistakably different from what she heard from the PA system.

But never mind all that. While the public felt deceived by the talentless Milli Vanilli duo, it was more forgiving of the talented Houston. Her fans weren't disappointed enough to forgo purchasing the single, which had Houston singing "America the Beautiful" on the flip side. More than $500,000 in proceeds from the single went to the American Red Cross Gulf Crisis Fund and the Whitney Houston Foundation for Children.

Perhaps hoping to distract the public from the Super Bowl mini-scandal, Arista announced that Houston would perform in a free "Welcome Home, Heroes" concert for troops returning from the Gulf. Thus, on March 31, 1991, Whitney stepped in front of an audience of 3,100 Gulf veterans and their families at the Norfolk Naval Station in Virginia. This time she not only sang the national anthem live, but she also sang it a capella, a strong and unmistakable rebuttal to critics who ridiculously claimed her powerful voice was actually a studio creation.

"Some people just don't have a clue, do they?" an exasperated Whitney Houston concluded to *Rolling Stone*. "What do they think I've been doing out here all of these years? I simply cannot explain what people have to say about me these days. And so I ain't even gonna try. . . ."

fourteen

When asked by the press what she most val-
ues in her life, what has most inspired her and con-
tributed to her success, Whitney Houston always
answers "God" and "family."

Yet being a high-profile family has had its share of
pitfalls for the Houstons. Over the years, personal and
family problems have surfaced in the press, leaving
Whitney and her family wishing perhaps that they were
all a bit less famous.

In early 1991, for example, Whitney's father began
dating Barbara "Peggy" Griffith, a twenty-nine-year-old
woman who was employed as a maid. . . by Whitney.
John Houston, who was seventy years old at the time,
had recently been granted a divorce from Cissy, finally
formalizing the separation that began when Whitney
was a young girl.

Though Whitney rarely speaks publicly of her father,
confidants say she has great love and respect for him.
In 1988, she had made it possible for him to leave his
unsatisfying part-time job with the City of Newark and

join her as a comanager of Nippy Inc., the corporate entity that handles her endeavors. Soon, he was CEO of the company, and with his experience in show business, he helped his daughter make millions. Nevertheless, John maintained a low profile, speaking out only when his daughter needed defending or when he was asked a specific question.

Barbara "Peggy" Griffith and her fifteen-year-old daughter, Alana, had come to America from Trinidad to escape a life of poverty. Recalled Griffith's uncle Regan Choonie, "Peggy was desperately poor and had a hard life as a girl, but she was always ambitious." Being hired as a domestic for Whitney Houston brought dramatic changes to her life, allowing her to live and work in a lavish environment.

Peggy met John Houston during an afternoon visit he paid to Whitney's home. When they began dating, close associates say Whitney was torn. Her maid dating her father? It all seemed so impossible. She had no choice but to dismiss Peggy Griffith.

Meanwhile, in April 1991, Whitney, Robyn Crawford, Whitney's twenty-nine-year-old brother (and now her bodyguard) Michael, and the rest of her twenty-member entourage traveled to Kentucky for a concert appearance, one of the first dates on the promotional tour for *I'm Your Baby*. The group checked in at the luxurious Radisson Plaza Hotel in Lexington, then decided to go to the famous Red Mile Harness Racetrack. Whitney was in a good mood, according to witnesses, feeling relaxed for the first time in quite a while following all of the distress at home in New Jersey.

After the evening at the track, the entire group made their way back to the hotel, where one of the men suggested they watch the Evander Holyfield/George

Foreman boxing match on the large-screen television in the hotel's lounge. Whitney and her entourage entered the lounge at approximately midnight, presumably intending only to watch the fight and have a few drinks before turning in.

According to one source who works for the hotel, Houston and her group "charged" into the lounge "casting a pall over everything with their snotty attitudes." Another employee remembers, "Anyone who tried to approach Whitney just to say 'hi' was met by frosty stares. Her bodyguards protected her like she was a fragile piece of china."

But, as often happens in such cases, members of Whitney's entourage deny those reports. While they may have appeared frosty to observers, they were basically just minding their own business. According to one of Whitney's friends, "We went into the lounge and tried not to make any fuss. We just wanted to enjoy the fight and have a few drinks. We didn't think that was too much to ask."

The few people who managed to approach Whitney for an autograph were refused, her team of beefy bodyguards making certain that fans were kept at a distance. Said an employee of the hotel, "Anytime anyone came near the group, one of the bodyguards, with a distinctive British accent, hissed in a loud voice, 'Piss off!' They simply would not let anyone near her."

Then, according to members of Whitney's camp, a group of men sitting in the lounge began to talk very loudly, ostensibly hoping Whitney would notice them. Suddenly, they began to taunt her, making racist and even sexual comments about her. Whitney and her group tried to ignore them, and finally left the bar.

Several members of the group went their own way, while Whitney, Robyn, and Michael climbed into the elevator, which took them to their rooms on the seventeenth floor. However, three of the men from the lounge had already made the same trip a few moments earlier and were sitting in the hospitality lounge when the elevator door opened.

There are two descriptions of what happened next—Whitney's version and the one recounted by the men with whom she crossed paths that fateful evening.

Whitney's version:

The three men from the lounge now seemed to be inebriated and continued to shout racist slurs at Whitney. Despite the taunts, Whitney and her bodyguard brother—who had told the men to "back off"—tried to ignore the situation and return to their rooms. But the men were persistent, until one of them attacked her brother. Whitney, never one to let anyone push her around, also became involved in the melee in an effort to protect her brother. Thus, there she was, punching out some stranger. In the end, the police had to be summoned.

The trio's version:

After Whitney and her brother stepped from the elevator, the men recognized her, said, "Hey, it's Whitney Houston!" and asked for an autograph. They were met with hostility from the star. Michael then lunged for one of the men and proceeded to pummel him. The man hit the floor, got up, and then began fighting Michael. Whitney, infuriated, jumped onto the back of the stranger to pull him off her brother. Then one of the stranger's friends, seeing the fight was now "two against one," became involved. Whitney turned around, so angry that tears were in her eyes, and swung a right hook, connecting with the face of the second man. "You will die tomorrow," Whitney supposedly threatened.

That week, the three men—one of whom was not involved in the fight but says he "saw the whole thing"—filed a lawsuit against Whitney and Michael. Whitney was charged with two misdemeanors, fourth-degree assault, and terroristic threatening. Michael Houston was charged with fourth-degree assault. Although Whitney's lawyers attempted to have the charges immediately dropped, the singer and her brother were served with summonses to appear in court.

Whitney retaliated by filing her own legal action against the two men who were directly involved in the fight, charging them with defamation, invasion of privacy, and assault and battery. She also alleged that they filed bogus charges after demanding $425,000 to keep the story out of the press. Michael Houston, meanwhile, filed assault charges against the men, claiming that the confrontation left him bleeding from the mouth and head.

All that's certain is that: *something* happened, and it wasn't pretty. Whitney got involved in a fistfight in a hotel. Not exactly becoming behavior for a star of her caliber, but very much in line with the way she was raised. Remember the little girl whose mother told her to go to school and beat up the leader of a gang of girls who had been tormenting her? "And if you don't kick her ass, I'm going to kick yours," was how Cissy put it.

"How could this have happened?" Whitney wondered to one associate. "This is so bad. How could Michael and I have gotten involved in this?"

An avalanche of embarrassing press about the incident forced John Houston to release a statement, saying, "I am very proud that Michael maintained his dignity and professionalism by not responding to the verbal abuse directed toward Whitney. In the face of this restraint, these men shrewdly concluded that the only way they could achieve a situation that would create the sensationalized media attention they desired, was to attack Michael physically without cause or provocation."

There was no choice but to admit that Whitney had been a willing participant in the fight. Said John Houston, "I am equally proud of my daughter, Whitney, who would not let any career concerns prevent her from protecting her brother. By exposing herself to potential physical harm, she risked career-threatening injuries."

Whitney was grateful for her father's words, particularly given the strain in their relationship caused by his involvement with her former maid. "It helped ease the tension between father and daughter," said one source. "Whitney definitely felt her father's support during this difficult time, even though she had found it somewhat difficult to be supportive of his relationship with Peggy. If any good came out of the situation in Kentucky, it's that it brought John and Whitney to some understanding."

After researching the allegations and interviewing witnesses from both sides, Fayette County Attorney Norrie Wake eventually dropped the charges against Whitney and Michael, stating that "contradictory evidence would have made conviction impossible." Indeed, the trio of strangers may have revealed their true motives by immediately calling the local press after the melee. Certainly, there was no need for them to have done so—unless they were looking for some short-lived—and perhaps financially rewarding—fame.

According to a source close to Whitney, she was both terrified and angry at what had happened. She felt it was a setup, a publicity stunt cooked up by the men who, she said, had attacked her and her brother. But it also led her to begin rethinking the issue of vulnerability to the very people who formed her audience.

Certainly fans were crucial to her career, but Whitney had been distraught in recent years at how aggressive some of them were. She couldn't help but wonder if she could ever go out in public again without a phalanx of bodyguards surrounding her.

While entertainers often seem more distant when they travel with protection, the fact is that they have no choice. "What am I supposed to do?" Whitney has asked. "Just go out and hope no one attacks me, or hassles me? Are you crazy? Am I?"

Some celebrities acknowledge fans by sponsoring special events, sending personal replies to letters, and speaking highly of fans to the press. But Whitney Houston has never been one of those performers. In her opinion, fans should appreciate her for her music and not pay attention to her private life. According to one industry insider, Whitney truly doesn't understand why many of her fans feel they need to scrutinize her every thought and movement.

"She finds it very restrictive," this executive states. "Whitney wants to have an anonymous life when she is not onstage. She does not want to be bothered by fans who want her autograph or want to talk to her. She is a very private person, and has always been a bit shy. Of course, she can't have a private life. She gave that up a long time ago, whether she likes it or not."

"I love my fans," Whitney has said, "but they should just want to see me on the stage. Other than that, they should just *get a life*!"

Particularly after the violent incident in Kentucky, many fans are reported to have had the opportunity to meet Whitney Houston only to suffer a harsh rebuff either from her bodyguards or from the star herself.

And because word gets around, her reputation among her fans is, generally speaking, not a good one. One plainly states, "Whitney does not care about her fans. She makes that very obvious. She makes you feel like you are some sort of weirdo because you've asked for her autograph."

According to "Linda" (who asked that her last name not be used), an administrator for the travel department of a large Fortune 500 company, she and a male friend, who is an avid Whitney Houston fan, saw the star in the lounge of a Holiday Inn in Canandaigua, New York, following a performance at the Finger Lakes Performing Arts Center in July 1991—three months after the incident in Kentucky. Whitney and her brother Michael were seated at the bar. Even though Whitney's voice had been extremely hoarse during her performance that night, she was smoking. While having a drink—whether or not it was alcoholic is not known—she began laughing loudly at whatever her brother was saying. She did not appear to be trying to hide her presence. Yet none of the thirty or so people in the small lounge approached her.

Because Linda's friend was too shy, Linda decided to approach the entertainer to ask if her friend could say hello. While her friend waited at their table she went up to Michael and said, "My friend just loves Whitney Houston, and he would be thrilled if he could just say hello before we leave."

Michael smiled at Linda and—as Whitney stared ahead and tried to ignore what was happening—earnestly told her, "I don't know. Whitney signed a few autographs earlier and she might be too tired."

Linda assured Michael of her friend's intention only to say hello. No autograph was necessary. Michael then leaned over to his sister and whispered the request into her ear. According to Linda, what happened next sent a chill down her spine. She remembered, "Whitney turned around and looked at me with the most awful expression, as if I was diseased. In my life, no one has ever looked at me with so much contempt."

Whitney then glared at her brother and spoke directly to him, completely ignoring the presence of the visitor. In a frosty voice, and with each word enunciated clearly, she said, "Tell *her* to tell *him*, 'Hello. I love him. *And good-night.*'" That said, Whitney turned back around.

Michael winced, shrugged, and appeared to be embarrassed.

Humiliated and angered, Linda went back to her table to get her friend. The two of them left immediately.

Of Whitney, Linda recalled, "She was so bitchy. I never really cared one way or the other about her myself, but to be treated like that—like I wasn't even a person—made me furious. What a diva! I wouldn't go to a concert of hers now even if I had free tickets."

Of course, Whitney Houston cannot give personal attention to each and every fan. Furthermore, her coldness may well be a protective device, one that allows her to feel she has some freedom to walk about and be *normal*. As she stated in the past, "I will not be a prisoner of my fame. I was born free."

Ironically, at that particular point in 1991, Whitney could have used a few more fans. Her *I'm Your Baby Tonight* world tour was off to a controversial start with the Kentucky incident. Subsequently, it was reported that Whitney was forced to cancel many dates because of a throat condition. But the fact is that across the United States and Canada, the unthinkable was happening. Ticket sales were slow. Stadiums and auditoriums were only half-sold by the time of scheduled performances, and a Canadian concert was canceled due to poor ticket sales.

Whitney's *I'm Your Baby Tonight* album sold over six million copies, but this was seen as dismal by Whitney Houston standards. (The record is now considered to be her least successful.) Concert promoters released a list of "The Bottom Ten," which was akin to "Box Office Poison," the film industry's blacklist of years gone by. Whitney Houston was listed as one of the acts that caused major concert promoters to lose, in all, over $4 million during the 1991 season alone. She was joined on the list by David Lee Roth, Huey Lewis, Diana Ross, Steve Winwood, the Doobie Brothers, Amy Grant, and others.

It had been a bad summer for concert tours in general. One of the main reasons some acts had become huge risks was the fees the artists demanded, regardless of ticket sales. The reasons for the small turnout at Whitney Houston concerts in particular seemed clear: bad press, backlash from fans after the Kentucky incident, and a poorly received album.

If this wasn't bad enough, 1991 ended with the marriage of her father to her former maid.

Indeed, when John Houston and Barbara "Peggy" Griffith married on December 28, 1991, it was almost more than Whitney could bear. "I can't believe this is happening," she told one former employee. "You know how much I love my father. But I don't know what to do about this . . . this . . . *situation*." Friends say that even after all these years, Whitney hoped her parents might reconcile and she had grown accustomed to having both parents near her, without the intrusion of others.

Cissy never dated. "Not interested" is all she would say when asked about men. If John had been social with women, he was so discreet that no one in the immediate family seemed to be aware of it. And so, as is common among children of divorce, as long as the parents do not remarry or become seriously involved romantically, the offspring may hold on to a slim hope that the situation could change. However, when one of the parents does remarry or become otherwise involved, the family suffers a severe jolt, forcing the child to admit that "Mom and Dad are never going to be together again." In a family as close-knit as the Houstons, John's marriage to an outsider—a domestic formerly employed by his daughter—created great turmoil.

The wedding service performed in front of only twelve guests by family friend Reverend Harry Spellman of Macedonia Church of Christ in Newark, took place in John's high-rise apartment in Fort Lee, New Jersey. "Whitney wasn't there," recalled Reverend Spellman. "None of John's relatives were there. I don't know why.

"Barbara was Whitney's maid. I can confirm that," continued the minister. "But now she's retired as a maid. She'll have a good life. I'd never seen John so happy."

"It's incredible," observed Peggy's uncle Regan Choonie. "[Peggy]'s gone from rags to riches."

And so it was that in December 1991, Whitney not only lost a pretty good maid, but she also gained a stepmother who was just barely older than she was.

Says one source, "In the end, Whitney decided that her father should have a fulfilling life, and that she would accept the marriage if it made him happy.

"But it was a difficult experience for her, and through it she learned she can't control everything that happens in her life when it involved other people's feelings and objectives. It was a good lesson."

fifteen

Kevin Costner was still waiting for a defini-
tive answer about the starring role in *The Bodyguard.*

Though she had been considering the film for some
time and said she wanted to do it, Whitney shied away
from actually committing to the time required to shoot
the movie while continuing to send revised versions of
the script back to Costner with requests for additional
changes. Meanwhile, she kept the door open for other
film opportunities.

One script that came her way was based on Tina
Turner's best-selling autobiography, *I, Tina,* which
recounted Turner's years with ex-husband Ike Turner.
The book and subsequent script (eventually retitled
What's Love Got to Do With It?) graphically depicted Ike's
abusive behavior, which eventually forced Tina out of
their relationship and into discovering new courage and
spirituality, along with a fulfilling life and a solo career.
Whitney was, in fact, close to signing the contract to
portray Tina Turner.

"Whitney loved the idea of the story," said a source,

"but was hesitant about the fact that she would be portraying someone who was still alive and had a thriving career. Still, for a time she thought the idea would work. But at the last minute she pulled back, leaving the producers to find a replacement." (The plum role went to actress Angela Bassett, whose exceptional performance was honored in 1994 with an Academy Award nomination for Best Actress.)

Finally, Costner telephoned Whitney and asked what he could do to convince her to take the role of singer/actress Rachel Marron in *The Bodyguard*. Whitney repeated that she felt the role was too overwhelming for her at this time, and that she was afraid she would fail at it. "I wanted to do it," she said later. "I made that clear at the very beginning. But I was stalling a little. I just wanted to be sure it was the right move for me. I prayed a lot over it."

"I promised her that I would be right there with her," Costner recalled, "and that she would not be bad in the movie because I refuse to let anybody fail around me. I promised that I would protect her."

Whitney was impressed with Costner's determination, and with his kindness. "Maybe I can pull this thing off after all," she told one associate. "With Kevin in my corner, maybe I can actually do it."

"It seemed impossible to her," said the associate, "but there was something driving her to do it, to be a movie star. It just seemed to be the next logical step.

"She had a talk with Cissy, and they talked about that old magic of believing. 'If you believe in yourself, then I believe you'll do a good job in a movie,' Cissy told her. 'But why *this* movie? Can't you do something else?'" The one issue that came up repeatedly was the interracial relationship between Frank Farmer (Costner) and Rachel Marron (Houston).

Early on, Costner and his partners had decided that race would not be played up in the film, which they envisioned as simply a love story. As Costner confirmed to a reporter, "I don't think race is an issue here. The film is about a relationship between two people, and it will be a failure if it is a film about interracial relationships. We're making a love story. Love doesn't know about race."

Her friends say that Cissy Houston is certainly not a racist. But she is a savvy public-relations strategist, and she feels that the public is, in fact, race-conscious and that it continues to embrace racist notions. "It's the way it is," she has said. "I wish it would change. But we have to recognize the way it is." She felt it would be a mistake for Whitney to make her acting debut in a film in which she would become intimate with a white man. "I don't think America is ready for it," she said. "And we've all worked too hard to take a chance like this."

But Whitney disagreed.

In fact, Cissy was beginning to find that she had little say in many areas of her daughter's life. Whitney's friend Robyn Crawford had actually taken her place as adviser in many areas, including those of Whitney's image, attire, and even hairstyles. And Whitney had surrounded herself with so many "administrative assistants" that it became difficult for Cissy to have an opinion about anything without a major confrontation with members of Whitney's staff. Though she continued to try to be involved in Whitney's hectic life and career, her daughter was becoming increasingly rebellious. She wanted to have control of her own life.

"This was hard for Cissy," says one observer. "She had always been there for her daughter, and her opinion had always mattered. But now her daughter was grown, an adult. It was time to let go. Whitney felt she should have the independence to do whatever she wanted to do, to make her own choices and decisions and not have any interference from anyone, including her mother. They were playing out an age-old struggle between mothers and daughters."

"I've decided I'm doing that movie," Whitney announced to her mother one day.

According to a witness, Cissy took a deep breath, raised her eyes to the heavens, and then exhaled deeply. "Then I guess you'll do what you have to do," she told her daughter, finally.

Filming for *The Bodyguard* began in early 1992. The movie was produced by Costner's production company, TIG Productions, which Costner ran with Jim Wilson. Mick Jackson, who had recently directed *L.A. Story,* was hired to direct.

Costner prepared meticulously for his role, consulting with several genuine bodyguards, including high-profile celebrity protection specialist Gavin DeBecker. Costner seemed to understand the intense pressure bodyguards experience while protecting their clients because he had himself employed a number of them. "I think the story rings true for many of us entertainers," he said. "There is a certain element that reminds us of our worst nightmare in terms of the public sometimes overstepping its bounds. It's something that we think about, but rarely have the chance to express."

Indeed, Whitney Houston could empathize with those emotions quite well. Her recent experience in Kentucky had left her wary of public appearances. She had begun to reevaluate all situations where she might find herself in danger, and she learned to rely heavily on bodyguards. In preparing for her role in the film, she observed, "I helped myself understand Rachel's relationship to Frank in the movie by remembering my own bodyguards and their devotion to their jobs. It is a deep concern to me that someone would sacrifice his life for mine, but these guys do it without thinking twice. They are really true heroes."

The Bodyguard is about a successful, spoiled, and stubborn superstar who is threatened by an unknown fanatic. Against the wishes of the beautiful singer/actress, a bodyguard is hired to protect her. Eventually, they fall in love. But, alas, the relationship is doomed. They are from different worlds. At the end, Rachel continues her fabulous life and thriving career . . . without Frank. "It's a sad but lovely story," Whitney would say. "I love the dramatic elements, and some of the emotions I had to express I was actually feeling at that time in my own life."

It was true that Whitney felt her personal life had taken a turn for the better, mostly as a result of her deepening relationship with singer Bobby Brown. Whitney said she was drawn to him like a magnet, despite what seemed to some to be major differences in their backgrounds and personalities.

Bobby Baresford Brown, who is six years younger than Whitney, was born in 1969 in the projects of Boston. According to his mother, Carole Brown, he was a mischievous child. She has recalled, "One time I was at a friend's house in the projects and the kids were playing outside. Somebody came to my girlfriend's house and said, 'Bobby is in the Dumpster and we can't wake him up.' I was so scared, I couldn't run. My legs gave out. I kept thinking he was dead. Well, when I got there, wouldn't you know it, Bobby jumps right up. It was all a joke. He was always doing things like that."

Carole Brown also recalled that, as a student, Bobby was primarily inconsistent. "He was just so-so.

Sometimes he would work. Sometimes not." She feels that the death of Bobby's grandmother is what sparked his troubled youth. "He just lost it," she says. "It was the first experience that he had with a family member passing, and he was close to my mother."

By the time Bobby was eleven years old, he was running with gangs in Boston. He had been shot, stabbed, and had seen a friend bleed to death on the streets of Roxbury. It was only the lure of show business that kept him alive, his innate talent allowing him to escape the mean streets and find life elsewhere.

That same year, he and friends Michael Bivens, Ralph Tresvant, and Ricky Bell (later Ronnie DeVoe as well) formed a singing group and entered a talent show. Music impresario Maurice Starr spotted the ragtag youths and transformed them into the group New Edition, an eighties version of the Jackson Five. Despite the success of the group—a few million-selling records that generated a huge teen following, according to Brown—they made little money, while Starr made quite a bit. Bobby claims, "I ended up with five hundred dollars and a VCR." He left the group in 1986 for a solo career, even though he was not the act's lead singer (Tresvant was).

Bobby is bitter about the consequences that early success had on his life. He told *US* magazine, "I left the household at a very young age. We were on the road alone. There was no time to grow up with my family. No time to grow up at all." This lack of parental supervision, along with a demanding touring schedule and huge success, may have caused him to become rebellious, and sometimes temperamental.

He left New Edition because Maurice Starr would not allow him to sing lead vocals. As a solo star, he finally scored with his second album, *Don't Be Cruel,* in 1988, which sold eight million copies (two million more than Whitney's *I'm Your Baby Tonight*), but despite his commercial success, the pain of his lost childhood remained, and the rebellious youth within him refused to grow up or go away.

During a 1989 world tour, Brown was arrested in Georgia for lewd conduct onstage. After that incident, he became a recluse, steadfastly denying rumors of drug abuse. Of the rumors, he told a reporter, "It bothers me. It hurt my mother even more because she raised her child different than everyone is making him out to be."

After the tour, Brown relocated to Atlanta with his young son, Landon, and his father, Herbert Brown (who was separated from Carole Brown). He lay low, taking the time to build a recording studio and forming his own record label.

But after Brown met Whitney Houston at the Soul Train Music Awards, his life was changed, and there was no looking back. He told the *Los Angeles Times,* "I may be a B-boy [slang for 'bad boy'] and she may be America's Sweetheart, but it's love." He added, "When it happens, you have to grab it. You can't let it go, no matter what anybody else thinks." Brown's father echoed his son's sentiments about Whitney Houston. Herbert Brown said, "He really loves this girl. He came up to me and he said, 'Daddy, this is it.'"

"Whitney is a proud black woman," says Bobby. "That's what really drew me to her. She's beautiful, not just outside, but on the inside. And she has some B-girl in her. After we finish a show, she puts on her jeans and we roll."

The fact is that Whitney and Bobby are really very much alike. While she may be, as Brown called her, "America's Sweetheart," she has a rough-and-tumble spirit that appealed to him. "They had a great passion from the start," said one associate. "They were too hot to cool down. Whitney's parents tried to ignore it, hoping the romance would just fade. But that wasn't to be. . . ."

In March 1992, Whitney announced to her family that she was pregnant—and that Bobby Brown was the father of the child.

John and Cissy were less than enthused. One source remembers their reaction. "Well, of course, they were furious. This was a strict Christian family. Whitney was raised in the church. Marriage and family were important. But Whitney wasn't married and had made no plans to correct this situation. And Bobby Brown seemed less than the ideal mate.

"Cissy and John were completely out of sorts. [Bobby] already had two children with two other women."

According to another source close to the family, John and Cissy did not hide their dislike and distrust of Bobby Brown. "Cissy really tried to stay out of it, but she couldn't," the source revealed. "She simply couldn't control herself.

"At first, there were just a few remarks made by Cissy to Bobby, which he disregarded. Then John Houston, who usually stayed away from these types of personal situations, began to tell Whitney what a mistake she was making. In the end, she wouldn't listen to her father, and she was definitely not listening to her mother at this time, either. When Whitney went to Miami to begin working on *The Bodyguard* in late February 1992, she left saying that she was going to be with Bobby and she didn't care what anyone thought. 'I love this man,' she said, 'I'm having his child. And that's that.'"

In March 1992, however, while filming the movie, Whitney began to experience some physical discomfort. She had started bleeding, leading to fears that she might miscarry. Terrified, she called her doctor, who ordered her to halt all activities and to rest.

Kevin Costner, concerned for his costar's health, told Whitney to try to relax. But how could she? She was making a movie, her first starring role, and surely must have been under great pressure. Between scenes, she had to be satisfied with frequent trips to her trailer—where she would sit with her feet up, drinking hot tea.

Unfortunately, two days after her visit to the doctor, she did have a miscarriage. Bobby immediately canceled a recording session in Atlanta and flew to Miami to be by her side. Said a friend, "Bobby told her, 'It's okay, baby. We lost this child because it wasn't meant to be. But that doesn't mean we can't have more children.'"

Whitney, though, was devastated. "She cried," said the friend. "She was so sad. She really wanted that child. It was such a loss. . . ."

But Whitney hardly had time to focus on the loss because of the consuming work of filming. Making matters more perplexing for her was that someone in her organization apparently leaked news of the tragedy to the tabloids.

"When Whitney read about the miscarriage in *The National Enquirer*, she couldn't believe her eyes," said one source. "'Pregnant Whitney Houston Loses Her Love Child' screamed out the headline. She hit the roof. 'Who did this?' she demanded to know. 'Who would betray me like this?' In the end, Whitney had to recognize that she could have no secrets. It still is not something she is used to. . . ."

A reporter from *USA Today* asked Whitney to confirm the report. At first, she couldn't believe the reporter's audacity. "I would rather not talk about my personal life," she began, "but what I will tell you is that [the tabloids] will take something as personal as this . . ." Her voice trailed off. After a beat, she continued, almost in resignation. "Let's say I did have a miscarriage. That's *my* business. You know what I'm saying?

"It just so happened that it happened while I was doing a movie, on a movie set. People get word and people call up the papers and say it. But [miscarriages] happen to women all the time. It's just that I'm this . . . this *person*. Whitney Houston."

"I'm eight years into this thing, man," Whitney finally said of her life in the spotlight. "You'd think this [kind of scrutiny] would be cool. No way."

The tragic miscarriage left Whitney and Bobby desolate, but it also served to bring them closer and make them more intent on solidifying their bond.

A year earlier, Bobby had asked her to marry him. She told him to "forget about it. It's just not in my plans." Then, in April 1992, after the miscarriage, while Whitney and Bobby were on a date, parked in an automobile, he pulled a small, unpretentious diamond ring from his vest pocket and handed it to her. Again he asked her to marry him.

Whitney was stunned, perhaps as much by the simplicity of the ring as by the question. At first, she was speechless. Then she said yes.

Bobby immediately took the cheap ring from her hand, put it back in his pocket, then gave her a magnificent diamond ring.

Whitney's eyes widened. "Oh, my God!" she exclaimed.

"I just wanted to see if you would say yes, even if I didn't have nothing," Bobby said.

"He is just so cute," Whitney would say when she recalled that evening's proposal.

The impending marriage did little to assuage Cissy and John's fears about the relationship. At the very least, it seemed to represent a break from the values with which Whitney had been raised.

In the past, Whitney had consistently reflected those values in her public and private statements. She had been vocal about her Christian upbringing. Her past relationships were mainly innocent dates with high-profile men, and she usually characterized those relationships as just "friendly." (Even though she seemed to be in love with Eddie Murphy, nothing much came of it.)

In a confusing 1991 interview, Whitney told *Ebony* magazine about her faith, and how it related to her love life. "I've had boyfriends all my life—very good-looking and very fine young men. And I've had great relationships.

"I was raised a Christian," she added, "and my mother was very strict with me as far as boys were concerned. She told me that the way to a man's heart is not by opening your legs. You let him get to know you first. All of that stuff has worked for me." The fact that Whitney had become pregnant out of wedlock suggested, however, that her values were undergoing some changes.

Perhaps the people who had installed her in front of the world as an idol, who assumed that because she had zillions of dollars she was certifiably mature, and who wanted her to be real then skewered her for actually becoming real . . . perhaps they had to remember that here was a young woman growing up in public. And they were going to see things they didn't expect to see, including contradictions, conflicts, unsettled emotions, and awkward self-revelations. There would be times when reporters, interviewers, and fans would not know when Whitney Houston was being candid, or when she was speaking only to protect her "Miss America" image. Perhaps even Whitney herself wouldn't know for sure.

But she was honest enough to do what she needed to do.

For one thing, Bobby Brown really did seem to be bringing out the so-called B-girl in her at every turn. Following the announcement of marriage, Whitney appeared to undergo a dramatic transformation. Her public persona suddenly took on a harder edge; she was now sounding decisively more "ethnic" in her interviews.

In place of family and church remembrances, she began to focus on her black heritage, roots, and— Bobby. "You know, Bobby and I basically come from the same place," Whitney said in one interview. "Bobby comes from Boston, out of the projects. I come from Newark, out of the projects."

(Well, she did *visit* the projects at various times as a child, staying there when her mother was on the road, and she wasn't unfamiliar with them. But for her to say she came "out of the projects" sounds a little excessive.)

"Bobby," she continued, "has two very strong parents. I have two very strong parents. Growing up, we all have a rebellious stage. Bobby's energy is street.

"You see somebody and you deal with their image, that's their *image*. It's part of them, but not the whole picture. I am not always in a sequined gown. I am *nobody's* angel. I can get down and dirty. I can get raunchy.

"I've learned to be freer from just being with Bobby.

I've learned to be a little more loose. Not so contained, you know?

"In fact, I wish I could move like him. He just naturally has this [she imitates Bobby's strut]. . . . And since I've been around him, I've gotten, you know, a little bit freer with my shit."

Filming of *The Bodyguard* continued into the spring of 1992. Although still a bit frightened about how the public would react, Whitney immersed herself in the project. Insecure about her performance, she had asked Kevin Costner if he felt she should take acting lessons. He quickly answered no, saying her personal charm and charisma would bring life to her character. He felt that acting lessons would only distract her.

"In Britain, I'd worked with a lot of actresses who are not particularly schooled," said director Mick Jackson when asked to comment on Whitney's acting. "And in this film it was either teach an actress to sing or, as with Whitney, teach a singer to act." As for working with Whitney, he noted, "Her life as a pop-music diva means that everything is set to her requirements, which is totally different from shooting a film. When she got a look at the schedule, the first thing she said was, 'I'm *not* a day person.'"

The script of *The Bodyguard* contained some lengthy scenes between Whitney's character and Costner's— Rachel and Frank—many of them deeply emotional and requiring a skilled actress. According to a source who worked on the film, some people involved in the production wished Whitney had a bit more acting experience. The source said, "Whitney just didn't have the acting skills to play some of those more dramatic scenes. She tried, God love her. But when the producers and director would view the dailies, they saw that it just wasn't happening."

Reportedly, the producers were forced to make a quick decision as filming progressed. They would either have to leave the scenes the way they were (and hope other elements—like camera angles and musical scoring—would help gloss over Whitney's acting) or cut them altogether, all the while rewriting the script so scenes yet to be filmed involved less emoting from her. They chose the latter route, scrapping some scenes to "protect" their female star—as Kevin Costner had promised.

One emotional scene that remained in the film has Rachel and Frank alone on the balcony of her Miami hotel room. After several attempts have been made on her life, Rachel has finally come to the conclusion that she does need a bodyguard. She admits to Frank, "I'm scared," and begins to express her fears.

Unfortunately, Whitney seemed to "freeze" during the scene, unable to connect with the emotions she was required to put over. (Perhaps some basic acting lessons could have taught her to find those emotions within herself, then use them to express the innermost fears of her character.) Still, Houston is nothing if not a trouper. But even though she gave her all to the scene, she just wasn't that convincing.

A scene on which she had to work hardest involved a confrontation between her character and Costner's. "I was supposed to be hysterical and it required a lot of emotions," she later said. "And I had to slap him several times. I kept saying to myself, 'Oh, God, I don't wanna hit this man, because this man didn't really do anything to me.' And I had to slap him really hard. That was very difficult. Very difficult."

Whitney used a form of "method acting" to pull this scene off. She recalled, "I had to reach down inside of me and bring it out, remembering times when I felt like slapping somebody, recalling times when I've been emotional and cried. It actually takes a lot for me to cry, a lot to make me mad. It took a lot of concentration to get through that scene.

"While music has rhythm that comes naturally to me, acting takes concentration. I would compare it to starting my music career and working in the clubs, really having to work at something. Doing the movie was like starting all over again in a new field."

It was rumored that Bobby Brown had serious reservations about his fiancée's interaction with Kevin Costner, a handsome Hollywood leading man. But this doesn't seem to have been the case.

In one interview, Whitney recalled, "I didn't go into this movie wanting to fall in love with Kevin Costner. I was already in love [with Bobby]. Being that he's my man, I talked to Bobby about the movie. I let him read the script. At some moments along the way, he did say, 'Well, how are these scenes going to be played? How much are you going to be involved with this?' and so on. But Bobby knew me and trusted me. I was not in the movie to be with a sex symbol. It wasn't about sex. Bobby was comfortable with that. You have to have a trust between the two of you. I think Bobby and I have that."

In reality, Bobby couldn't justify any apprehension at all about Whitney's work with Kevin, especially since his own recent music videos graphically portrayed sexual messages much stronger than any of those found in *The Bodyguard*. In many of them, an abundance of beautiful scantily clothed women dance around Brown, "bumping and grinding" with him.

Whitney has observed, "I look at Bobby's videos and I say, 'Oh honey, God!' But I know that that person in the video loves me. And all of that bumping and grinding is his business; that's what he does for a living. That's part of his entertainment, his career."

As filming of *The Bodyguard* drew to a close, Whitney needed to turn her attention to her next big role—that of Bobby Brown's wife. Initially, the couple had every intention of eloping, in order to throw off the press. A close friend of Bobby's revealed that the lovers secretly made elaborate plans to sneak away, marry, and then announce the event to the media. But when Whitney confided the plans to Cissy and John Houston, their reaction stopped her cold. Despite their ambivalent feelings about the union, they wanted to give their only daughter a grand send-off into married life. Whitney decided not to disappoint them.

Making matters more complicated for Whitney was the tension that had always existed between Bobby and her longtime friend Robyn Crawford. Crawford made no attempt to hide her distrust and dislike of Brown, even when he was present. One friend said, "[Robyn] just didn't get along with him, and he really didn't make any effort to change her opinion of him, either. Robyn just doesn't like the type of 'bad boy' Bobby represents."

The friend continued, "When Whitney got pregnant, Robyn just about had a cow. She thought Bobby was up to his old tricks again, and that soon after the baby was born, he would just end up with someone else."

It didn't take long for Crawford's prophecy to come true.

Before long, it was revealed that Bobby had become a father once again—by another woman.

Bobby Brown and the mother of his newborn son (who was also the mother of his two-year-old daughter) had grown up together in Boston's Orchard Park housing project. According to Bobby, he and the woman had once been involved, but had ended their romance. He added that they had not dated since Whitney came into his life.

However, the fact remained that Whitney and Bobby had been seeing each other for over a year, and Whitney thought they were in a monogamous relationship. Bobby had to scramble to salvage his relationship with Whitney, and—apparently—he was successful. "Somehow, he convinced her that the relationship with that other woman was over long before the child was born," said a source. "But he felt that he should have an obligation to his son, and that Whitney should respect that obligation. She should *want* him to be responsible.

"Then, Whitney found herself bombarded by flowers from Bobby. What's a girl to do when she's madly in love?

"She put up the white flag and told her family she intended to go on with the wedding as planned."

sixteen

"My private life is mine," Whitney Houston said in 1992. "You can't establish a life in the public. They'll rip you apart."

It was clear that Whitney was not happy with her role as a public figure. As much as she enjoyed her success and fame, the accompanying invasion of privacy was almost more than she could handle. How ironic, then, that in May 1992, while filming her first motion picture and planning an elaborate wedding, Whitney starred in an ABC-TV special entitled "Whitney Houston: This Is My Life."

The program was promoted by the network as "An inside look at the many sides of Whitney Houston, in her first network special," and was to contain behind-the-scenes footage of the making of *The Bodyguard*, interviews with family members (including John and Cissy), along with narration and "personal thoughts" from the star herself. Whitney would be seen preparing for a concert, working out a scene for the movie, lounging in her home, working in her office, driving her car. . . . all of which was apparently intended to demonstrate to the viewer that she does, indeed, do these things.

During one portion of the program, Whitney's mother said, "I think this is the real Whitney—to a point. There's a real grown-up side, and there's a very young side, which she shows you most of the time. But she's also a human being, and if you push the wrong button, she can be something else."

Of the special, the *New York Post*'s David Bianculli wrote, "It's so superficial and safe, this portrait of a glamorous pop singer on the road should have been called 'No Truth, No Dare.'" Comparisons with Madonna's controversial feature film *Truth or Dare* were inevitable, and if viewers were expecting startling revelations and backstage fights, they would have been disappointed. Most observers agree, however, that the real point of the television special was to promote the upcoming film. In that respect, since Whitney was seen rehearsing and filming scenes, perhaps it was useful.

As production of *The Bodyguard* wound down and the film could be viewed as a whole, problems began to surface. Kevin Costner was unhappy with the chemistry between its main characters, Rachel and Frank, whose relationship was the central focus of the entire story. According to one source close to the production, Costner had wanted desperately to spend more time with Whitney prior to the filming, in order to establish an off-screen rapport with her that could translate into on-screen passion.

"He did *not* want to have an affair with Whitney, as some in her camp thought," said the source. "Whitney is surrounded by so many people, all of whom are trying to protect her and many of whom are suspicious. There were some who thought, 'Oh, this guy is like so many other guys who just want to sleep with Whitney.' But Costner couldn't have cared less about sleeping with Whitney. He's all business. He just wanted to *know* her so he could relate to her better.

"This just didn't happen," continues the source. "Kevin invited Whitney out on several occasions, but she was basically unreachable. He liked Whitney and had great respect for her, but there was nothing for him to be attracted to, to be passionate about. She never gave him anything to work with." Perhaps this explains why, when watching *The Bodyguard,* the viewer has the impression that Rachel and Frank are two friends who care for each other, but definitely not two lovers engaged in a torrid romance.

Costner decided to reedit the final cut of the film, as a clause in his contract gave him the option to do. Director Mick Jackson, who had been involved in *The Bodyguard* for more than a year, including twelve weeks of editing and two successful preview screenings, was not pleased with this decision. But producer Jim Davis and screenwriter Lawrence Kasdan agreed with Costner that there were some serious problems with Jackson's so-called director's cut, which he had submitted to the studio.

Although it is not unusual for producers to reshape a director's cut, one source said, "It is surprising, though, that the studio basically allowed a director of some note like Mick Jackson to be partially removed from his own movie. But Kevin Costner has a lot of power. He did the same thing on another Warner Bros. project, *Robin Hood: Prince of Thieves,* and he is basically credited with saving the film."

In actuality, Costner was fulfilling his promise to protect Whitney. He had assured her upon her acceptance of the role that she "would not be bad." And according to many sources, he was reediting some of the scenes so Whitney would be seen in her best light.

Such acts of kindness don't happen that often in an industry where throat-cutting and backstabbing are regular features of daily life. While one could argue that he was protecting himself as well, Costner could just as easily have let the film be released as it was. After all, the other studio executives and production people thought it was fine.

But Whitney had more on her mind at this point than *The Bodyguard*. During the summer of 1992, reports of increasing behind-the-scenes strife and bickering among Whitney, Bobby, and members of Whitney's staff continually surfaced. In June, rumor had it that Whitney, Bobby, and Robyn had come to physical blows over the upcoming wedding. "Robyn even tried to beat up Bobby, who is four inches shorter than her," one writer reported.

Whitney had to laugh when she read that story. "First of all, if that were true, Robyn would have been knocked out," she told Hillary de Vries of the *Los Angeles Times*. "But my husband is a gentleman. He would never fight a woman.

"She's my best friend who knows me better than any woman has known me," Whitney told De Vries, *again* trying to clarify her relationship with Robyn Crawford but only adding fuel to the fire of speculation. "By the time I met Bobby, Robyn and I had had enough time together." Whitney then said that Robyn had been living in the New Jersey mansion but had now moved "into her own place, about thirty minutes away."

It seemed that everyone was concerned about Whitney's welfare. An employee of hers recalls that Cissy, John, and even Clive Davis were seeking "some assurances" from Bobby Brown before they would let the wedding take place.

The employee tells of an evening that John Houston and Bobby Brown spent together, a dinner arranged by Whitney so her future husband could become better acquainted with her father. "This evening was supposed to put to rest any fears that John [might] have had about Bobby's reputation and intentions," the employee has said. "The evening began on an easy note, with Bobby and John talking casually about various topics, but never really getting down to brass tacks. They both had a couple of drinks and then sat down to dinner. Bobby was very nervous about being there with John.

"And then, right in the middle of dinner, Bobby abruptly announced that he had to use the phone. So he left the table. Upon returning, he said that he had to cut the meal short and take off—something about having to meet with his manager."

John Houston was confused and unhappy about this turn of events and immediately told Cissy about it. What was *that* all about? the Houstons wondered. When Cissy confronted her daughter, Whitney said she knew for a fact that Bobby had, indeed, gone to have an emergency meeting with his manager. Her parents were not convinced. And they had no idea at all of what to think about Bobby Brown.

Clive Davis, the president of Arista, had a meeting with Whitney shortly after this dinner to ask her if she truly believed Bobby Brown was ready to settle down. Davis also had a lot at stake. Whitney was—is—Davis's most successful artist. All of the media coverage about her fiancé's erratic behavior only served to muddy Arista's clean, wholesome, Miss America, image of Whitney. Arista had spent millions of dollars over the years creating and polishing that image; now that she was a major star, maintaining it was more important than ever. By becoming involved with someone who seemed as rebellious and uncontrollable as Bobby Brown, she was courting trouble.

The public-relations problem created by Whitney's relationship with Bobby reminded some industry observers of what happened in the early 1970s when Cher—also perceived at that time as one of America's most treasured stars—dumped her mate and singing partner Sonny Bono to marry Gregg Allman, a long-haired rock star who had openly admitted to being a drug addict. Ratings of her solo television series plummeted, and the show was soon canceled. Then Cher starred in a new series with ex-husband Sonny while she was pregnant with new husband Gregg's child. That show was quickly canceled, also. In retrospect, Cher blames this downslide in her career on the American public's reaction to her marriage to Gregg. "America could not accept it," she said. "They could not accept that I was living my own life, and involved with some-one like Gregg Allman."

During her meeting with Davis, Whitney reportedly recognized and appreciated the executive's feelings, also understanding that his concern was as much personal as corporate. Davis did, in fact, care for Whitney and did not want her to get hurt. As their meeting ended Whitney embraced Clive warmly, thanked him for his concern, and told him she and Bobby Brown were in love and that she knew what she was doing.

Clive, in what she must surely have regarded as a measure of respect, did nothing to try to talk her out of the relationship.

The wedding day was drawing nearer. Soon, those close to Whitney began repeating two words over and over—"prenuptial agreement." Whitney's advisers wanted her to consider having Bobby sign such an agreement, in order to protect her money and other assets. While no bride or groom finds the possibility of a future, messy divorce very appealing, a person in Whitney's financial position who is about to be married is often advised by attorneys and business managers to draft an agreement that, in the event of divorce, assures her ability to leave the marriage with the finances, investments, and holdings that were hers before the union.

At this time, Whitney's financial worth was estimated at about $30 million, while Bobby Brown's was estimated at just over $5 million. Brown had made a small fortune in the few years he was recording, but had little to show in the end, save a few investments and his $2 million estate. He blamed bad management for his serious financial problems and would finally sue some of his representatives, claiming they had mismanaged his funds.

But despite Bobby's financial problems, Whitney was not interested in having him sign any kind of prenuptial agreement. "She kept saying she was in love, and that she wouldn't consider having him sign a paper that planned for the end of the marriage," said a source. "A lot of people thought this was extremely naive of her. It's safe to say that some members of her family were less than enthused about her decision. But Whitney Houston does what Whitney Houston wants to do, and it was her decision. 'If I can't trust my own husband,' she said, 'then who can I trust?'"

In June 1992, some of Whitney's friends and other family members surprised the bride-to-be with a wedding shower at the Rihga Royal Hotel in Manhattan.

Cissy Houston, Natalie Cole, Valerie Simpson, CeCe Winans, Dionne Warwick—seventy-five guests in all—toasted Whitney with a bash that was hosted by maid of honor Robyn Crawford. The guests were treated to Dom Perignon and Cristal champagne, and were served crab, jumbo shrimp, caviar, and assorted pastas.

The theme of the party seemed to be "sexy items to keep Bobby's interest," with Whitney receiving a set of velvet handcuffs, see-through negligees, and a glow-in-the-dark condom. There was one serious gift—a Bible—presented by some of the nuns from the Catholic high school Whitney had attended.

According to one attendee, Whitney was as happy as she had ever been. "She was absolutely beaming," the friend observed. "No matter what anybody else has said, Whitney Houston was looking forward to being Mrs. Bobby Brown. She really considered this to be the pinnacle of her life.

"She always said her life would be complete with a great career, a great husband, and a couple of kids. And now she was on her way to having all of these things. I'd say she was pretty satisfied with her life. . . ."

Shortly after the engagement party, Bobby complained, during a dinner in which wedding plans were being finalized, about habits of Whitney and Robyn that he considered inappropriate. "Bobby told Robyn he thought it was ridiculous for her and Whitney to be sharing clothes. That's how another fight started," an observer said. "And then it got really out of hand, with Robyn and Bobby yelling and pointing fingers at each other. Whitney actually had to stand between the two of them, to act as referee."

Even with Bobby's claims to be a changed man, one must wonder why Whitney Houston—a successful, powerful, and beautiful woman—would put up with his behavior. A Los Angeles-area psychologist explained it this way: "I have seen many cases in which a woman who is powerful in the business world or in the arts, has relationships with men who are destructive, oftentimes immature, and truly not ready for marriage."

She continued, "Although these women control their business personas quite well, inwardly, they are extremely insecure. This makes them prime targets for men who manipulate by giving and pulling back without notice, or for men who abuse them either physically or emotionally—only to come back afterwards even more loving and adoring than before. It is similar in some ways to the 'battered woman' syndrome."

Also, Whitney seemed often to be playing the "rebellious daughter" role with family and friends. The more they all warned her about Bobby, the more determined she became. "I see this a lot with children of highly religious households," the psychologist added. "Those who grow up in the church often rebel against their parents and the church in order to assert their own personalities. It is their way of dealing with a repressive upbringing. They are really saying, 'Now that I am an adult, I do what I want to do and not what you or the church tell me to do.'"

Whitney Houston clearly felt she should be allowed to live her life, making her own choices and mistakes—and she, no doubt, was right. "My husband is extremely respectful of me," she told Lynn Normant of *Ebony* magazine, "And you know what? If I felt Bobby was the kind of man who was not faithful to me, I would not be with him."

On July 18, 1992, Whitney Elizabeth Houston walked down the aisle on the arm of her father, John, to marry Bobby Baresford Brown. The ceremony took place at Whitney's lush, five-acre, $2.8 million estate in Mendham Township, New Jersey. As a seventeen-piece orchestra from the New York Metropolitan Opera played Richard Wagner's traditional wedding march, Whitney and her father made their way down the aisle. Guests gasped at Whitney's stunning wedding gown.

The $30,000 gown, made of French Lyon lace, with iridescent beads, white pearls, and sequins, trailed to the floor. Its front was a bodice cut, with soft lace covering Whitney's neck and shoulders, leading to a pearl choker with drop beads. The gown featured a four-foot train— the lace alone costing over $4,000. Whitney wore a matching, beaded skullcap, to which a veil was attached. Simple, white, low-heeled shoes ensured that she did not appear taller than her husband.

To say that Whitney Houston was radiant on her wedding day is an understatement. "She was positively glowing," reported an eyewitness. "I've never seen her so happy, nervous, excited, perhaps scared. She lit up from within, that's all I know."

John Houston could not help but become emotional as he walked his daughter down the aisle. Later, Whitney would reveal that he had tears in his eyes. "This is the hardest thing that I have ever done," Whitney recalled him whispering to her as they walked arm in arm.

Whitney smiled at him. Crying, she said, "I know this is hard. But, you know what? You are the first man that I was ever in love with."

John nodded. "I know it," he said. Then, in a tone that was nothing if it was not serious, he added, "He'd *better* take good care of you."

The wedding was attended by a number of celebrities, including Dionne Warwick, Patti LaBelle, Aretha Franklin, Gladys Knight, Valerie Simpson, Dick Clark,

Natalie Cole, Leslie Uggams, Donald Trump, and Marla Maples. Stevie Wonder and Luther Vandross also attended; both would perform at the reception. Kevin Costner was noticeably absent.

Security for the affair was tight, with guests having to pass through five checkpoints. Bodyguards stood in front of members of the bridal party at all times. Guests were asked to forgo bringing gifts, and instead to make a contribution to the Whitney Houston Foundation for Children. It is reported that over half a million dollars was raised.

Bobby, who seemed extremely nervous, wore a white suit with tails. Robyn Crawford, Whitney's maid of honor, had elaborate beads woven into her hair and, according to one guest, looked better than she ever had. (One reason for her smile may have been the black Porsche Robyn found waiting for her in her driveway as she left for the ceremony. The car was a gift of appreciation from the bride, her childhood friend and present employer.)

The service was conducted by Reverend Marvin Winans. Bobby Brown wept openly during most of the ceremony, interrupting Winans several times with emotional outbursts such as "Yes, yes, *yes!*"

Whitney spoke her vows in a soft voice, many times praising the Lord as she repeated the minister's words. A lighter moment came when she placed the platinum ring on Bobby's finger. Brown lifted his hand high into the air, shouting, *"Yeah!"* He then smiled mischievously at the guests.

With the speaking of the final vows and the announcement that Bobby Brown and Whitney Houston were "man and wife," seven white doves— Whitney's lucky number—were released into the pale blue skies over the Houston estate.

When Reverend Winans finally told Bobby he could kiss the bride, Bobby lifted the fragile veil and kissed Whitney passionately. The kiss was clocked at over three minutes.

Following the ceremony, Whitney, Bobby, the wedding party, and families joined eight hundred other guests for a reception under an outdoor canopy, which had been carpeted and air-conditioned. Robert Clivilles and David Cole of C&C Music Factory kept the dance floor crowded, never stopping for a breath between songs.

Whitney and Bobby were inseparable on the dance floor, their bodies pressed together even for the up-tempo songs. Bobby had taken off his tuxedo jacket to reveal a short-sleeved white cowl-collared shirt, clasped at the neck by a silver jewel. Eventually, he somehow ended up with a woman's pearl earring dangling in his left ear as he twirled his new bride on the dance floor. As is traditional with newly married couples, the cutting of the wedding cake led to a mock fight in which frosting was squished into the faces of both bride and groom, while the crowd roared with approval.

Whitney and Bobby partied with their guests until two o'clock in the morning, some twelve hours after the festivities had begun. Later, the newlyweds flew aboard the Concorde to Europe for a ten-day Mediterranean cruise aboard a luxurious 140-foot yacht with a crew of nine, whose job was to anticipate their every need. The honeymoon was a wedding gift from Arista and MCA Records.

The ship's main stateroom, which the Browns rarely left, was equipped with a television, VCR, stereo, his-and-hers showers, and a Jacuzzi.

Whitney told a friend that she had every intention of becoming pregnant on their wedding night. "She really wanted to start a family right away," the friend recalled. "When she told Bobby this, he said he would have her pregnant 'before the ink had dried on the thank-you cards.'"

In fact, Whitney began experiencing morning sickness even before the four-week honeymoon was over. And the newlyweds hadn't even come *close* to sending out those cards.

seventeen

    Now that Whitney Houston was a married woman and *The Bodyguard* was finished and nearly ready for release, she had to face the prospect of going back to work. She had recorded six songs, which she performed in the movie. After the movie was finished, she had to go back to the studio and polish up the vocal performances, both for the film's final print and for the movie's album soundtrack. Choosing which songs would finally be used had been an arduous task. Whitney, Clive Davis, and producer/arranger David Foster were responsible for most of the decisions, though Kevin Costner also had much input.

Several songwriters and producers had submitted material, including the popular and successful team of L. A. Reid and Babyface, who had produced and written the song "I'm Your Baby Tonight." Along with Daryl Simmons, they wrote an upbeat song, "Queen of the Night," which Whitney performed during a club scene in the film. (Whitney collaborated on the song as well, adding some lyrics.)

Whitney also decided to record the classic R&B song "I'm Every Woman," originally sung by Chaka Khan. (Back in the seventies, Cissy had performed backup vocals on the hit, and according to the family, young Whitney had trailed along for the recording session and added her voice to the mix.)

Chaka Khan had been a close friend of the family for years. Many rock-and-roll and rhythm-and-blues purists consider her "I'm Every Woman" (written by Valerie Simpson and Nicholas Ashford) one of the most uplifting, optimistic songs ever produced, and her version is still played on radio stations. Most critics agree, however, that Whitney's raucous version on *The Bodyguard* soundtrack is superior.

The Bodyguard soundtrack would also contain a solo version of Whitney's first gospel song, "Jesus Loves Me," which she performs in the film with Michele Lamar Richards (the actress who portrayed Rachel Marron's sister, Nikki). Whitney's gospel roots are very apparent in the track, and one can almost see the singer at the age of twelve as she stood before her congregation on that hot summer day when she first realized the power of her voice.

In addition, producer David Foster and his wife, Linda Thompson, wrote the stirring ballad "I Have Nothing," a strong, moving song with emotional lyrics that are used in the film to portray the relationship between Rachel Marron and Frank Farmer. Foster also produced "Run to You," (written by Allan Rich and Jud Freidman) for the soundtrack, as well as Whitney's remake of the Dolly Parton love song "I Will Always Love You."

"I Will Always Love You," which was recorded by Parton in the seventies and by Linda Ronstadt on her *Prisoner in Disguise* album, would become one of the biggest hits of Whitney Houston's career. The song's simply expressed message seemed perfect for the star-crossed-lovers theme of *The Bodyguard.* Dolly Parton sang the song in her trademark casual, yet lilting style, with the singer vowing to hold her lover in her heart forever, although fate has kept them apart. Whitney's version is much more determined. Whereas Dolly sounds like a hopeless victim, Whitney sounds strong and resolved, as if she knows she'll survive this difficult moment.

Interestingly enough, Whitney's version was almost not recorded. David Foster had his mind set on having her do "What Becomes of the Broken Hearted?", which was originally recorded in 1966 by Motown recording artist Jimmy Ruffin. That song, written by Paul Riser and William Witherspoon, is a soulful ballad that tells of a love spurned and of dreams broken by reality. Whitney and Clive Davis agreed with Foster that it would be an excellent choice, with Whitney's vocals illuminating an already haunting melody. So Whitney recorded the song.

However, when Paul Young released a rendition of the oldie-but-goodie and it became a chart hit, the film's producers decided to hold back Whitney's version, and began to look for a replacement. Costner suggested Dolly Parton's "I Will Always Love You." When Whitney heard the Parton song, she thought it was superb. Of course, it became a huge number-one hit for Whitney, staying on top of the charts for an unprecedented fourteen weeks—the longest-running number-one song in the history of the *Billboard* charts.

Estimates indicate that Dolly Parton earned more than $3 million in royalties for the remake. (The song had also been featured in the film *The Best Little Whorehouse in Texas,* starring Parton and Burt Reynolds.)

The version of "I Will Always Love You" that

appears in *The Bodyguard* begins a cappella. There is a slow build, and as the emotional content of the lyrics takes hold of the listener, the music blends seamlessly with Whitney's voice. That's the version everyone in the world has heard and bought and goes around humming, but it is not the version Whitney Houston, Clive Davis, or David Foster intended to release. "The version they had all agreed upon was very different than the final product," says one source close to the production of "I Will Always Love You."

"Originally, they planned that the song would open with a musical interlude—as practically every song does—and then go immediately into Whitney singing the refrain, 'I will always love you. . . .' That version completely left out the opening verse, 'If I should stay / I would only be in your way. . . .'

"It was Kevin Costner who made the suggestion that the song open with Whitney singing the beginning of the arrangement a cappella. None of the others liked the idea but, somehow, Kevin seemed to have an instinct about this. He really is a musical person. To think that he conceived not only the idea to record the song but also the noteworthy, memorable a cappella arrangement that the world now knows so well is quite amazing. Of course, everyone involved now agrees that Costner was dead-on right."

The producers of *The Bodyguard*, after meeting with Dolly Parton, reportedly struck an oral agreement that she not sing "I Will Always Love You" during the time the movie and film were being promoted. The producers wanted Whitney's version to take hold with the public. Unfortunately, when "I Will Always Love You" became a hit, Parton apparently could not resist the various opportunities to sing it once again. After all, she probably figured, she did write it.

So Dolly often sang "I Will Always Love You" on television. However, her version of the song, with its sweet simplicity, is so dramatically different from Whitney's that hearing it is almost jarring. It actually makes the listener wonder if, perhaps, Whitney overdid her own version.

Whitney was not happy about this turn of events. In fact, on two specific occasions she turned down invitations to attend events honoring Dolly Parton's songwriting skills. According to one friend, Whitney said, only half joking, "I tell you something, I will *not* always love Dolly Parton or Sandy Gallin [Dolly's manager]."

After two months, much to the amazement of the tabloids, Bobby and Whitney were still married. Whitney was growing ever more pregnant, and pregnancy seemed to agree with her. As her face filled out it took on a dreamy quality and seemed to have a Marilyn Monroe–like glow.

Bobby Brown told the press he enjoyed married life, and mentioned to one reporter that dating during the era of AIDS and other sexually transmitted diseases had, in part, spurred him to walk down the aisle. "You got to settle down," he said. "There's too much going on in the world today to be alone."

Whitney also beamed, saying, "I love being married. I want to spend my whole life with [Bobby], to give to him and take from him."

She defended his supposed "wild" life-style by telling music writer Anthony DeCurtis, "I want to get something straight. I've heard a lot about my husband being this womanizer. You know: 'He's a womanizer, he's got three illegitimate children, da-da-da-da-da-da'—you know that whole thing? I just want people to understand something: My husband has never, never disrespected any woman. Any woman that he's wanted has wanted him.

"And I want people to know that my husband's a good person. He's a respectable human being. He was raised with respect.

"And I just wish they would try to stop making him out to be this man who just goes around and arbitrarily says, 'I want her and I'm gonna screw her.'"

Whitney concluded, "He loves being married and he's respectful to his marriage. He respects me, and I respect him. I'm tired of people talking about him like he's this bad guy and he has no respect for his marriage. That's bullshit.

"He does [have respect for the marriage]. And anybody who knows him knows that's true."

One can hardly blame Whitney for coming to the defense of her new husband, yet her statements seem oddly naive. After all, Bobby's reputation was sullied long before she came into the picture. Her need to deliver this spirited defense of his character must have brought sadness to those who cared about her.

Interestingly, though, in terms of her public persona, Whitney's tumultuous marriage started taking on a Liz Taylor–like air of sensationalism, as the tabloids began reporting about it on a weekly basis. The tabloid media started referring to "Whitney and Bobby" the way they used to refer to Liz and Dick and to Roseanne and Tom. The public began to empathize with Whitney Houston and wonder about her trials and tribulations. "Why in the world did she marry Bobby?" her fans often asked.

Truly, while she would be loath to admit it, all of the reportage devoted to Whitney and her chaotic life experiences actually served to widen her appeal.

The marriage did little, however, to change John and

Cissy Houston's view of Bobby Brown, even after the birth of the couple's first child. According to a source close to the Houston family, Bobby's ever-present entourage brought about the first major conflict between Cissy and her new son-in-law. The source revealed that after only a few months of marriage, some of Bobby's friends had invaded Whitney's New Jersey estate.

"These guys were always in the house, whether Bobby and Whitney were there or not," says the source. "One day, Cissy came into the home and found some of Bobby's friends snorting cocaine in the kitchen, right off of the counter. [Bobby Brown has steadfastly denied any involvement with drugs.]

"Cissy really hit the roof and threatened to call the police. Whitney and Bobby were out of town. It took a long talk with Whitney by telephone to convince Cissy that calling the police wouldn't be a good idea. But Cissy never got over that. She hated any kind of drugs, especially in her daughter's house."

Meanwhile, Robyn Crawford admitted that Whitney's marriage had placed a strain on her relationship with her employer/friend, stating that it had become more businesslike and less friendly over the years. As she told one reporter for a European publication, "The foundation that we had years ago, the friendship that we shared, is pretty much back there in the past.

"Now it's business. Those of us who work with her have to change to accommodate what happens. I would say that, as a person, Whitney has pretty much stayed the same. I think that it's the people around her, myself included, who have had to make the change to adjust to the fact that she is now so famous, so in demand. . . ."

Robyn continued, "A lot of times you get your feelings hurt. I may look at her in a room and think, 'That was my best friend.' But it's not about being that personal anymore. It's about going as far as she wants to go [in her career]."

Robyn also realized that Whitney's marriage changed things for everyone. "None of us around her, not her mother or father or me, could be to her what a husband can be. In a marriage it seems to me that it is always the woman who has to do more—commit herself more, devote herself, always be there. And Whitney is going to be that kind of wife: she's very traditional."

In another interview, Robyn offered these insights into Whitney's character. "She is not high-handed or temperamental or arrogant, but although she walks softly, she carries an invisible stick. If you back her up against a wall, you will be sorry. In the nicest way, she will make you feel [very small]."

If anyone in the world, outside of Whitney's family, knows the *real* Whitney Houston, it's Robyn Crawford. She had been close to Whitney since their teen years, but found herself slowly relegated to behind-the-scenes status. Somehow, it all seemed so sad. Nothing was the same anymore.

Midway into her pregnancy, Whitney became fearful that her tight concert schedule might cause complications. She was still reeling from her miscarriage, and friends say she became obsessed with the thought that she might not deliver a healthy baby.

"She would always talk about it, and worry about it," one friend said. "She was gaining a lot of weight, which is to be expected with most pregnancies—and she felt sick a lot of the time, so she was always running to the doctor to make sure everything was normal."

Her doctor told Whitney she needed to slow down

during the final months of her pregnancy. So, to the dismay of fans across the United States, Whitney canceled several concerts and hoped the public would be understanding about her situation. These cancellations, however, did little to improve her image with her fans. She could only hope that the release of *The Bodyguard* would make things better and also satisfy their insatiable appetite for her.

The Bodyguard premiered on Monday, November 23, 1992, at Mann's Chinese Theater in Hollywood. The event doubled as a fund-raiser for both Whitney's Children's Foundation and the Magic Johnson Foundation, which offered funding for pediatric AIDS causes. The stars, including Kevin Costner, turned out in force. Whitney looked resplendent in a black billowy gown that fell over her protruding stomach.

Reviewers provided the public with little or no reason to anticipate the film. In fact, the reviews were dismal.

The *Los Angeles Times:* "Just about everything that can go wrong with this film does, and yet it's compulsively watchable. (But so is a train wreck.)"

Variety: "No wonder this Lawrence Kasdan script has been on the shelf for more than a decade: In the custody of director Mick Jackson, it proves a jumbled mess with a few enjoyable moments, but little continuity or flow."

USA Today: "Whitney Houston's acting [is] sub-Connie Francis. Costner, allegedly smitten with his client, had more chemistry with the Warren Commission in *JFK*."

Even Kevin Costner had to admit that he didn't understand the ending of the movie. (It's not clear whether Frank Farmer and Rachel Marron plan to continue their romance, or not.) "The movie went on to make $400 million, and the end doesn't even make sense," Costner lamented. "I know that that's hard for critics and the public. It would be hard on me if I wasn't in *The Bodyguard*. I mean, you go, 'Damn! I don't get it.' "

Despite the fact that Costner was involved in the final cut of the film, once it was released and he saw it in the theater, he didn't like much of it. "[Director] Mick [Jackson] did a very good job of filming it," Costner recalled, "but when the movie was released, it wasn't as good as it could have been. Some things, I feel now, we needed to massage because they felt embarrassing to me. And they felt embarrassing to Whitney, and I owed Whitney on a promise that she would look as good as she could in that film."

The jury was split on the issue of the film's interracial romance. Many reviewers found it disconcerting that the subject was never broached by any character in the film. Surely, these reporters felt, Rachel Marron's son, mother, sister, or *someone* close to her would have noticed that her aggressive bodyguard, Frank Farmer, was white.

And what of Frank's woodsy father, who owned the cabin where Frank secreted Rachel and her family in order to protect them from a terrorist? Wouldn't Frank's father logically have pulled Frank aside upon their arrival at the cabin and pointed out to his son, or just sort of indicated his own awareness, that these folks were . . . black? Maybe. Maybe not.

In retrospect, Costner's insistence that the issue not be even mentioned in the film caused more rather than less attention to be drawn to the characters' racial differences. Perhaps Rachel's son could have looked up at his mother and simply said, "Momma, Frank's white." Rachel then could have soothed her son with, "Yes, Fletcher, he is." And that would have been the end of that.

When the film opened to the public two days after the premiere, fans swarmed the theaters for a look at Whitney Houston on the big screen. Despite the negative reviews, the movie did extremely well at the box office, due in large part to the success of the single "I Will Always Love You," which had been issued several weeks before the film and soared to the top of the charts.

"It's an odd thing when you're very dissatisfied with what you make and it's very successful," Costner observes. "Just as it's very unnerving when you think something is very good and it's not successful."

The Bodyguard soundtrack also moved quickly up the charts and became a number-one hit early in 1993. Throughout the next year, the album would spawn hit records and compelling videos for Whitney with "I'm Every Woman," "I Have Nothing," and "Queen of the Night."

Coinciding with the release of the film and the soundtrack, *Vanity Fair* magazine featured a story about Whitney Houston by Lynn Hirschberg titled "Thoroughly Modern Whitney." The magazine's editors, apparently envisioning an upbeat story about Whitney's marriage, her impending motherhood, and *The Bodyguard*, secured Whitney's agreement to an interview—as long as she was guaranteed the magazine's cover.

The resulting story is actually standard fare about Whitney's family history, rise to the top, and dealings with fame. One of the more amusing anecdotes has Whitney reading the tabloids, obviously as interested in other celebrities and their unusual lives as the rest of America is in hers.

Hirschberg reported that during the interview, Whitney read aloud from the *National Enquirer.* "Nicollette married Harry Hamlin so that she could get a green card?" she is quoted as musing incredulously. "Fergie's pregnant?" she intoned, then turned to her hairstylist, Ellin Lavar, who was curling the hair on Whitney's wig while the *Vanity Fair* interview was taking place. "My, oh *my,*" Whitney exclaimed.

She continued leafing through the tabloid, eventually stopping at an article on Madonna. Whitney read aloud, "Madonna says k.d. lang looks so much like Sean Penn she could fall in love with her." She then turned from the pages of the *Enquirer* and told Hirschberg, "You know, I like to read the tabloids. It's either me or Oprah they're writing about. They take turns."

When that *Vanity Fair* article was published in 1992, it caused more than a small problem for Whitney. Ironically enough, she was, again, having her hair styled in her home when she was handed an advance copy. Surrounded by her hairdressers and makeup staff—and with Robyn Crawford standing nearby—Whitney began to read.

"She was reading the story aloud in some parts," remembers one eyewitness. "At first, she thought it was well-written and she was enjoying the pictures of Bobby and herself.

"Suddenly, she stopped reading aloud. Her face took on a very serious tone. It was clear that something was wrong."

The source compared it to a calm before a hurricane. "Whitney became very quiet for a minute and then all hell broke loose," said the eyewitness. "She smacked the magazine against the make-up mirror and suddenly began to scream, 'Robyn! They're doing it to us again! Damn it, they're doing it to us again.'

"Then, Whitney started to sob.

"Everybody was told to leave the room, which we all did in a real hurry."

Apparently, Whitney had been assured by the magazine that the reporter would not mention any unsubstantiated rumors about her relationship with Robyn Crawford. But, as it turned out, the subject was raised several times in the five-page story. Hirschberg wrote, "There are the persistent rumors that Houston is gay (which she has repeatedly denied) and that Brown is a crackhead (which he has repeatedly denied)."

Then several paragraphs later: "Her rumored affair with Robyn Crawford was a main point of gossip. It is easy to see why conclusions were drawn: Houston and Crawford have been the best of friends for fifteen years and are virtually inseparable. Crawford counsels her on all aspects of her career—from what dress to wear at a photo shoot to how loud the vocal should sound on a particular track from *The Bodyguard.*

"They watch each other constantly. 'Doesn't Robyn look thin?' Houston will ask as she sees Crawford's reflection in the makeup mirror.

"Whether or not they were ever lovers (again, Houston denies this), their relationship is fascinating for its fierce intensity. It is difficult to imagine anything— even Houston's marriage—coming between them."

According to Whitney's staff member, this sent her through the roof. Whitney felt that any questions about her sexuality took on a certain legitimacy when they were raised by a magazine that is considered to be so respectable.

"How dare she?" Whitney screamed, referring to the writer. "*How dare she?*"

Members of her staff, who were now standing on the other side of a closed door, could clearly hear Whitney crying. "It's just not fair," she sobbed. "And to think, I *cooperated* with this story. And *this* is what happens.

"When is this ever going to stop?" Whitney sobbed as Robyn tried to console her.

Many celebrities in the past have been accused of various sexual practices though in the majority of instances, the rumor has a shelf life of only a few months and then dies off as another, and even more shocking story takes its place. But the Whitney/Robyn whisperings seem to have nearly as much durability as sightings of a still-living Elvis Presley.

Truly, Whitney had asked a very good question: *when is this ever going to stop?* The answer, unfortunately, is that it probably never will—not as long as Whitney Houston is famous, anyway. Rumors and innuendo are the price of fame.

"If I could go back to who I was before I became this *person*," Whitney Houston once claimed, "I can't say I wouldn't do it. I can't say that at all. . . ."

eighteen

        "I know all the rumors," Whitney Houston has said. "I'm supposed to be a lesbian, and Bobby is supposed to be gay, and we got married to cover this whole thing up. It's so ludicrous. How could people think that anyone would go through so much trouble! This is a *marriage*. It's supposed to be *sacred*. I do not take it lightly."

Of course, it's unlikely to the point of being farcical to imagine that Whitney Houston and Bobby Brown married each other for publicity or in order to protect their heterosexual images. Still, this story of an "arranged marriage" has been a favorite of Hollywood gossipmongers.

"This ain't about publicity," Whitney says angrily when asked whether there were ulterior motives for her marriage to Bobby Brown. "I don't want to spend the rest of my life with somebody I thought was just going to give me *publicity*. I've got enough of that on my own. And so does he. People don't live like that. Especially black people who were raised in families with morals, standards, and integrity. But the press isn't going to sell papers if writers say, 'Well, Whitney and Bobby are doing great.'

"You know how nasty it is that I'm a married woman and they're still calling me gay?" Whitney has asked. "If I was gay, yes, I hope I would have enough integrity to say I like women. But, see, I don't think it's anyone's business. If I have sex with snakes, should I sit down in an interview and tell you I have sex with snakes?" she asked a reporter.

"No," she said answering her own question. "If I'm a good person, if I don't hurt anybody, what does my sexual preference have to do with anybody. If I was gay, I swear I would say it. But I ain't ever liked a woman in my bed. I swear to *God*.

"I'm so fucking tired of that question. And I'm tired of answering it," she concluded.

The coupling of Whitney and Bobby showed every sign of being a passionate one—a passion enhanced by their obvious differences. Each seemed to have something that was not fully developed in the other, something that drew them together. They were impassioned not only about each other, but also about their careers individually and as a couple, and about the impending birth of their child.

According to a Los Angeles–based marriage and family counselor, the intensity of the couple's arguments suggests a hot-blooded love. "Couples who only consider themselves to be friends rarely display passion toward each other, even in arguments," she notes. "There is no reason to get to a passionate level, because the stakes are low.

"I have found, however, that those couples who are experiencing highly intense, romantic, sexual, passionate feelings for each other tend to fight in an equally intense fashion. It is the other side of the coin: love and hate of equal measure. It seems to be unlikely that Whitney and Bobby are just friends *acting* like they are married. No one can act that well."

Whitney Houston and Bobby Brown have certainly had some rather volatile arguments—and in public, no less. "We don't just have arguments," Whitney once confided. "Bobby and I have good ol' knock-down drag-'em-out *married people* fights. *Oooooh*, he makes me so mad. But I love him so."

When Whitney joined her husband on his 1992 album, *Bobby*, for a duet entitled "Something in Common," it was clear that the couple was hoping to impart a personal message. During the instrumental opening, Bobby dedicates the song to "All of those who don't believe in love—*especially* ours." It seemed more a dare than a prayer, with Mr. and Mrs. Bobby Brown's message coming through loud and clear: "We are in love, whether you believe it or not."

Always the subject of much controversy, Brown was now finding it difficult to enjoy a private relationship with one of pop music's greatest divas. If anything, his romance with Whitney shone the spotlight more brightly on him and on his private affairs. Old rumors of drug abuse surfaced upon the release of the *Bobby* album, with the entertainer once again strongly denying the allegations. His label, MCA Records, came to his defense in an interview. Said Ernie Singleton, president of the Black Music division of MCA, "I have heard stuff like this over the years on numerous occasions, but I can tell you, I have never had an experience with Bobby that painted a drug picture to me and I think I'm pretty streetwise. You don't have to be around me when you do it. I can tell when you're whacked. I've also confronted Bobby . . . and he said 'no.'"

"I wish they'd just leave me alone," Bobby Brown would say of the media, echoing Whitney's sentiments.

To complicate matters, the *Bobby* album, which was poorly reviewed and did not sell particularly well, did nothing for Brown's career, but did provoke comparisons with his more famous wife. "It made things even tougher for him," said one friend. "It was natural for Bobby to want to be as successful as his wife. But it was becoming clear that this would never happen. He was going to be living in her shadow . . . unless a miracle occurred in his career. This frustration began to cause some stress between the two of them. It was the unspoken reason behind a great many of their battles."

To complicate things further, Bobby's relationship with his in-laws had not improved. A friend reports that by Christmas 1992, Bobby and his mother-in-law were barely on speaking terms. Whitney spent much of her own time trying to keep them apart. And that friction caused Christmas 1992 to be a very chilly holiday at the Houston home.

By January 1993, *The Bodyguard* had grossed over $272 million at theaters worldwide. It was perfect holiday fare and had women flocking to buy tickets, outnumbering male patrons by more than four to one. Mike Clark of *USA Today* said of the film, "It's tapping into what was, until two or three years ago, an audience taken for granted—women twenty-five and over . . . the whole *Fried Green Tomatoes* thing." It was reported that some female ticket buyers were seeing the film two and three times. One writer observed, "The motivating force of romantic movies is a female audience dragging men along. And it's not only hard-working females who have the fantasy of being swept off their feet; young girls want it as well."

Whitney, however, had other matters on her mind than the success of *The Bodyguard.* "I was flat on my back," she recalled. "People were talking about me, the movie, the song ['I Will Always Love You'] and I was totally disinterested. I just wanted to have my baby. That's where my focus was. . . ."

By February 1993, in her ninth month of pregnancy, Whitney Houston reportedly weighed in at almost two hundred pounds, close to double her prepregnancy weight. She was miserable. "Oh, God, how much longer," she lamented. "Please. *Please.* I can't take it another day."

Because of the prodigious weight gain, she was forced to wear special elasticized tights to aid circulation in her legs, and she had trouble walking. Her legs and feet became so swollen that at a baby shower thrown by family and friends, she was forced to sit with her feet elevated and wrapped in slippers—*satin* slippers, of course.

Over two hundred friends attended Whitney's baby shower, including Aretha Franklin, whose gift—a pink, motorized Cadillac large enough for the baby to ride around in—was the hit of the party. But the event was interrupted by Whitney's doctor, who took one look at her and ordered her back to bed. The singer was helped to her feet by Cissy; then, obviously uncomfortable in a standing position, she smiled weakly at her guests, sighed her thanks for their presence, and was led upstairs to her room.

"Lord, let this baby be born. . . *now,*" Cissy implored during the shower.

By the end of February, Whitney was under around-the-clock care by her doctor, with a live-in nurse responding to her every need. The pregnancy had become a difficult one. Whitney reportedly developed toxemia, a condition that causes a sharp rise in blood pressure as well as swelling in the tissues. Cissy, too, was said to have suffered from this during her pregnancies, so she was especially empathetic.

Finally—on Thursday, March 4, 1993, at 11:38 A.M., at the St. Barnabus Medical Center in Livingston, New Jersey—Houston gave birth to a six-pound, twelve-ounce girl by Cesarean section, a procedure that became necessary as a result of complications during labor. (Whitney had intended to have a natural delivery.) The child was named Bobbi Kristina Houston Brown. Bobby Brown was at Whitney's side for the birth.

Cissy and John Houston paced nervously in the waiting area, anxious for news from the delivery room. When a member of the hospital staff announced that they were the grandparents of a lovely baby girl, the former spouses hugged each other joyfully.

Cissy spoke to Bobby Brown only once at the hospital, after she had seen her grandchild. A friend revealed, "Cissy could only bring herself to say one thing to Bobby at the hospital, and that was, 'The baby is beautiful.'"

In July 1993, Whitney Houston resumed her concert schedule, her first stop being the James L. Knight Center in Miami, Florida. With a hit movie, a number-one album, a controversial marriage, and a beautiful new daughter, the opening night of a major tour should have been momentous. But such was not to be the case.

The evening began with fans being forced to wait

in a tight pack outside the arena until just ten minutes before showtime. They were practically crushed against the doors that led inside. Once they were allowed into the concert hall and hurried to their seats, a sound check of the audio equipment (which should have been completed before the doors opened) took another hour. By this time, the impatient audience was not in any mood for surprises. Yet the surprises kept on coming.

Although an opening act had not previously been announced, the show—which finally started two hours late—began with a performance by Houston's friends and protégées, Angie and Debbie (members of the gospel-singing Winans family). These performers were in an unenviable position, taking the stage to face a crowd of unruly, angry fans who wanted only to see the person they had paid their money to see, and who had already waited two extra hours for the privilege.

As the two young Winanses tried to perform, incensed audience members began to stomp their feet, drowning out the performance. Finally, the entertainers left the stage.

Then, as if that had not been enough, there was *another* opening act, a sax player named Kirk Whalum. It was all too much for some of Whitney's fans.

Recalled one of her dancers, "Whitney was in her dressing room, livid, during the opening acts' performances. She was already tense because of the delay, which hadn't been her fault. The fact is that there was a problem with one of the computers that operated the lights. They had to fix it before the show went on. When she heard the crowd's mean reaction to the opening acts, she saw red. It really pissed her off. She didn't see any need for that kind of behavior from the audience.

"Out of respect for her, she felt the crowd should have treated the opening acts fairly. Whitney felt protective of them."

A backstage worker said Whitney appeared to be agitated before she came onstage. "She sighed several times," recalled the worker, "as if she was saying, 'Oh well, I've got a job to do, and here I go. But I ain't happy. I ain't happy at all.' And then she just went out there and into her first song—with a bad attitude."

According to one fan who attended the concert, "Whitney finally came onstage about 10:00 P.M., and we all expected her to apologize and try to compensate for the long wait and unexpected opening act by giving the best concert that she had ever given in her life. But much to our surprise, instead, she had this . . . this *diva* attitude.

"It was clear from the moment she took the stage that she was really pissed at the audience."

After the opening number, an eager fan appeared at the lip of the stage with a autograph pad, hoping to secure her signature. Most entertainers have ways of calming a crowd. But Whitney's demeanor this evening did not make matters better for her. She glared down at the fan, pointed out toward the auditorium, and said—into the live microphone so everyone in the auditorium could hear—"Your ticket definitely *does* say 'seat' on it, doesn't it?"

The humiliated fan quickly retreated.

At that remark from Whitney, the audience turned against her. Boos and catcalls filled the arena.

"If you had to sum up their mood just then," wrote Leonard Pitts of the crowd in his *Miami Herald* review, "it would be something like this: 'Excuse us, Miss Thing, but we pay your salary, remember?'"

Whitney was disgusted. "Look, I've been booed

before," she told the crowd arrogantly. "And it really doesn't faze me."

There was a collective gasp from the audience, followed by more sounds of disapproval. By intermission, a line of people demanding refunds had formed at the box offices.

"It was like an attitude thing toward the audience," said Sam Johnson, a ticket holder from Miami.

"She needed an attitude adjustment," agreed Bobby Banaeian of Boca Raton.

"I will never come to another concert by her," agreed fan Susan Robson of Fort Lauderdale. "I think she's gotten too big for her britches."

Indeed, this disastrous concert created a buzz rarely heard in low-key Florida. The next day, from Homestead to West Palm Beach, many conversations seemed to center on Whitney Houston's temperamental behavior. In fact, local radio call-in shows were dominated by listeners who felt Houston's behavior was unacceptable.

"Houston took the stage with an attitude that smelled like rotting fish," Pitts continued in his scathing *Miami Herald* review. "It was the Hindenburg of pop concerts. Her behavior was tacky, unprofessional, arrogant and beneath the dignity of a singer of her talent and stature."

"Whitney's position was clear," said one of her associates. "'*So what?*' It was her first show after the baby was born. She was tired and the audience was unruly. She was in no mood to take any shit from them. 'I do the best I can do,' she said after the show. 'But I ain't no robot. And that crowd pissed me off.'"

Members of Arista Records' promotional staff, the concert's promoters, and other executives from the Knight Center spent the next day in consultation with

Houston, aimed at avoiding a repetition of the disaster at the next night's show.

"Oh, *puh-leeze*!" Whitney told one worried record-company executive. "Stop overreacting. That was just one night, and I'm not going to worry about it. Things will be better tonight."

True to her forecast, Tuesday night's sold-out performance went off without complication. Fans appeared willing to forgive their fiery diva for her behavior the night before. In fact, they seemed soothed by her majestic voice and by songs that spoke personally to them. Whitney received a series of standing ovations. But the press remained unimpressed and unforgiving.

Wrote Pitts, "Toward the end of the set, Houston dragged out the old Sunday school chestnut, 'Jesus Loves Me.' And surely He does. But then, He probably didn't go to Monday night's show."

"I don't know what to make of any of it," Whitney Houston said later, her voice filled with resignation. "I don't understand fame at all. I don't know what makes an audience happy, what makes them sad. I don't know what people want. All *I* want is to sing."

Yes, after the birth of her child, Whitney Houston was back on the concert trail. But the question would remain: did she really want to be there?

At her next stop, in Vienna, Virginia, a female fan was so irate at having to wait for Houston during Kirk Whalum's opening-act sax performance that she jumped from the balcony onto a ledge where the lights were hung. There, she exposed herself from the waist up and started screaming, "Where is Whitney? She'd better get out here!" She was quickly arrested.

"Oh, Lord," Whitney said backstage after that incident. "Lord, have mercy on all of us."

When Whitney finally appeared, she attempted to

ignore the occurrence. Instead, she addressed the crowd about her private life, noting among other things that "Bobby and I have been married for almost a year. Some people didn't think we would last six months. My husband and I and the baby are very happy. You heard it from the horse's mouth. Don't believe what you hear and what you read."

"Work it, girl," someone shouted out from the audience.

"I'm trying, baby," Whitney responded.

Later, Whitney spoke candidly to Barbara Walters on one of Walters's prime-time specials and admitted that she had never planned to become the center of so much attention, to have worldwide fame and intense public scrutiny. "I knew that I wanted to sing," she said to Walters, "but now, looking back on it, I think I *really* just wanted to be a background singer, like my mother. . . ."

"The price of fame is a great one," Cissy had once said. "I don't know anymore if it's worth it. I really and truly don't."

How ironic. When Cissy Houston was her daughter's age, she wanted nothing more than major stardom. Instead, she watched in awe as her dream unfolded . . . for Whitney. And now that they had experienced this brand of frenzied, international celebrity, both mother and daughter had to wonder if it was worth it.

"You can't really plan fame," Whitney observed, "or what you'll do with it once you have it. Or how you'll handle it. Or how you'll feel about your audiences. Or how they'll feel about you.

"I just want to sing. I wish people would concentrate more on my singing than on my life and on my so-called temper. It's my life, my *person*, my moods, and I don't choose to share each and every bit of it with the entire world."

Tough? Sort of. Hard-edged? Maybe. Unrepentant? For sure. But . . . selling her soul and smiling sweetly for the sake of her public image? No. Definitely not that. She was playing it honestly. You had to give her credit for that.

Whitney concluded, "You know what? I didn't ask for this, all of this attention and invasion of privacy. They say it comes with the territory . . . well, I don't think it does. Nor do I think it should have to."

nineteen

On August 9, 1993, Whitney Houston turned thirty years old. In the twelve years since she had signed with Arista Records, she had recorded four top-selling albums—*Whitney Houston, Whitney, I'm Your Baby Tonight,* and *The Bodyguard*—which sold over sixty million copies worldwide. She had performed in countless concerts, costarred in a blockbuster film, become embroiled in a high-profile and controversial marriage, given birth to a child, and begun her own very successful management organization—Nippy, Inc. "It has been some life, I have to tell you," the thirty-year-old star said. "Honey, I am *exhausted*."

She was also becoming a vital force in charitable work, her benefit performances confirming her true gift for emotional commitment to her music and her audience. When she sings to raise money for philanthropic purposes, a different light seems to come into her eyes. She has performed for the United Negro College Fund, is an AIDS activist, and established the Whitney Houston Foundation for Children, Inc., which is dedicated to promoting a positive self-image in America's youth.

Says Whitney, "I believe that when you become famous and successful you have a responsibility to those who are looking to you for inspiration and encouragement. I definitely feel a responsibility, especially to our young people. My mother raised me to believe that I should be of service to others. It's not enough for me to just be a 'star.' That's a label that others put on you, anyway. For me, I have to be able to *give* something back."

On the day of her birthday, Whitney was performing in Monte Carlo on the French Riviera. To celebrate the event, Bobby Brown hosted a small, elegant surprise gathering on a yacht in the Mediterranean.

Six-month-old Bobbi Kristina had, by this time, grown into a lovely child, and in order to spend every waking moment with her, Whitney turned the backstage areas of her concert venues into what one observer called "a day-care center." Audiences at her concerts became accustomed to appearances by Bobbi Kristina—and often by Bobby Brown. Whitney was sending mixed messages, however. At one moment she would complain that her fans wanted so much more from her than just her voice—that they wanted her *life.* Then, in the next moment, she would present her husband and child onstage during a concert, only encouraging the media feeding frenzy in her private life. One could practically hear the whispers rising from the crowd: "Oh, yeah, I forgot about him. But now that you put him in our faces, Whitney, it reminds me of all those stories. Are you really happy, or are you just acting?"

Perhaps she simply couldn't resist demonstrating her

pride in her family, regardless of the price she would pay when photos of her baby cooing onstage later found their way onto the covers of the *Star* and the *National Enquirer*. During one concert in Atlanta, Whitney swept her young daughter into her arms and joyously announced to the crowd, "Here she is: The most important thing in my world. My baby, Bobbi. B.K. [her nickname for Bobbi Kristina]." During another appearance, this one in London, the child began to gurgle and laugh into the microphone, for all to hear.

"Like mother, like daughter," Cissy said backstage. She couldn't help but laugh.

Cissy, of course, had fond memories of her own daughter onstage with her as she and the Sweet Inspirations cast their magic spell over standing-room-only audiences. By bringing Bobbi Kristina to her own concerts and briefly introducing her to the world, Whitney seemed to be carrying on a family tradition. Perhaps, as Cissy had done, Whitney was sharing with Bobbi Kristina the irresistible allure of show business.

One thing began to seem absolutely certain to those who saw her perform. Whitney Houston was not posturing or trying to prove anything by her behavior. She was expressing feelings that arose from her soul. In a funny way, one observer said, almost surprised by the genuineness of her own reaction, "It's enough to give you a feeling of hope about things."

In early October 1993, after an overseas tour, Whitney's plane landed at John F. Kennedy Airport in New York. With Bobby Brown and Bobbi Kristina in tow, the singer and her entourage piled into a limousine, then sped off. Coincidentally, Port Authority police were staking out a limousine that belonged to the reputed head of a drug cartel. The authorities became confused and raced after Whitney's limousine instead (even though it had the vanity plate NIPPY 3 prominently displayed).

Suddenly Whitney's vehicle was surrounded by five police cars and ten uniformed policemen, their guns drawn. A frightened Whitney Houston slowly rolled down her window.

Calmly—she certainly didn't want any trouble with her baby in the limousine—Whitney said, "Officers, I am Whitney Houston. My child is here. Whatever you want, *please* be careful. . . ."

Then she flashed the peace sign.

Noted one observer, "It was probably everything she could do to keep her husband from exploding and causing a bigger scene."

"Hey, that *is* Whitney Houston," one of the officers announced, astonished.

"May we see some ID?" another officer asked.

The policemen remained with their guns poised and ready to fire as one of the squad checked Whitney's identification. After he was convinced of her identity, the officer apologized profusely. The others nodded in agreement and went on their way.

"She's one cool cookie," an officer was overheard saying. "Could have been killed . . ."

She may have had the good sense to keep a cool head while guns were pointed at her and her family, but later, Whitney was infuriated by the occurrence. "How could this have happened?" she demanded of her entourage. "My God. Is this 1993 or 1963?"

"Oh, she was riled up over that one," said an associate. "And with good reason. A limousine full of black people stopped by the police. And even though—as we would later learn from police reports—they clearly knew who she was, they had their guns drawn just the same. She was livid."

Whitney's father recalled, "The cops recognized Whitney. And still they didn't drop their guns. If anyone in that car would have made a sudden movement, they would all have been wiped out."

The Houstons insisted that they be shown an official report of the incident, and when Whitney saw it she could not believe her eyes: it stated that only two police cars had been involved—and no guns.

"Liars!" Whitney shouted as she tore the report in half.

Pressed to reveal the truth, the Port Authority admitted that their official report was "erroneous." Charles Knox, the superintendent of public safety, in a prepared statement, apologized to Houston and her family. "Upon further investigation undertaken at my behest, we have found that the initial police reports were erroneous in indicating that only two police officers and two police cars pulled over Ms. Houston's limousine." The statement continued, "In fact, we have found that there were at least five police cars and at least nine officers, several of them with weapons drawn, present when the vehicle was stopped."

Knox also explained that the police thought they were witnessing a drug-smuggling deal. He noted that Whitney's limo had taken off in a hurry and that the plainclothes policemen did not want to blow their cover, and therefore decided to follow the car instead of simply inspecting it when it was parked at the airport.

"This did nothing to appease Whitney," said a former associate. "She couldn't help but think this dangerous incident was a result of fame causing her trouble, again. Many people in her camp felt full well that the cops knew the limousine had Whitney and Bobby in it.

Some felt the couple was set up, that the authorities were told there'd be drugs, which, of course, was not the case. 'This can never, ever happen again,' Whitney announced. And then she beefed up her security even more. . . ."

Despite her recurrent encounters with the dark side of fame, Whitney's career continued to spiral upward. As of late 1993, *The Bodyguard* had grossed over $411 million worldwide. The soundtrack album had sold over twenty-four million copies, making it the biggest-selling soundtrack ever.

Critics and fans felt the upcoming awards season would be more than kind to Whitney Houston. They weren't wrong, as she swept the annual Billboard Music Awards by winning in eleven categories, with "I Will Always Love You" meriting the Number One World Single, the Number One Hot Single, and the Number One R&B Single awards. During the ceremony, Whitney wowed the audience with a scintillating version of her hit "I Have Nothing," dedicating it to "everyone watching at home, because there would be no me without you." Her rousing vocals brought the usually reserved awards-show crowd to its feet for a wildly enthusiastic ovation during the final verses of the song.

The plaudits continued with the twenty-first annual American Music Awards, in early 1994. In fact, some record-industry observers felt that the honors that year should have been renamed "The Whitney Houston Music Awards." Whitney scored an impressive sweep of eight awards, becoming the top winner of the night. Wearing a figure-flattering white satin gown with a high neckline, her hair pulled back into a demure bun with curls framing her face, Whitney flashed a joyous smile for each win.

At one point, she noted to the crowd that Bobbi

Kristina was in the audience. "I couldn't leave her, 'cause she started cryin'," Whitney told the delighted audience. She then sang "I Have Nothing" and followed it with "I Loves You, Porgy" (from *Porgy and Bess*) and "And I'm Telling You I'm Not Goin'" (from *Dreamgirls*).

Although Whitney had often performed "And I'm Telling You I'm Not Goin'" in her stage shows, this was the first time she did so on national television. A few days later, Jennifer Holliday—the singer/actress who originated the role of Effie White in *Dreamgirls* and made "And I'm Telling You I'm Not Goin'" her signature song—complained to a New York radio station disc jockey that Whitney had "stolen" her song. "I felt that, of all the songs that she could do, it wasn't necessary for her to do one of mine," Jennifer grumbled. "I didn't take it as a compliment at all, mostly because I don't think I'm dead yet."

Whitney's unfazed reaction when she heard of this: "Girl, *please*."

The Grammy Awards ceremony in early 1994 offered Whitney even more recognition. She was honored by winning Best Pop Female Vocalist for "I Will Always Love You," with the hit song also taking the prize for Record of the Year. *The Bodyguard* soundtrack won for Album of the Year.

At the end of January 1994, Whitney, Bobby, and Bobbi Kristina left for a brief vacation on Williams Island off the coast of Florida. One afternoon, Bobby and Whitney returned to their lavish condominium to find a hastily written note from Bobbi Kristina's nanny. A friend described what happened. "Whitney picked up the note and screamed. Something had happened to the baby. The note said the nanny had taken Bobbi

Kristina to a local hospital. Without hesitation, Whitney and Bobby raced out of the door and sped to the hospital.

"Once there, they discovered that Bobbi Kristina had suffered a serious burn, caused by a curling iron. Apparently, the nanny, who had been using it, unplugged the red-hot curling iron and set it on a counter with the cord dangling to the floor. Bobbi pulled herself up high enough to grab at the cord, and brought the scorching instrument tumbling down on her bare arm."

According to a nurse at the hospital, Whitney was upset, but remained polite toward the staff. "She just wanted treatment for her baby right away," said the nurse. "She was very mature about it, though it hurt her to see her baby in such pain. She paced back and forth outside of the nurses' station as the treatment was being administered. She was obviously very worried. But she never raised her voice, or anything like that. In other words, she didn't behave like a Hollywood bigshot."

Bobbi was treated for her burns and released immediately into her mother's arms. The burn was, in fact, not a serious one.

"This could have been a lot worse. The tongs were obviously very hot. Whitney and Bobby are lucky that their daughter was not more seriously injured," noted one hospital official. The nanny was not fired, incidentally, but was reprimanded by Whitney and instructed on how to better baby-proof any area in which Bobbi Kristina might be playing.

On February 4, 1994, Whitney hosted a surprise twenty-fifth birthday party for her husband at Tavern on the Green restaurant in New York. According to magazine publisher Jamie Foster Brown (*Sister 2 Sister*), who attended the party with singer Freddie Jackson, this was "the bash to end all bashes."

Whitney arrived at the restaurant dressed in a smart two-piece black combination, with a V-neck jacket and an elegant, form-fitting skirt hemmed just above the knee. She seemed to radiate her happiness at having planned such a party for her husband. Unfortunately, the big news of the evening was an altercation between Bobby Brown and a photographer.

"It supposedly started when Bobby, his mother Carol, and Whitney all got up onstage to welcome and thank the guests for coming out," recalled Brown in her magazine report. "Bobby's mom was happy. She spoke very emotionally, and disjointedly, and she said that she loves all of her children. She also said that she loves Whitney, not because she's *Whitney Houston* but because she's her daughter-in-law. Bobby got up and said, 'No matter what anybody thinks, my marriage to Whitney is real. And if you don't respect it, then fuck all of you.'"

Such a lovely birthday sentiment!

Brown's report continued, "Bobby's mother then said that although she wouldn't use that kind of language, she agreed. Then Bobby and Whitney sang a duet."

Afterward, Whitney and Bobby went into the press room, where a photographer hired by Whitney to commemorate the event made a sarcastic comment to Bobby, suggesting that his mother should get her own talk show. Bobby thought the photographer was being "a smart-ass." So he smacked him across the face with the back of his hand. This, of course, caused quite a scene. Whitney was visibly upset with Bobby for almost ruining the party, but other guests helped to calm the easily riled Brown.

Certainly, by the time Bobby turned twenty-five,

Whitney Houston knew the kind of volatile and unpredictable personality he had. Lately she had seemed to spend a great deal of her time either calming him down or insisting to the press and public that her relationship with him was solid and true. As a result of all the controversy, fan magazines were rife with reader comments, mostly negative, about the Whitney/Bobby union.

Fresh! magazine, targeted at a young black audience, has printed several letters that one might imagine would give Whitney cause for some alarm. An example: "Dear *Fresh*: Whitney Houston spends all of her time trying to convince people how wonderful her dumb husband is, and gets upset because people say she's married to the wrong kind of person. What did she expect? She used to be so nice and good, and he spends half of his time getting someone pregnant and then dumps them. The only reason that he didn't dump her is because she's rich and she can do a lot for his career."

According to those who know her best, Whitney Houston is not a naive, easily exploitable woman. Surely she understands that her relationship with Bobby Brown is fraught with problems. One can be fairly certain that whatever has been reported in the press—and whatever Mr. and Mrs. Bobby Brown have acknowledged as accurate—is but a fragment of the larger chaos that reigns in the emotional lives of these two celebrities.

But who can explain matters of the heart? Who knows why a person stays in a relationship that seems completely dysfunctional to the outside world? Who knows how Bobby Brown feeds Whitney Houston's soul? And who knows how she feeds his?

• • •

Despite turmoil in her personal life, Whitney
Houston's career had not suffered. By the spring of 1994,
every major film production company and Hollywood
studio seemed to be on the lookout for the next
"Whitney Houston movie." Whitney's own company,
Nippy, Inc., announced several projects in development,
including remakes of various film classics. In May 1994,
Daily Variety announced that incoming CBS-TV president
Peter Tortorici was planning to mount a production of
Rogers and Hammerstein's *Cinderella*, with Whitney
Houston playing the lead. According to Broadway and
network sources, the project was being quietly organized
for CBS by Storyline Productions, the company that pro-
duced the successful 1993 television version of *Gypsy*,
which starred Bette Midler.

Cinderella had played the small screen twice in the
past, in 1957 with Julie Andrews and again in 1965
with Lesley Ann Warren; both were highly rated.
Because of Whitney's popularity, the producers were
confident that the latest version would be another
record breaker.

At the same time, other sources announced that
Whitney was interested in a remake of *The Bishop's Wife*,
a weepy 1940s film starring David Niven, Cary Grant,
and Loretta Young. The story concerns a bishop and
his spouse, who attempt to raise money for a much-
needed new church during the Christmas holidays. The
situation seems hopeless until the miraculous appearance of an angel, who assists the couple. In this odd
love story the wife finds herself attracted to the angel.
However, contrary to what one might anticipate from
the nonangelic, this attraction somehow manages to
strengthen the bond between the bishop and his wife,

with the angel heading back to heaven after a job well done. Denzel Washington is expected to be cast as the angel.

Of course, in the timeworn tradition of public-relations hype, Whitney and her staff consistently denied working on these film projects, insisting that "no deal has been made yet and so there is nothing to discuss." This kind of statement, whatever else it accomplishes, heightens the public's curiosity about what has been so hotly denied, which is, of course, exactly what the principals want.

Whitney's life seemed to be slipping into the usual snake pit of rumors, anyway. After so many years of turmoil, sorting out rumor from fact was becoming increasingly difficult. Was the public expected automatically to disregard every report of marital strife between Whitney and her husband? Whitney continued emphatically denying any stories of trouble on the home front; however, the stories persisted, often supported by public sightings of the feuding couple.

One factor that was adding significant strain to the Browns' marriage was Bobby's recent financial woes. In early 1994, he was served with a writ from the Internal Revenue Service, claiming he owed over $3 million in back taxes. Reacting to this, Bobby filed a lawsuit against his former business management company, which he claims defrauded him of $10 million.

A family friend expressed her concern. "Bobby could lose everything," she said, "including his $3 million Atlanta estate. He doesn't know what he's going to do. He's got all of these relatives and friends living in his mansion and they're all going to have to go somewhere else."

In his own lawsuit, Bobby claimed that his former business managers had failed to act in his best interests, charging them with malpractice, breach of contract, and negligence. He added, in legal documents, that he was so broke that "it had become impossible to pursue [my] singing and dancing career, which has been materially damaged."

By 1994, Bobby Brown had made an estimated $27 million from his recording career. According to well-placed sources, it would seem that his generosity to friends and lavish tastes in jewelry, cars, and gifts had contributed substantially to his current difficulties. However, court papers indicate that Brown trusted his managers implicitly in all of his financial affairs, even giving them signature rights over his bank accounts. "But [the managers'] accounting records were so poor, it was impossible for anyone to determine Brown's financial condition," said the court records. "[The managers] led Brown to believe that he was still in a financially secure position, when in fact, he was not."

Whitney was not pleased with this turn of events, says a friend. She knew she would never allow herself to be taken advantage of in this manner, and was not sure how such a thing could happen to Bobby.

And Bobby now turned to his wife for financial assistance, which did not annoy Whitney as much as it did her advisers. "It was all very stressful," said a former associate of Whitney's. "The public thinks it's all a bed of roses, being stars. But they have the same real problems—money and otherwise—as the rest of the world, only bigger."

In order to halt foreclosure on his 14,000-square-foot home in Atlanta, a second mortgage—for $850,000—was arranged via Nippy, Inc.

Despite this evidence of apparent harmony, other conflicts in their relationship continued. In March 1994, a quarrel between the couple and Robyn Crawford at

the posh Peninsula Hotel became the talk of Beverly
Hills. According to hotel sources, Brown and Houston
had been arguing for over a week when, on the morning of March 24, Robyn Crawford called hotel security
for assistance.

"When we arrived at the hotel room, Robyn
Crawford answered the door," said one security guard.
"She had a scratch on her hand and red marks on her
arms and neck. Although she played down any incident
that may have happened, something was clearly wrong.
After a few moments, Whitney Houston's own security
personnel, who had apparently also been summoned,
arrived."

As all of the security men watched and wondered
what to do, Brown, according to the guard, began curs-
ing at and threatening Crawford. "We asked Ms.
Houston if she would like us to stay until the police,
who had also been called by this time, arrived," the
security officer reported. "But she said she could handle
the situation from here.

"We noticed, by his behavior, that Mr. Brown had
been apparently drinking. It seemed that Brown,
Houston, and Crawford had all been involved in some
sort of physical altercation."

Whatever happened is a mystery to this day, though
every new report of the matter had its own spin on
details. The indisputable fact, however, is that another
"incident" had occurred, and circumstances did not
appear to be rosy for Bobby and Whitney.

The rest of the spring of 1994 was worse, with more
public spats and more reported accusations—including
one to the effect that Bobby had had an affair with a
female rap singer. (The woman in question insisted,
however, that while she was with Brown in his hotel

room, all they discussed was how much he loved Whitney and Bobbi Kristina.) Other reports, in tabloid magazines and on television, stated that Whitney had caught Bobby "in the act" with a cheerleader.

They separated.

They reconciled.

They separated again. (When Bobby fell into arrears on the $850,000 mortgage that Nippy, Inc., had arranged for him on his Atlanta home, no further help seemed to be forthcoming from Whitney. The home went into foreclosure again, and a public auction was set. The IRS also had two tax liens against the property totaling more than $1.3 million.)

Then they reconciled again.

Who knew what to think or believe anymore? More to the point, who really cared? The existence of irreconcilable differences between the Browns seemed beyond doubt; it didn't take a psychiatrist to figure that out.

Anyone who is weary of the constant rumors and speculation can only hope that the couple either finds a way to live together harmoniously or separates, thereby sparing the public any more of the melodrama that arises around them wherever they go.

Given the circumstances, it would seem that Whitney would be in no frame of mind for her latest bombshell: she was pregnant again.

She and Bobby had told the press they planned to have three children and hoped the next one would be a boy. But Whitney may have felt this wasn't the best time for her to have a second child. (Would they name it yet another variation of "Bobby"? Already, in addition to Bobbi Kristina, Brown had another child, from a previous relationship, named Bobby. At least evidence of his having passed this way would not be lacking.)

Nevertheless, during a concert appearance in June 1994, Whitney called Bobby onto the stage and, in a variation of "Lucy Tells Ricky She's Pregnant," broke the news in front of 18,000 hysterical fans. Indeed, never a private moment for Whitney—at, seemingly, her own insistence.

Whitney had previously told Bobby that the pregnancy test came back negative, so her news was a surprise. Bobby hugged her, the two kissed passionately, then Whitney sang "The Greatest Love of All" as Bobby watched, his face glowing with pride.

What to make of these two lovebirds?

Unfortunately, in July 1994, Whitney suffered a miscarriage.

She was, according to her associates, devastated and deeply depressed. Bobby was there for her. He and Whitney flew to Colorado, where she was able to spend time recuperating. Her spokesperson, Lois Smith, admitted to *USA Today*, "[Whitney] and Bobby spent a couple of days in the mountains. She's not very happy right now, but they'll have more children. She wants more children. The pregnancy was in the earliest stages, so there were no complications."

Bobby had certainly proven that he can be a supportive partner. He had been at Whitney's side during a number of grave emergencies: her two miscarriages; her difficult pregnancy and the birth of their daughter; and the emotional aftermath of Bobbi Kristina's burn accident in Florida. Perhaps Whitney felt that he was actually dependable, that he had been there when she needed him most.

Meanwhile, Whitney had proven herself to be a vital partner in the relationship. To some, it seemed as if she was performing a tightrope act: balancing a marriage, a baby, and a thriving career. She even became a loving mother to the three children Bobby had fathered—Landon, seven; LaPrincia, four; and Robert, two and a half. She was apparently willing to do it all for her husband. In truth, Whitney Houston dearly wanted this marriage to be a success. "Until the end of time," as she told Barbara Walters, "whenever that is."

In the summer of 1994, when asked what she wanted most from her life, Whitney told *McCall's* magazine, "Really, it has nothing to do with business, whatsoever. It's my family. To raise children. To raise decent human beings. To keep my husband happy. To keep him strong. Things of that nature. They are very simple things."

Even Whitney Houston's strongest detractors could not wish her any less. Certainly, she must remember a time when things were simpler. . . and, perhaps, more fun. A time when a nervous but excited young girl sang out for the first time to a captivated audience in a church in New Jersey. A time when "the magic of believing" was the key to personal happiness. Could she ever go back to such a time?

"Probably, never," Whitney has lamented. "But, still, I thank God for my life and for all of His blessings. Goodness, what a road I've traveled," she concluded with a wry smile. "Still, when I close my eyes to pray, I can't help but wonder about where I'm headed . . . and what I will find once I get there."